IFRS® MADE EASY

IFRS® MADE EASY

Steven M. Bragg

WILEY

John Wiley & Sons, Inc.

Published by John Wiley & Sons, Inc., Hoboken, New Jersey.

Published simultaneously in Canada.

For general information on our other products and services or for technical support, please contact our Customer Care Department within the United States at (800) 762-2974, outside the United States at (317) 572-3993 or fax (317) 572-4002.

Wiley also publishes its books in a variety of electronic formats. Some content that appears in print may not be available in electronic books. For more information about Wiley products, visit our web site at www.wiley.com.

Library of Congress Cataloging-in-Publication Data:

ISBN 978-0-470-89070-7 (book); 978-1118003626 (ebk); 978-1118003633 (ebk); 978-11180003640 (ebk)

Printed in the United States of America.

10 9 8 7 6 5 4 3 2 1

Contents

Preface   vii

About the Author   ix

PART I – REVENUE AND EXPENSES

Chapter 1   Revenue Recognition   3

Chapter 2   Employee Benefits   17

Chapter 3   Share-Based Payments   33

Chapter 4   Income Taxes   43

PART II – ASSETS AND LIABILITIES

Chapter 5   Financial Instruments   61

Chapter 6   Interests in Joint Ventures   81

Chapter 7   Investments in Associates   87

Chapter 8   Inventory   93

Chapter 9   Property, Plant, and Equipment 103

Chapter 10   Intangible Assets   117

Chapter 11   Asset Impairment   129

Chapter 12   Provisions and Contingencies 143

PART III – THE FINANCIAL STATEMENTS

Chapter 13   Financial Statements Presentation   153

Chapter 14   Consolidated and Separate Financial Statements   169

Chapter 15   Related Party Disclosures   175

Chapter 16   Events after the Reporting Period   179

Chapter 17   Financial Reporting in Hyperinflationary Economies   183

PART IV – PUBLIC COMPANY REPORTING

Chapter 18   Operating Segments   189

Chapter 19   Earnings per Share   197

Chapter 20   Interim Financial Reporting   205

PART V – BROAD TRANSACTIONS

Chapter 21   Business Combinations   215

Chapter 22   Changes in Accounting Policies, Estimates, and Errors   225

Chapter 23   Discontinued Operations and Non-Current Assets
             Held for Sale   233

Chapter 24   Effects of Foreign Exchange Rate Changes   241

Chapter 25   Leases   247

Index   261

Preface

IFRS Made Easy is designed to give you answers to the most common accounting questions arising from international financial reporting standards. The accountant, controller, and chief financial officer can learn about such key topics as:

- Revenue recognition rules
- Defined benefit and defined contribution pension plans
- Payments based on an entity's share price
- Deferred tax assets and liabilities
- Cash flow hedges and fair value hedges
- Investments in associates and joint ventures
- Inventory revaluations
- Fair value adjustments for property, plant, and equipment
- Asset impairment
- Contingent liabilities
- The proper structure of financial statements
- Disclosures for related party transactions
- Financial restatements in a hyperinflationary economy
- Operating segment thresholds
- Basic and diluted earnings per share
- Accounting principles in interim reporting periods

- Business combinations
- Restatements caused by accounting errors
- Accounting for assets held for sale
- Foreign currency translation
- Lease accounting by the lessee and lessor

IFRS Made Easy is divided into five sections, each dealing with the main categories of IFRS: revenue and expenses, assets and liabilities, the financial statements, public company financial statements, and broad transactions.

Part I, Revenue and Expenses (Chapters 1-4) delves into a variety of revenue and expense topics. These include revenue recognition, employee benefits, share-based payments, and income taxes.

Part II, Assets and Liabilities (Chapters 5-12) addresses IFRS for accounting issues related to assets and liabilities. There are separate chapters covering the accounting for financial instruments, interests in joint ventures, investments in associates, inventory, property, and intangible assets. A separate chapter addresses the key issue of asset impairment, and we conclude Part II with a discussion of provisions and contingencies.

Part III, The Financial Statements (Chapters 13-17) addresses IFRS for the construction of financial statements. Part III is divided into separate chapters to address the basic form of the financial statements, how to consolidate them, and how to report on special situations. These situations address disclosures, including related-party disclosures and the reporting of events occurring after the reporting period. Finally, Part III covers financial reporting in hyperinflationary economies.

Part IV, Public Company Reporting (Chapters 18-20) addresses IFRS that are specific to additional information required to be disclosed by public companies as part of their financial statements. Separate chapters address the reporting of operating segments, earnings per share, and interim reporting.

Part V, Broad Transactions (Chapters 21-25) addresses a broad range of accounting transactions. These include business combinations, changes in accounting estimates, discontinued operations, the effects of foreign exchange rate changes, and leases.

Throughout, *IFRS Made Easy* has been structured to give the user a clear understanding of those IFRS topics that the accountant is most likely to encounter on an ongoing basis.

About the Author

Steven Bragg, CPA, has been the chief financial officer or controller of four companies, as well as a consulting manager at Ernst & Young. He received a master's degree in finance from Bentley College, an MBA from Babson College, and a Bachelor's degree in Economics from the University of Maine. He has been the two-time President of the Colorado Mountain Club, and is an avid alpine skier, mountain biker, and certified master diver. Mr. Bragg resides in Centennial, Colorado. He has written the following books:

Accounting and Finance for Your Small Business

Accounting Best Practices

Accounting Control Best Practices

Accounting Policies and Procedures Manual

Advanced Accounting Systems

Billing and Collections Best Practices

Business Ratios and Formulas

Controller's Guide to Costing

Controller's Guide to Planning and Controlling Operations

Controller's Guide: Roles and Responsibilities for the New Controller

Controllership

Cost Accounting

Cost Reduction Analysis

Essentials of Payroll

Fast Close

Financial Analysis

GAAP Guide

GAAP Policies and Procedures Manual

GAAS Guide

IFRS Made Easy

Inventory Accounting

Inventory Best Practices

Investor Relations

Just-in-Time Accounting

Management Accounting Best Practices

Managing Explosive Corporate Growth

Mergers and Acquisitions

Outsourcing

Payroll Accounting

Payroll Best Practices

Revenue Recognition

Run the Rockies

Running a Public Company

Sales and Operations for Your Small Business

The Controller's Function

The New CFO Financial Leadership Manual

The Ultimate Accountants' Reference

The Vest Pocket Controller's Guide

The Vest Pocket GAAP Guide

The Vest Pocket IFRS Guide

Throughput Accounting

Treasury Management

Free On-Line Resources
by Steve Bragg

Steve issues the Accounting Best Practices podcast. You can sign up for it at www.accountingtools.com, or access it through iTunes. The accountingtools. com Web site contains hundreds of accounting tips, best practices, and book reviews.

IFRS® MADE EASY

PART ONE

REVENUE AND EXPENSES

1

REVENUE RECOGNITION

INTRODUCTION

Many entities stretch the boundaries of how much revenue they can recognize within an accounting period, since they want to show exceptional revenue growth to their investors and creditors. This tendency has resulted in a number of IFRS rulings regarding the appropriate recognition of revenue. Most such rulings are relatively simple, single-paragraph statements, but others are more complex. The next section deals with the simpler revenue recognition rules, while other, more complex areas are addressed later in separate sections.

REVENUE RECOGNITION RULES

This section contains the bulk of all revenue recognition rules under IFRS, in alphabetical order. More complex revenue recognition situations, such as construction projects and customer loyalty programs are dealt with later, in separate sections. The simpler revenue recognition rules are:

- *Admission fees*. The fees generated from artistic performances and other special events are recognized when the event takes place. If the seller is selling subscriptions to a number of events, then it allocates the subscription to each event covered by the subscription, based on the extent to which services are performed at each event.

- *Advance payments*. The buyer may send either full or partial payment to the seller in advance of the delivery of goods. The seller may not yet have the items in inventory, they may still be in the production process, or they will be drop shipped by a third party. Under these circumstances, the seller should not recognize revenue until the goods are delivered to the buyer.

- *Barter exchange*. A transaction does not generate revenue if it involves the exchange of goods or services of a similar nature or value. If the exchange is for dissimilar goods or services, the transaction *does* create revenue; this is measured at the fair value of the goods or services received, as modified by the amount of any cash transferred. If the fair value of received goods or services cannot be reliably measured, then use instead the fair value of the goods or services given up, as modified by the amount of any cash transferred.

- *Bill and hold*. In a bill and hold sale, the buyer requests that delivery be delayed, but accepts billing and takes title to the goods. The seller recognizes revenue when the buyer takes title and the following conditions are satisfied:

  ○ Normal payment terms apply to the transaction

  ○ The buyer acknowledges the delayed delivery instructions

  ○ It is probable that delivery will be made

  ○ The goods are identified, on hand and ready for delivery

  The seller cannot recognize revenue related to a bill and hold transaction if there is only an intention to acquire or produce the goods in time for delivery, as opposed to actually being on hand.

- *Cash on delivery terms*. If a seller is selling goods based on cash on delivery terms, then it should recognize revenue when it delivers the goods and collects the cash from the transaction.

- *Deferred payments*. In the event of a deferred cash payment, the fair value of the consideration received may be reduced. When a delayed payment effectively constitutes a financing transaction, recognize revenue as the discounted cash flow of the transaction, using an imputed interest rate that is the more clearly determinable of either a) the

---

Example

Snoring Sofas is offering a year-end deal for its luxury leather sofas, under which customers can either pay €2,000 in cash or a zero-down payment with 24 monthly payments of €100 each, totaling €2,400. Since there is a difference of €400 between the cash price and the extended terms, the zero-down payment deal is essentially comprised of separate financing and sale transactions. For any sale under the zero-down payment plan, Snoring should record a sale of €2,000, which is the amount of consideration attributable to the sofa. The difference between the cash price and the total payment stream is interest revenue, and Snoring should record it under the effective interest method over the two-year payment period.

prevailing interest rate for a similar transaction by an entity with a similar credit rating; or b) a rate of interest that discounts the transaction to the current cash price of the underlying goods or services.

- *Goods sold.* If goods are sold, then measure revenue at the fair value of the consideration received, taking into account the amount of any trade discounts and volume rebates accepted by the entity. When paid in cash, recognize revenue only for the amount of cash received or receivable. You can only recognize revenue from the sale of goods when all of the following conditions have been recognized:

  - *Benefits assured.* The economic benefits associated with the transaction will flow to the entity.

  - *Costs measurable.* The costs related to the transaction can be reliably measured.

  - *Ownership relinquished.* The entity no longer retains management control over the goods sold.

  - *Revenue measurable.* The amount of revenue to be recognized can be reliably measured.

  - *Risks and rewards transferred.* All significant risks and rewards associated with the goods have been transferred to the buyer. This usually coincides with the transfer of legal title or possession to the buyer.

- *Initiation fees.* If an initiation or membership fee only creates a membership condition, then the seller can recognize revenue when there is no significant uncertainty regarding fee collectability. However, if the fee entitles the buyer to services or publications or discounted purchases from the seller during the membership period, then the seller recognizes revenue on a basis that reflects the timing, nature, and value of the benefits provided.

- *Installation fees.* When a seller charges an installation fee associated with a delivery of goods, the seller recognizes revenue in accordance with the stage of completion of the installation. However, if the installation fee is incidental to the sale of goods, then the fee is recognized when the goods are sold.

- *Installment sales.* The buyer may send a series of payments to the seller in exchange for the immediate delivery of goods from the seller to the buyer. In this case, the seller can recognize revenue once the goods are delivered; however, the amount recognized is the present value of all payments, which the seller calculates by discounting the payments at the imputed rate of interest. The seller recognizes the interest portion of the payments as it earns them, which it calculates using the effective interest method.

- *Layaway sales*. Layaway sales occur when goods are delivered to the buyer only when the buyer has completed the final payment in a series of installment payments. In a layaway sale, the seller only recognizes revenue when it delivers the goods. However, if the seller's historical experience shows that most layaway transactions are converted into sales, it can recognize revenue when it receives a significant deposit, provided that the goods are on hand, identified, and ready for delivery.

- *Royalties*. Recognition is in accordance with the terms of the relevant agreement, unless the substance of the agreement calls for a different method. From a practical perspective, recognition may be on a straight-line basis over the term of the agreement. If the agreement is an assignment of rights in exchange for a fixed fee or non-refundable guarantee where the licensor has no remaining performance obligations, the licensor can recognize revenue at the time of sale. If payment under the agreement is contingent upon the occurrence of a future event, revenue should be recognized when it is probable that the fee or royalty will be received.

- *Servicing fees*. A seller of goods may include in the selling price a fee for subsequent servicing or product upgrades. If so, the seller should defer the amount of revenue related to the servicing fee, which should cover the servicing cost and a reasonable profit. It should then recognize the associated revenue over the servicing period.

- *Subscriptions*. When the seller makes deliveries of publications and similar items to the buyer under a subscription agreement, it normally recognizes revenue on a straight-line basis over the period when the items are issued. However, if the items vary in value by period, then the seller should recognize revenue based on the sale value of each item in proportion to the total estimated sales value of all items included in the subscription.

- *Tuition fees*. The provider of educational services should recognize revenue from tuition fees over the period of instruction.

IMPACT OF GOODS OWNERSHIP ON REVENUE RECOGNITION

If an entity retains significant risks of ownership in ostensibly transferred goods, then it cannot recognize related revenue. Examples of significant retained ownership risks are:

- *Contingent conditions*. The buyer of the goods must in turn sell the goods before it pays the entity for the sale.

- *Installation conditions*. Installation is a significant part of the contract, and it has not yet been completed. The seller can recognize revenue immediately after the buyer accepts delivery if the installation process is simple, or when the inspection is performed only for purposes of final determination of contract prices.

- *Performance obligations*. The entity retains an obligation for unsatisfactory performance that exceeds normal warranty provisions.

- *Return rights*. The buyer is entitled to rescind the purchase, and the probability of such return is uncertain. The seller can recognize revenue when the buyer has formally accepted delivery or when the time period allowed for rejection has expired.

Example

Diamond Flatware sells its tableware through the Garnet retail chain. Garnet purchases tableware from Diamond under a consignment agreement. Diamond should recognize revenue from the sale of its tableware only when the goods are sold by Garnet.

If an entity retains an *insignificant* risk of ownership, it can recognize revenue. For example, if an entity has transferred the significant risks and rewards of ownership, except for legal title in order to protect collectibility, then revenue may be recognized. Similarly, a retail establishment can recognize revenue even when customers have a refund right, as long as the retailer can reliably estimate future returns, and recognizes a related liability.

ADVERTISING BARTER TRANSACTIONS

An entity may enter into a barter transaction to provide advertising services in exchange for receiving advertising services from its customer. This can involve the exchange of no cash at all, or approximately equal amounts of cash or other consideration. Two forms of revenue recognition can arise from this scenario:

1. *Similar services*. If there is an exchange of similar advertising services, then the exchange does not result in revenue recognition by either party.

2. *Dissimilar services*. If there is an exchange of dissimilar advertising services, the seller can recognize revenue. It is not allowable to do so based on the fair value of advertising services received. Instead, the

seller can measure revenue based on the fair value of the advertising services it provides, by reference to non-barter transactions that:

a. Involve advertising similar to that included in the barter transaction

b. Occur frequently

c. Involve a different counterparty than in the barter transaction

d. Involve cash or other consideration that has a reliably measurable fair value

e. Represent a predominant number of transactions and amounts as compared to the barter transaction

---

Example

Trouser TV enters into an advertising barter transaction with Macho magazine, where Trouser advertises Macho on its cable network in exchange for similar coverage in Macho magazine. Trouser is providing Macho with five advertising spots of 30 seconds duration. Trouser normally provides such coverage at a rate of $10,000 per spot, and does so frequently with other parties, who pay cash. The proportion of transactions where Trouser is paid cash for advertising is approximately 90 percent of all of its advertising transactions. Accordingly, Trouser TV can recognize the fair value of its advertising as revenue, which is $10,000 multiplied by five coverage spots, or $50,000.

CONSTRUCTION CONTRACT REVENUE RECOGNITION

The contractor can recognize the revenues and expenses associated with a contract, through the stage of completion of the contract at the end of the current reporting period (the *percentage of completion method*), when it can reliably estimate the outcome of the contract.

If the contract is fixed price, the contractor can consider the contract's outcome to be reliably estimated when the following four conditions are satisfied:

- All contract revenue can be reliably measured.
- The benefits of the contract will probably flow to the contractor.
- The remaining contract costs and the stage of completion at the end of the reporting period can be reliably measured.
- Costs attributable to the contract can be identified and reliably measured, so that costs actually incurred can be compared to prior cost estimates.

If the contract is cost plus, the contractor can consider the contract's outcome to be reliably estimated when the following two conditions are satisfied:

- The benefits of the contract will probably flow to the contractor.

- Contract costs, whether or not reimbursable, can be reliably measured.

If the contractor cannot reliably estimate the outcome of a contract, then it can only recognize revenue to the extent of contract costs incurred that it will probably recover, with no profit recognition.

Under the percentage of completion method, the contractor matches revenues with contract costs incurred in reaching a designated stage of completion; this results in the reporting of both revenue and expenses that can be attributed to the proportion of work completed. If the contractor has incurred costs that relate to future contract activity, then it categorizes these costs as an asset (assuming that the costs are recoverable) designated as Contract Work in Progress.

A contractor can use a variety of methods to determine the stage of completion of a contract, including the following:

- Surveys of work performed.

- Completion of a physical proportion of the work.

- The contract costs incurred to date as a percentage of the estimated total contract costs. This calculation should exclude contract costs related to future activity on a contract and payments made to subcontractors in advance of work performed.

Example

Wolf Construction is working on a contract for Mr. Grimm, involving a main house and guest house. The first segment of the contract is for the main house. Wolf spends €180,000 for building materials that have been delivered to the construction site, but which are designated for the guest house, for which no work has yet begun. Wolf has also made an advance payment of €25,000 to Piglet Concrete for the construction of an Olympic-size swimming pool. In both cases, Wolf cannot include the expense in its percentage of completion calculations, since they do not reflect work performed to date.

The percentage of completion method involves making ongoing changes in accounting estimates. As such, changes in estimate are recognized in the period in which the change is made and in subsequent periods; it does not alter the accounting in prior periods.

Example

Wolf Construction enters into a fixed price contract with Amiens Prefecture to build a suspension bridge. The amount of revenue listed in the contract is €5,800,000. Wolf's initial estimate of project costs is €5,000,000 over the expected three-year term of the project.

At the end of Year 1, Wolf revises its estimate of project costs upward to €5,100,000.

In Year 2, Amiens approves a change in the contract scope to include temperature sensors on the bridge surface that will transmit a warning when the road temperature drops below freezing. The scope change calls for a revenue increase of €300,000, and Wolf estimates additional contract costs of €250,000. At the end of that year, Wolf has spent €150,000 for materials that are stored at the construction site, but which are intended for use in the following year.

Wolf calculates its revenue recognition based on the percentage of completion method. A summary of its calculations follows:

	Year 1	Year 2	Year 3
Initial revenue in contract	€5,800,000	€5,800,000	€5,800,000
Contract scope changes	–	300,000	300,000
Total contract revenue	€5,800,000	€6,100,000	€6,100,000
Costs incurred to date	1,785,000	4,013,000	5,350,000
Estimated costs to complete	3,315,000	1,337,000	–
Total estimated contract costs	5,100,000	5,350,000	5,350,000
Estimated profit	€ 700,000	€ 750,000	€750,000
Stage of completion	40%	80%	100%

Wolf calculates the 80% stage of completion at the end of Year 2 without the €150,000 of contract costs related to materials stored for use in Year 3.

Based on the preceding information, Wolf recognizes revenue and expenses by year in the following amounts:

	Project to Date	Prior Years Recognition	Current Year Recognition
Year 1			
Revenue (€5,800,000 × 40%)	€2,320,000	–	€2,320,000
Expenses (€5,100,000 × 40%)	2,040,000	–	2,040,000
Profit	280,000	–	280,000
Year 2			
Revenue (€6,100,000 × 80%)	4,880,000	€2,320,000	2,560,000
Expenses (€5,350,000 × 80%)	4,280,000	2,040,000	2,240,000
Profit	600,000	280,000	320,000
Year 3			
Revenue (€6,100,000 × 100%)	6,100,000	4,880,000	1,220,000
Expenses (€5,350,000 × 100%)	5,350,000	4,280,000	1,070,000
Profit	750,000	600,000	150,000

The contractor should recognize an expected loss immediately when it is probable that total contract costs will exceed total contract revenue. The amount of the loss recognized is not impacted by the stage of project completion or the amount of profits that the contractor may earn from contracts that are not treated as part of the same contract. Examples of situations where contract recoverability is in doubt are:

- Contracts that are not enforceable

- Contracts that are subject to litigation or legislation

- Contracts for property that are likely to be condemned or expropriated

- Contracts where the customer is unlikely to meet its obligations

- Contracts where the contractor cannot meet its obligations

CUSTOMER LOYALTY PROGRAM REVENUE RECOGNITION

A customer loyalty program is used by a company to give its customers an incentive to buy its goods or services. Customers earn award credits by buying from the company, which they can then use to obtain free or discounted goods or services.

A company that issues award credits shall treat them as a separately identifiable component of the sales transaction in which they are granted. The company must allocate the sale between the award credits and the other components of the sale. The amount of the allocation to the award credits shall be based on the fair value of credits, which is the price at which the credits can be sold separately, or the fair value of the awards for which they can be redeemed. In the latter case, the fair value of the awards should be reduced to account for the proportion of award credits that the company does not expect its customers to redeem. If customers can select from a number of awards, then the fair value analysis should reflect an average of the award fair values, weighted for the frequency of expected award selection. If an allocation of consideration to award credits is not possible based on fair values, a company may use alternative methods.

If the company pays out awards itself, then it recognizes revenue for the consideration allocated to the award credits when customers redeem the awards and the company delivers the awards.

Example

Manchester Electronics has a customer loyalty program. It grants participating customers award points every time they purchase from Manchester. Customers can redeem their points for free oil changes at any Manchester store.

(continued)

(*continued*)

The points are valid for three years from the date of each customer's last purchase, so that points essentially have no termination date as long as customers keep buying from Manchester.

During February, Manchester issues 80,000 award points. Management expects that 75% of these points, or 60,000 points, will eventually be redeemed. Management estimates that the fair value of each award point is ten cents, and so defers revenue recognition on €6,000.

After one year, customers have redeemed 30,000 of the award points for oil changes, so Manchester recognizes revenue of €3,000 (30,000 redeemed points/60,000 estimated total redemptions × €6,000 deferred revenue).

During the second year, management revises its redemption estimate, and now expects that 70,000 of the original 80,000 award points will be redeemed. During that year, 20,000 points are redeemed, so that a total of 50,000 points have now been redeemed. The cumulative revenue that Manchester recognizes is €4,286 (50,000 redeemed points/70,000 estimated total redemptions × €6,000 deferred revenue). Since Manchester already recognized €3,000 in Year 1, it now recognizes €1,286 in Year 2.

During the third year, customers redeem an additional 20,000 award points, which brings total redemptions to 70,000. Management does not expect additional redemptions. Accordingly, Manchester recognizes the remainder of the deferred revenue, which is €1,714.

If a third party pays out the awards, the company is essentially collecting the consideration allocated to the awards on behalf of the third party. In this scenario, the company measures its revenue as the difference between the consideration allocated to the award credits and the amount payable to the third party for supplying the awards. The company can recognize this net difference as revenue as soon as the third party becomes obligated to supply awards and is entitled to be paid for doing so. This recognition may arise as soon as the company grants award credits. However, if customers can claim awards from either the company or the third party, revenue recognition only occurs when customers claim awards.

Example

Real Fruit, a purveyor of organically-grown farm produce, participates in the customer loyalty program operated by Icarus Airlines. Real Fruit grants its participating customers one air travel point for every dollar they spend on farm produce. These customers can then redeem the points for air travel with Icarus. Real Fruit pays Icarus €0.008 for each point. During the first year of the program's operation, Real Fruit awards 3 million points.

(*continued*)

Real Fruit estimates that the fair value of an award point is €0.01. It therefore allocates to the 3 million issued points €30,000 of the consideration it has received from the sale of its produce. Real Fruit has no further obligation to its customers, since Icarus is now obligated to supply the awards. Accordingly, Real Fruit can recognize the €30,000 of revenue allocated to the award points at once, as well as the €24,000 expense payable to Icarus (€3,000,000 × €0.008).

If Real Fruit had acted as an agent for Icarus and simply collected funds on behalf of Icarus, then it would only recognize revenue as the net amount it retains, which is €6,000 (€30,000 allocated to the awarded points - €24,000 paid to Icarus).

If the cost of the obligation to supply awards exceeds the consideration received, the company should recognize a liability for the excess amount. This situation can arise, for example, when the cost of supplying awards increases, or when the proportion of award credits redeemed increases.

FRANCHISE FEE REVENUE RECOGNITION

Franchise fees are recognized based on the purpose for which they were charged. The following types of fee recognition can be used:

- *Assets.* The franchisor recognizes fees as revenue either when it delivers assets to franchisees or when it transfers title.

- *Services.* The franchisor recognizes revenue associated with continuing services over the period during which the services are rendered. If the related fee is not sufficient to cover the franchisor's provisioning costs and a reasonable profit, then it must defer the necessary additional amount from its initial franchise fee and recognize it as revenue over the servicing period. The franchisor can recognize the remainder of any initial fee when it has performed all of its obligations to the franchisee.

- *Continuing franchise fees.* When the franchisor charges a fee for various continuing rights or services, it recognizes revenue over the applicable period.

- *Agency transactions.* If the franchisor acts as an agent for a franchisee, such as when it orders supplies on behalf of the franchisee at no profit, this transaction cannot be recognized as revenue.

If franchise fees are collectible over an extended period and there is significant collection uncertainty, then the franchisor recognizes revenue as it collects cash installments.

If the franchisor's obligations under an area franchise agreement depend on the number of outlets established, revenue recognition should be based on the proportion of outlets for which services have been substantially completed.

PROFESSIONAL SERVICES REVENUE RECOGNITION

Commissions can be earned for a variety of transactions. Here are the recognition criteria for several types of commissions:

- *Advertising*. An advertising agency can recognize commissions when the related advertisements are released. If it earns commissions for production work, it recognizes revenue based on the stage of completion of the project.

- *Financial services*. Revenue recognition of fees earned for financial services requires the seller to distinguish between the following:

  ○ Fees that are really part of the interest rate of a financial instrument, which should be treated as an adjustment to the effective interest rate.

  ○ Fees earned for services to be rendered, such as a loan servicing fee or an investment management fee.

  ○ Fees earned upon the completion of a significant act, such as a loan placement fee or a loan syndication fee.

- *Insurance*. An insurance agent is not normally obligated to render further services once the policy commences. If so, the agent can recognize the commission as revenue on the policy commencement date. If the agent is required to render further services during the policy period, then the agent must recognize the commission over the policy period.

SERVICES REVENUE RECOGNITION

An entity is usually able to make reliable revenue estimates after the parties to the transaction have agreed to the terms of settlement, consideration to be exchanged, and each party's rights regarding services to be provided and received. An entity can recognize the revenue associated with services provided when it satisfies all of the following conditions:

- *Revenue measurable*. The amount of revenue to be recognized can be reliably measured.

- *Benefits assured*. The economic benefits associated with the transaction will flow to the entity.

- *Completion measurable*. The stage of completion at the end of the reporting period can be reliably measured.

- *Costs measurable*. The costs related to the transaction can be reliably measured, as can the costs to complete it.

The following issues drive the calculation method used to recognize services revenue:

- *Straight-line recognition*. If the services provided are comprised of an indeterminate number of acts over a specified period of time, revenue should be recognized on a straight-line basis over the designated time period, unless some other method better represents the provision of services.

- *Significant activities*. If a specific activity is substantially more significant than other activities, then an entity should defer revenue recognition until that activity has been completed.

- *Unreliable estimates*. When an entity cannot reliably estimate the outcome of services, it should only recognize revenue to the extent of the expenses recognized that are recoverable. Under this scenario, no profit is recognized. If it is not probable that the costs incurred are recoverable, then the entity does not recognize revenue and it recognizes all costs incurred as expenses.

DISCLOSURES

An entity should disclose the following items:

- *Policies*. The revenue recognition policies the entity has adopted, including the methods it uses to determine stages of completion for the provision of services.

- *Revenue categories*. The amount of revenue associated with each of the following categories:
  - Sale of goods
  - Rendering of services
  - Interest
  - Royalties
  - Dividends

- *Exchanges*. The revenue caused by exchanges of goods or services in each of the preceding categories.

2

EMPLOYEE BENEFITS

INTRODUCTION

There are many types of employee benefits, including compensated absences, bonus plans, and pension plans. This chapter discusses all types of employee benefits and how to account for and disclose them, with particular attention to defined benefit plans.

TYPES OF EMPLOYEE BENEFITS

Short-term employee benefits are those due to be settled within 12 months of the period in which employees render the related service. *Post-employment benefits* are those payable following the completion of employment. *Termination benefits* are payable as a result of either the entity's decision to terminate employment prior to the retirement date, or an employee's voluntary acceptance of redundancy in exchange for those benefits. *Other long-term benefits* are those other than post-employment and termination benefits that will be settled after the 12 months following the period when employees render the related service.

DEFINITIONS

The following terms are central to an understanding of employee benefits:

- *Actuarial gains and losses.* These include adjustments for the differences between previous actuarial assumptions and what has actually occurred, and changes in actuarial assumptions.
- *Defined benefit plan.* A post-employment benefit plan under which an entity provides specific benefits to current and former employees.

17

- *Defined contribution plan.* A post-employment benefit plan under which an entity pays a fixed contribution into a fund.

- *Group administration plan.* An aggregation of individual employer plans that are combined so that participating employers can pool their assets to reduce investment and administration costs. Employee claims within the plan are segregated by employer. From an accounting perspective, a group administration plan is identical to a single employer plan.

- *Multi-employer plan.* A defined contribution or benefit plan that pools the assets contributed by various entities, and uses the assets to provide benefits to the employees of multiple entities. A plan is a defined benefit multi-employer plan if participating entities contribute just enough to it to pay the benefits due in the same period, and employee benefits are determined by the length of their service, and participating entities cannot realistically withdraw without paying an additional contribution for benefits earned but not yet paid.

- *Past service cost.* The change in the present value of defined benefit obligations caused by employee service in prior periods. This cost arises from changes in post-employment benefits or other long-term employee benefits. The change in this cost may be either positive or negative.

- *Post-employment benefit plan.* An arrangement whereby an entity provides post-employment benefits for its employees.

- *Qualifying insurance policy.* An insurance policy issued by an insurer that is not related to the employing entity. The proceeds of the policy can only be used to pay or fund employee benefits under a defined benefit plan, and are not available to the entity's creditors. The proceeds cannot be paid to the entity, unless the proceeds are surplus assets not needed to meet benefit obligations, or the proceeds are reimbursing the entity for benefits already paid.

- *State plan.* A plan established by legislation and operated by a government, which covers all entities or a subset thereof. An entity accounts for its participation in a state plan in the same manner it would account for a multi-employer plan. A state plan is usually a defined contribution plan.

- *Vested employee benefits.* Benefits granted to employees that are not conditional on any future employment.

SHORT-TERM EMPLOYEE BENEFITS

Short-term employee benefits include:

- *Absences.* Compensated absences where payment is settled within 12 months of when employees render related services. Examples are vacation, short-term disability, jury service, and military service.

- *Base pay.* Wages and social security contributions.
- *Non-monetary benefits.* Includes medical care, housing, cars, and various subsidies for other goods or services.
- *Performance pay.* Profit sharing and bonuses payable within 12 months of when employees render related services.

The entitlement to compensated absences can be accumulating or non-accumulating. An *accumulating compensated absence* is carried forward and can be used in future periods. An accumulating compensated absence can be vesting, so that employees are entitled to a cash payment for unused entitlement when they leave the entity. If an accumulating compensated absence is non-vesting, then employees do not receive such a cash payment when they leave the entity.

ACCOUNTING FOR SHORT-TERM EMPLOYEE BENEFITS

Recognize the cost of short-term employee benefits in the period incurred. There is no need to incorporate actuarial assumptions in these costs. Also, do not discount these costs with a present value calculation.

Record a short-term employee benefit as an accrued expense, after deducting any amount already paid. If the amount paid exceeds the undiscounted benefit cost, then record the overage as a prepaid asset to the extent that it will reduce the amount of a future payment or yield a cash refund.

ACCOUNTING FOR A SHORT-TERM COMPENSATED ABSENCE

Recognize the expected cost of a short-term compensated absence when employees render service that increases their entitlement to future compensated absences. Conversely, do not recognize a liability or expense for a non-accumulating compensated absence until the absence occurs.

You must recognize the cost of a compensated absence even if it is non-vesting, though it is permissible to incorporate the possibility of employee departures in the cost calculation.

Example

Jive Mural Company has 50 employees, and all are entitled to three days of paid sick leave each year, which they can carry forward for five years. At the end of the first year, the average unused entitlement accruing during that year is one day per employee. Jive's experience is that all carried forward sick days are used before the end of the five-year period. Thus, Jive expects that it will pay an additional 50 days of sick pay in a future period (50 employees x 1 unused sick day each), and it recognizes a liability for this amount.

ACCOUNTING FOR A PROFIT SHARING OR BONUS PLAN

Recognize the expected cost of a profit sharing or bonus payment only when the entity has a legal obligation to make such a payment based on past events, and if it is possible to reliably estimate the obligation. To have a reliable estimate, there should be a formal plan containing a benefit formula, or the amounts to be paid are determined before the financial statements are authorized for issuance, or the entity's past practices clearly indicate the amount of the obligation.

Example

Sulphur Solutions, the maker of sodium-sulphur batteries, has a profit sharing plan under which it pays 5% of its net profits to those employees who have worked for the company for all 12 months of the year. Sulphur retains the profit distribution for any employees who are not still working for the company at the end of the year. Based on its historical 10% employee turnover rate, Sulphur estimates that it will pay out 4.5% of its profits, and so it recognizes a liability and expense for that amount.

An entity may not be legally required to pay a bonus, but has done so in the past, which creates a constructive obligation to do so in the future. If so, recognize the expected cost of the profit sharing or bonus payment, while also factoring in the possibility of a liability reduction caused by the departure of employees who leave without their profit sharing or bonus payments.

ACCOUNTING FOR A MULTI-EMPLOYER PLAN

If a multi-employer plan is a defined benefit plan, then an entity within the plan accounts for its proportionate share of the defined benefit obligation, assets, and costs associated with the plan in the same way as for any other defined benefit plan.

If there is not enough information to account for the entity's share of a defined benefit plan as such, then account for it as a defined contribution plan.

It may also be necessary to disclose a contingent liability for actuarial losses relating to other entities participating in the plan, or if the plan makes participating entities liable for any shortfalls that arise if other entities stop participating.

ACCOUNTING FOR A DEFINED CONTRIBUTION PLAN

The entity's obligation matches the amount it contributes to the plan in a period, so recognize the contribution amount as an expense. This should be an accrued expense, after deducting any contributions already paid. If the contribution paid exceeds the amount due, then recognize the excess as a prepaid expense, if the prepaid amount reduces future payments or will result in a refund.

Do not use any actuarial assumptions to measure the obligation, since there is no possibility of an actuarial gain or loss. Do not measure obligations on a discounted basis, unless they are due later than 12 months from the period when employees render the related service.

ACCOUNTING FOR A DEFINED BENEFIT PLAN

Follow these six steps to account for each separate defined benefit plan:

1. *Benefit estimation.* Use actuarial methods to estimate the amount of employee benefits earned in the current and prior periods. This requires the use of demographic variables such as employee turnover and mortality, as well as financial variables, such as future changes in salaries and medical costs, that influence benefit costs.

2. *Discounting.* Discount the resulting benefit using the Projected Unit Credit Method. This results in the present value of the obligation, as well as the current service cost.

3. *Fair value.* Determine the fair value of any plan assets.

4. *Gains and losses.* Determine total gains and losses, as well as the amount of those actuarial gains and losses that can be recognized.

5. *Past service cost.* If the plan has been introduced or changed, calculate the past service cost.

6. *Settlement cost.* If the plan has been curtailed or settled, calculate the resulting gain or loss.

Example

Mr. Trent Nectar, president of Ambergris Cuisine, will receive a benefit upon his retirement from Ambergris of 20% of his final annual salary, for each of his remaining years of employment. He will retire in three years. Ambergris expects his salary in each of the three remaining years to be €200,000, €220,000, and €240,000. The discount rate is 4%. The current service cost, pension liability, and interest cost associated with Mr. Nectar's retirement benefit follows:

(continued)

(*continued*)

Year	Salary	Current Service Cost*	Discounted Current Service Cost	Interest Cost**	Year-end Liability***
1	€200,000	€24,000	€22,189	€ –	€22,189
2	220,000	24,000	23,077	888	46,154
3	240,000	24,000	24,000	1,846	71,077
		€72,000	€69,266	€2,734	

*20% of the final-year salary
**4% of the year-end liability
***Cumulative discounted current service cost plus cumulative interest cost

The amount an entity recognizes as a defined benefit liability at the end of a reporting period is the net total of:

+ Present value of the benefit obligation
+ Any unrecognized actuarial gains
− Any unrecognized actuarial losses
− Any unrecognized past service costs
− Fair value of any plan assets from which obligations are to be directly settled
= Amount recognized as a defined benefit liability

If this calculation results in an asset, then measure it at the lower of the calculation or the total of any cumulative unrecognized net actuarial losses and past service cost and the present value of any refunds from or reductions in future contributions to the plan.

An entity only has a right to a refund if it has an unconditional right to it during the plan lifetime irrespective of whether the plan liabilities are settled, or on the assumption that the plan will be gradually settled until there are no members left in the plan, or assuming the full settlement of liabilities in a single event. Do not recognize a refund if the right to a refund depends on a future event. Measure a refund net of any associated costs, such as taxes and professional fees.

The amount of the reduction in future contributions to a plan is the lower of the plan surplus and the present value of the future service cost to the entity for each year over the shorter of the expected life of the plan or the entity. Future service costs shall assume no benefit changes and a stable workforce, unless there are specific commitments that will change these items.

If there is a future minimum funding requirement, and that contribution exceeds the future service cost in any year, the present value of that excess reduces the amount of the asset available as a reduction in future contributions.

ACCOUNTING FOR ACTUARIAL GAINS AND LOSSES

Actuarial gains and losses arise from changes in the present value of a defined benefit obligation, or in the fair value of related plan assets. Such gains and losses are caused, for example, by changes in rates of employee turnover, early retirement, altered rates of mortality, and changes in the estimates of these items for future periods.

When measuring a defined benefit liability, recognize a portion of actuarial gains and losses as income or expense if the net cumulative unrecognized actuarial gains and losses at the end of the reporting period exceed the greater of 10% of the fair value of any plan assets, and 10% of the present value of the defined benefit obligation. These 10% boundaries create a corridor within which actuarial gains and losses are likely to vary over time, and which do not require ongoing recognition.

Calculate and apply these limits separately for each defined benefit plan.

It is allowable to recognize these gains and losses in other comprehensive income, as long as the entity does so for all defined benefit plans and all actuarial gains and losses. Also, do not reclassify these gains and losses to profit or loss in a later reporting period.

If an entity has a surplus in a defined benefit plan, and it cannot recover the surplus under the plan terms through a reduction in future contributions, then take the following steps to recognize actuarial gains or losses in the current period:

- *Actuarial losses.* Immediately recognize any net actuarial losses and past service costs of the current period to the extent that they exceed any *reduction* in the present value of any refunds from or reductions in future contributions to the plan. If there is no reduction, then immediately recognize the net actuarial losses and past service cost of the current period.

- *Actuarial gains.* Immediately recognize any net actuarial gains of the current period after reducing it by the past service cost of the current period to the extent that it *exceeds* any increase in the present value of any refunds from or reductions in future contributions to the plan. If there is no increase, then immediately recognize the net actuarial gains of the current period after deducting any past service cost of the current period.

ACCOUNTING FOR THE RETURN ON PLAN ASSETS

The expected return on plan assets is based on market expectations at the beginning of the period for returns over the life of the related obligations. The difference between the expected and actual rate of return on plan assets is an actuarial gain or loss.

> **Example**
>
> The actuarial assumptions for Ambergris Cuisine's defined benefit plan include an expected return of €150,000 in Year 1. The actual return during that period is €165,000, which produces an actuarial gain of €15,000.

ACCOUNTING FOR PAST SERVICE COST

Past service cost is the change in the present value of defined benefit obligations caused by employee service in prior periods. This cost arises from changes in post-employment benefits or other long-term employee benefits. The past service cost can be negative if an entity changes its benefits so that the present value of the obligation declines.

You should recognize past service cost as an expense on a straight-line basis over the average period until benefits vest. If benefits vest immediately, then recognize the associated expense immediately. There should be no need to amend the amortization schedule unless there is a benefit curtailment or settlement.

> **Example**
>
> Nolan Thermal Energy operates a pension plan for its employees that provides a pension of 1% of final salary for each year of service, following a ten-year vesting period. Nolan increases the pension to 1.5% of final salary. At the date of this change, the present value of the additional benefit for service up to that point for the past ten years is:
>
> | | |
> |---|---:|
> | Employees with more than 10 years of service | €180,000 |
> | Employees with less than 10 years of service | 92,000 |
> | (average remaining vesting period is 4 years) | |
> | | €272,000 |
>
> Nolan must recognize the €180,000 benefit increase immediately, because that benefit is entirely vested. It recognizes the €92,000 portion of the benefit on a straight-line basis over the next four years.

If the entity reduces benefits payable under a defined benefit plan, then recognize the resulting reduction in the benefit liability as past service cost over the average period until the benefits become vested. If there is a combination of some benefit increases and decreases under a defined bene-fit plan, then treat the changes as a single net change.

Past service cost *does not* include:

- Benefit improvement estimates resulting from recognized actuarial gains, if there is an obligation to use plan surpluses for the benefit of plan participants

- Incorrect estimates of discretionary pension increases when there is a constructive obligation to grant the increases

- Increased benefits resulting from employee completion of vesting requirements

- Plan amendments that reduce benefits related to future service

- The impact of the difference between actual and previously assumed salary changes on the benefit obligation for prior years

ACCOUNTING FOR PLAN ASSETS

You should deduct the fair value of any plan assets when calculating the amount to be recognized in the statement of financial position. If there is no market price available for making this determination, then estimate their fair value. For example, you can estimate the fair value by discounting the expected future cash flows arising from the plan assets.

Do not include unpaid contributions from the entity to the fund when making this determination, nor any non-transferable financial in-struments issued by the entity and held by the fund. Also, reduce plan assets by any fund liabilities not relating to employee benefits, such as trade payables.

ACCOUNTING FOR CURTAILMENTS AND SETTLEMENTS

A *curtailment* arises when an entity reduces the number of employees cov-ered by a plan, or amends a benefit plan so that future service by employees will yield reduced benefits; a corporate restructuring is a common cause of a curtailment. A *settlement* occurs when an entity conducts a transaction that eliminates an obligation to pay future benefits; a common scenario is when employees receive a lump-sum cash payment in exchange for their rights to receive post-employment benefits.

You should recognize a gain or loss on a curtailment or settlement of a defined benefit plan when the event occurs, following the re-measurement of the obligation and/or assets using current actuarial assumptions. The gain or loss includes:

- *Fair value*. Any change in the fair value of the plan assets.

- *Gains and losses*. Any actuarial gains and losses and past service cost not previously recognized.

- *Present value*. Any change in the present value of the defined benefit obligation.

When a curtailment or settlement includes only some of the employees covered by a plan or when there is only a partial obligation settlement, you should recognize a proportionate share of the previously unrecognized past service cost and actuarial gains and losses. You calculate the proportionate share on the basis of the present value of the obligations before and after the event, unless there is another more rational basis.

Example

Ambergris Cuisine discontinues its Canola Oil production facility; the employees of that segment will earn no further benefits. Under current actuarial assumptions as of the curtailment date, Ambergris has a defined benefit obligation with a present value of €100,000, plan assets having a fair value of €75,000, and net cumulative unrecognized actuarial gains of €5,000. The curtailment reduces the present value of the obligation by €10,000, to €90,000. 10% of the net cumulative unrecognized actuarial gains relate to the part of the obligation that was eliminated by the curtailment. These changes result in the post-curtailment figures in the following table:

	Prior to Curtailment	Curtailment Gain	Post Curtailment
Obligation present value	€100,000	€(10,000)	€90,000
Plan assets fair value	(75,000)	–	(75,000)
	25,000	(10,000)	15,000
Unrecognized actuarial gains	5,000	500	4,500
Net liability in statement of financial position	€ 30,000	€ (9,500)	€10,500

Ambergris records the curtailment gain with the following entry:

Accrued pension cost	9,500	
Curtailment gain		9,500

DEFINED BENEFIT PLAN AMOUNTS APPEARING IN PROFIT OR LOSS

You should recognize the net total of these amounts in profit or loss:

Actuarial gains and losses	Interest cost
Current service cost	Net actuarial gains or losses
Effect of any curtailments or settlements	Past service cost
Expected return on plan assets and reimbursement rights	

DISCOUNT RATE USED IN ACTUARIAL ASSUMPTIONS

You should refer to the market yields at the end of the reporting period on high quality corporate bonds when determining the discount rate on post-employment benefit obligations. If there is no deep market for such bonds, then use the market yields at the end of the reporting period for government bonds. In either case, use corporate or government bonds whose currency and term are consistent with the currency and estimated term of the post-employment benefit obligations. It may be necessary to estimate the discount rate for longer maturities by extrapolating the current market rate along the yield curve.

You can calculate the interest cost associated with a defined benefit obligation by multiplying the discount rate at the start of the period by the present value of the defined benefit obligation throughout the same period.

PRESENT VALUE METHOD USED FOR DEFINED BENEFIT PLAN CALCULATIONS

Use the Projected Unit Credit Method (PUC method) to calculate the present value of defined benefit obligations, related current service costs, and past service cost. Under the PUC method, each period of service creates an additional unit of benefit entitlement, and measures each unit individually; you then aggregate the units to reach the final obligation amount.

Example

Under Watson Supercomputer's defined benefit plan, a lump sum benefit is payable upon termination of an employee's service, and equals 2% of an employee's final salary for each full year of service. Mr. Bond has a salary in Year 1 of £80,000, which Watson assumes will increase at a compounded rate

(continued)

(*continued*)
of 5% per year. Watson uses an annual discount rate of 8%. The following table shows the increase in the obligation to Mr. Bond over a four-year period, where the pay increases result in a pay level of £92,610 at the end of Year 4:

Year	1	2	3	4
Benefit attributed to:				
- Prior years	0	1,852	3,704	5,556
- Current year (2% of final salary)	1,852	1,852	1,852	1,852
- Current year and prior years	1,852	3,704	5,556	7,408
Opening obligation:	–	1,470	3,176	5,145
- Interest on opening obligation at 8%	–	118	254	412
- Current service cost*	1,470	1,588	1,715	1,852
Closing obligation	1,470	3,176	5,145	7,409
Discount rate	0.79383	0.85734	0.92593	1.0000

*The current service cost is the current year benefit multiplied by the present value discount rate.

ATTRIBUTING BENEFIT TO PERIODS OF SERVICE

The general rule for attributing benefit to periods of service is to do so in accordance with the plan's benefit formula. However, if employee service in later years leads to a materially higher benefit level than in earlier years, then attribute benefit on a straight-line basis from the date when employee service first leads to benefits under the plan, until the date when further employee service leads to no material additional plan benefits (other than from additional salary increases).

Example

The Samson Shoe Company has a defined benefit plan that pays retirees €2,000 for each year of service, payable on their retirement date. Under the terms of the plan, Samson must attribute €2,000 to each year. The current service cost is the present value of €2,000, while the present value of the defined benefit obligation is the present value of €2,000, multiplied by the number of years of employee service through the end of the reporting period.

    Samson offers a different plan to the employees in a labor union, under which they receive a monthly pension payment equaling 0.5% of their final

(*continued*)

full-year wages for each year of service, with pension payments starting at age 70. Under the terms of this second plan, Samson recognizes a benefit equal to the present value, at the expected retirement date of each employee, of a monthly pension of 0.5% of the estimated final salary, which is payable from the expected retirement date to the expected date of death. The current service cost is the present value of this benefit, while the defined benefit obligation is the present value of monthly pension payments, multiplied by the number of years of employee service through the end of the reporting period.

Samson offers a third plan to its management group, under which it pays them a lump-sum benefit of €200,000 that vests after 20 years of service. There is no further benefit for service exceeding the 20-year vesting period. In this case, Samson attributes €10,000 to each of the first 20 years of each manager's employment. Samson adjusts the current service cost in each of the 20 years for the probability that managers will not complete the service period.

Samson also has a post-employment medical plan that reimburses 5% of retiree medical expenses if employees work for the company at least 10 but less than 20 years, and reimburses 40% of these costs if they work for the company for 20 years or more. The 20-year vesting period leads to a materially higher benefit level, so for employees expected to stay with the company that long, Samson attributes the benefit on a straight-line basis for 20 years, which is 2.0% (40% ÷ 20 years) of the present value of the expected medical costs. For those employees expected to leave after 10 years but before 20 years, Samson attributes 0.5% (5% ÷ 10 years) of the present value of the expected medical costs. Samson attributes no benefit for those employees it expects to leave within 10 years.

ACCOUNTING FOR OTHER LONG-TERM EMPLOYEE BENEFITS

Other long-term employee benefits include sabbatical leave, long-term disability benefits, and deferred compensation paid 12 months or more after the period in which they are earned. There is little uncertainty related to these benefits, so accounting for them is simplified. The principal simplifications are that an entity immediately recognizes actuarial gains and losses, as well as all past service costs.

To account for other long-term employee benefits, recognize as a liability the net total of the present value of the defined benefit obligation, minus the fair value of plan assets from which obligations are to be settled. Also, recognize as expense or income the net total of the current service cost, interest cost, expected return on plan assets and reimbursements rights, actuarial gains and losses, and any curtailments or settlements.

If the other long-term employee benefit is for long-term disability and the benefit level depends on the length of service, then recognize the benefit over the service period, factoring in the probability that payment will be required and the period of time over which the entity expects to make payments. If the benefit level is the same irrespective of a service period, then recognize the expected cost when a disability event occurs.

ACCOUNTING FOR TERMINATION BENEFITS

You should recognize termination benefits as a liability and an expense when the entity commits to either terminating employment before the normal retirement date or providing termination benefits due to an offer to encourage voluntary redundancy; if the latter, measure termination benefits based on the number of employees you expect to accept the offer. An entity is committed to a termination only when it has a detailed formal plan for doing so and it is not realistically possible to withdraw from the plan. The formal plan should include the location and function of the affected employees, as well as the approximate number to be terminated, the termination benefits for each job classification, and when the entity will implement the plan.

If termination benefits are due for payment more than 12 months after the reporting period, then record their present value using a discount rate that is based on market yields, at the end of the reporting period, on high quality corporate bonds. If there is no deep market in such bonds, then use the market yields on government bonds instead.

DISCLOSURES FOR A DEFINED BENEFIT PLAN

Disclose the following information for an entity's defined benefit plan. This information can be presented in total for all plans, individually, or in other groupings that are more useful.

- *Accounting policy.* The accounting policy for recognizing actuarial gains and losses.

- *Actuarial assumptions.* The actuarial assumptions in use at the end of the reporting period, including discount rates, expected rates of return on plan assets and on reimbursement rights, salary rates of increase, medical cost trends, and other material actuarial assumptions.

- *Comparative periods.* The present value of the defined benefit obligation, the fair value of plan assets, and the surplus or deficit in the plan for the current annual period and the previous four annual periods. For the same periods, also note the experience adjustments separately for the plan liabilities and assets, expressed as either an amount or a percentage of the period-end liabilities and assets, respectively.

- *Contributions*. The best estimate of contributions the entity expects to be paid into the plan during the annual period beginning after the reporting period.

- *Fair value proportions*. The percentage or amount that each major category of plan assets constitutes, of the fair value of total plan assets; this should at least include equity instruments, debt instruments, and the entity's own financial instruments or property.

- *Funding*. Split the obligation into amounts arising from unfunded plans and from wholly or partly funded plans.

- *General*. The nature of the plan and the financial effects of any changes in the plan during the period.

- *Other comprehensive income items*. The amount recognized in other comprehensive income for actuarial gains and losses, and the cumulative amount of actuarial gains and losses so recognized.

- *Profit or loss items*. The amount recognized in profit or loss for the current service cost, past service cost, interest cost, expected return on plan assets, expected return on reimbursement rights, actuarial gains and losses, the effect of curtailments or settlements, and the line items in which they are included.

- *Rates of return*. The basis for determining the overall expected rate of return on assets, incorporating the effects of major categories of plan assets. Also separately note the actual rates of return on plan assets and any reimbursement rights recognized as an asset.

- *Reconciliation–assets*. Reconcile the opening and closing balances of the fair value of plan assets and reimbursement rights, showing the separate effects attributable to the expected return on plan assets, actuarial gains and losses, effects of foreign exchange rates, employer contributions, plan participant contributions, benefits paid, business combinations, and settlements.

- *Reconciliation–general*. Reconcile the present value of the defined benefit obligation and the fair value of the plan assets to these categories recognized in the statement of financial position, showing net actuarial gains and losses not recognized in the statement, the past service cost not recognized in the statement, any amount not recognized as an asset, and the fair value of any reimbursement right recognized as an asset.

- *Reconciliation–obligations*. Reconcile the opening and closing balances of the present value of the defined benefit obligation, showing the separate effects attributable to current service cost, interest cost, plan participant contributions, actuarial gains and losses, effects of foreign exchange rates, benefits paid, past service cost, business combinations, curtailments and settlements.

- *Sensitivity analysis.* The effect of a one percentage point increase and decrease in the assumed medical cost trend rate on both the aggregate of the current service cost and interest cost components of post-employment medical costs, and the accumulated post-employment benefit obligation for medical costs. Keep all other assumptions constant for this analysis.

3

SHARE-BASED PAYMENTS

INTRODUCTION

An entity may base its payments for goods or services on the price of its shares. The accounting for such transactions varies, depending upon whether the payments are actually settled with equity or cash. This chapter discusses how to recognize these transactions, as well as the impact of a variety of related issues on the transactions, such as vesting, the modification of terms, and reload features.

SHARE-BASED PAYMENTS SETTLED WITH EQUITY

In general, if you settle a share-based payment with an equity instrument, measure the goods or services received at the fair value of the goods or services received. If you cannot reliably estimate this fair value, then measure them at the fair value of the equity instruments issued. The treatment of two subsets of these transactions differ somewhat:

- *Employee services*. Measure the fair value of employee services received in exchange for equity at the fair value of the equity instruments granted at their grant date.

- *Suppliers*. First measure the transaction at the fair value of the goods or services received. If this measurement is not reliable, then measure instead based on the fair value of the equity instruments granted as of the date when the goods are delivered or services rendered.

Example

The Sontag Supercomputer Company orders a specially-designed computer chip from a supplier, and receives delivery on July 31. The supplier has

(continued)

(*continued*)

agreed to accept 10,000 of Sontag's ordinary shares as payment. The chips are custom-designed for Sontag, so it is impossible to directly determine their value. Instead, Sontag assigns a value to the transaction based on the market price of its shares on July 31 (the delivery date) of €5.50. Thus, Wilkerson records an expense of €55,000 on the delivery date.

SHARE-BASED PAYMENTS SETTLED WITH CASH

When an entity settles a share-based payment in cash, measure the goods or services received at the fair value of the offsetting liability. You should re-measure the liability's fair value at the end of each reporting period and at final settlement, and recognize in profit or loss any incremental changes in fair value following each measurement.

Example

The Roadrunner Tire Company grants 10,000 restricted share units (RSUs) to its chief executive officer, Mr. Coyote, under which Roadrunner will pay Mr. Coyote, in cash, the net increase in the RSUs during their vesting period. The grant date is January 1, and the vesting date is December 31 of the same year. On January 1, Roadrunner's stock sells for £5. On April 30, the share price has increased to £6, so Roadrunner records compensation expense of £10,000. On October 31, the share price has dropped back to £5, so Roadrunner reverses the £10,000 charge to compensation expense. On December 31, the settlement date, the share price has risen to £7, so Roadrunner records compensation expense of £20,000 and pays the amount in cash to Mr. Coyote.

If employees must render services in exchange for cash-settled share-based payments, then recognize the services received and the offsetting liability as the employees render service. Again, you should re-measure the fair value of the instruments at the end of each reporting period and at settlement, and recognize any incremental changes in profit or loss.

Example

A-Frame Construction issues two grants to its chief executive officer, Ms. Charis. The first is share appreciation rights worth €50,000 that vest immediately and that require cash payment. Since Ms. Charis has no service period requirement, A-Frame should recognize the full amount of the compensation expense at once.

(*continued*)

The second grant is for share appreciation rights worth €100,000 that vest over 36 months, and which will be paid in cash. Due to the implied 36-month service period, A-Frame should recognize the €100,000 compensation expense ratably over 36 months.

SHARE-BASED PAYMENTS SETTLED WITH CASH ALTERNATIVES?

An entity may enter into a share-based payment transaction where either the entity or the payee can opt for payment in cash or in the entity's equity. You should account for such transactions as cash-settled share-based payments (see the preceding section) if the entity has incurred a cash settlement liability. If there is no such liability, then treat it as an equity-settled share-based payment (see the Share-Based Payments Settled With Equity section).

An entity may grant a payee the right to choose whether the transaction is settled in cash or equity instruments. This is a compound financial instrument, where you treat the right to receive a cash payment as the debt component and the right to receive an equity instrument is the equity component. The accounting treatment varies, depending upon whether the payee is an employee or a supplier:

- *Employee*. If the transaction is with an employee, measure both components at their fair value on the measurement date, taking into account all terms and conditions of the grant.

- *Supplier*. If the transaction is with a supplier, measure the equity component as the difference between the fair value of the goods or services received and the fair value of the debt component as of the receipt date.

For either scenario, on the settlement date, re-measure the liability to its fair value. If the settlement is with an equity instrument, rather than cash, then transfer the liability to equity. If the settlement is with cash, then the offsetting entry is to the liability.

Example

Micronesian Linens buys a flax spinning machine for €500,000. The supplier can choose payment in the form of either 100,000 Micronesian ordinary shares in one year, or a cash payment in three months that equals the market price of 80,000 Micronesian shares. Micronesian estimates that the one-year option has a fair value of €600,000, and the three-month option has a fair value of €450,000.

(continued)

(*continued*)
Upon receipt of the equipment, Micronesian should credit a liability account for €450,000 and credit an equity account for €50,000. The €50,000 represents the difference between the value of the spinning machine and the fair value of the liability.

In other circumstances, the entity has the right to choose whether the transaction is settled in cash or equity instruments, rather than the payee. Accounting for this is a four-step process:

1. Determine whether you have an obligation to settle in cash. This may be the case if there is a past practice of always settling in cash, or if the entity is legally prohibited from issuing more shares. If so, then account for the transaction as a cash-settled share-based transaction.

2. If there is no obligation to settle in cash, but the entity pays in cash, then deduct the payment from equity.

3. If there is no obligation to settle in cash, and the entity pays with an equity instrument, then there is no further accounting transaction.

4. If the entity picks the payment alternative with a higher fair value, then record the excess value given as an additional expense.

DETERMINING THE FAIR VALUE OF AN EQUITY INSTRUMENT

If you measure a share-based payment based on the fair value of the equity instrument granted, then determine fair value using one of the following two methods, in declining order of preference:

1. *Market prices*. Take into account the terms and conditions attached to the granted equity instrument, since they may vary from the equity instruments for which market prices are available.

2. *Valuation technique*. Use a valuation technique to estimate what the price would have been on the grant date between knowledgeable and willing parties.

If there are vesting conditions attached to an equity instrument, do not take them into account when estimating the fair value of the equity at the measurement date. Instead, adjust the number of equity instruments used to measure the transaction, based on the best available estimate of the number of such instruments that will vest. You should revise this estimate if subsequent information indicates that the number of equity instruments likely to vest differs from previous estimates.

On the vesting date, alter the current estimate of the number of equity instruments to vest to match the actual amount that does vest.

In rare cases, it is not possible to measure a share-based transaction based on the fair value of the underlying equity instruments. If so, measure them at their *intrinsic value*, at the initial service date and at the end of each subsequent reporting period as well as the final settlement date. Intrinsic value is the difference between the price a party must pay for the right to receive shares, and the fair value of those shares.

Example

The Mallard Roast Duck franchise chain pays for the services of a legal firm with share options. Each option has an exercise price of €10 and a fair value of €15. The intrinsic value of each option is €5, which is the difference between its fair value and exercise price.

If there is any change in the intrinsic value between the various measurement dates, record the difference in profit or loss. The final settlement date for share options can be the exercise date, forfeiture date, or the end of the option's life.

Meanwhile, measure the goods or services received based on the number of equity instruments that vest or are exercised. For share options, recognize an amount for goods and services received during the vesting period that is based on the number of share options that you expect to vest, which you should periodically update if there is better information, and eventually match to the actual number exercised. If settlement occurs during the vesting period, recognize at once all remaining unrecognized amounts.

If, upon settlement, you pay some additional amount, record the payment as an equity reduction; however, if the payment exceeds the intrinsic value of the equity instruments, recognize the excess as an expense.

After the vesting date, and *only* when the equity instruments are measured at their intrinsic value, reverse all amounts recognized for goods or services received, if the related share options are forfeited or lapse.

THE IMPACT OF VESTING ON SERVICE RECOGNITION

If an entity settles a share-based payment in equity and the equity vests immediately, then the entity presumes that the related services have also been completed, and should recognize the full amount of the transaction at once.

If an entity settles a share-based payment in equity and the equity *does not* vest at once, then the entity presumes that the related services will be provided over the vesting period, and accordingly recognizes the services over the vesting period. There are three conditions under which you can estimate the vesting period:

- *Fixed period*. If the vesting period is fixed in the agreement, then use the stated vesting period over which to recognize the related expense.

- *Market condition*. If the vesting period is dependent upon a market condition, then estimate the expected vesting period, ratably recognize the expense over that period, and do not subsequently revise it.

- *Performance condition*. If the vesting period is based upon the completion of a performance condition, then estimate the vesting period at the grant date, using the most likely outcome. You should revise the vesting period if subsequent information indicates that a different vesting period is more likely.

MODIFICATION OF THE TERMS OF A SHARE-BASED PAYMENT

You may sometimes modify the terms and conditions of an equity instrument, such as altering an option exercise price or the vesting period. These changes can alter the fair value of the equity instrument. The primary measurement concept is to, at least, always recognize goods and services received based on the fair value of the equity instruments on their grant date, unless vesting is not yet complete. This applies even if the instruments are later modified, cancelled, or replaced. In addition, you should recognize instrument modifications that incrementally *increase* the fair value of the instruments. Here are the key accounting issues related to terms modifications:

- *Extra payments*. If the entity makes any payment to an employee or supplier upon the settlement of the instrument, account for it as an equity deduction. If the payment exceeds the fair value of the equity instrument, then recognize the incremental difference as an expense.

- *Liability component*. If a share-based payment arrangement contains a liability component, then re-measure the liability's fair value at the settlement date. If there is a payment to settle the liability, account for it as a liability extinguishment.

- *Replacements*. If an entity grants new equity instruments to an employee and identifies them on the grant date as replacements for cancelled instruments, then recognize the incremental increase (if any) of the fair value of the new instruments on their grant date over the old instruments immediately prior to their cancellation.

- *Settlement*. If an equity instrument is settled during the vesting period, treat it as vesting acceleration, and immediately recognize all remaining expenses that would otherwise have been recognized later in the vesting period.

This answer has assumed that terms modifications are being applied to an equity instrument granted to an employee. If it is granted to a supplier, the accounting treatment is the same, except that you replace the grant date with the date when the entity obtains goods or services from the supplier.

Example

Mr. Smith is the president of High Fidelity Distributors. High Fidelity's board of directors granted him 100,000 restricted stock units (RSUs) on January 1 of Year 1, and they will fully vest on December 31 of Year 3. The RSUs were initially valued at £3.60 each, or £360,000 in total. Since Mr. Smith is assumed to be providing services during the vesting period, the company charges £10,000 to compensation expense in each of the 36 months.

After 10 months, the board of directors decides to modify the terms of the RSUs, so that they vest immediately. At this point, £260,000 of the related expense remains unvested, so High Fidelity must charge the remaining £260,000 to expense as of the date of the modification.

OTHER SHARE-BASED PAYMENT ISSUES

This section contains several minor topics pertaining to share-based payments:

- *Forfeited or not exercised instruments*. There is no subsequent adjustment to total equity after the vesting date of an equity instrument. Thus, if an employee does not exercise share options or a supplier forfeits vested shares, you should not reverse the related amounts recognized for services received.

- *Reload feature*. A reload feature automatically grants additional share options whenever an option holder exercises previously-granted options using an entity's shares to satisfy the exercise price. If a share option contains a reload feature, do not include it in an estimate of the fair value of options granted. Instead, account for it as a new option grant.

- *Repurchase of an equity instrument*. If an entity repurchases a vested equity instrument, account for the payment as a deduction from equity. If the payment exceeds the fair value of the equity instruments that the entity purchased as of the repurchase date, then recognize the excess as an expense.

DISCLOSURES

The disclosure of information about share-based payments is generally to give the users of an entity's financial statements an understanding of the extent and type of such arrangements. More specifically, disclose the following:

- *Description*. Summary of each type of share-based arrangement in existence during the reporting period, and its general terms and conditions.

- *Expenses*. The total expense recognized in the reporting period related to share-based payment transactions, where the goods and services received under such arrangements are recognized at once as an expense. Separately disclose that portion of the expense caused by transactions accounted for as equity-settled share-based transactions.

- *Fair value*. If the fair value of goods or services received were measured directly, then disclose how this determination was made. If the fair value was measured based on the value of equity instruments issued, then disclose the weighted average fair value of the equity instruments granted during the period, as well as the following:

  ○ *Options*. If share options were granted, note the pricing model used, inputs to the model, volatility assumptions and the usage of historical volatility information, and whether other option features were incorporated into the fair value calculation.

  ○ *Other equity instruments*. If equity instruments other than options were granted, note how fair value was determined, the inclusion of dividends in the fair value calculation, and whether other instrument features were incorporated into the fair value calculation.

  ○ *Modified arrangements*. If equity instruments were modified during the period, explain the modifications, the incremental fair value of changes caused by the modifications, and how the incremental fair value of the modifications were measured.

- *Liabilities*. For any liabilities caused by share-based transactions, note the total period-end carrying amount, as well as the total intrinsic value of liabilities at the end of the period where the payee's right to payment has vested.

- *Option pricing*. The number and weighted average exercise prices of share options, broken out for the options outstanding at the beginning and end of the period, exercisable at the end of the period, and for those options granted, forfeited, exercised, and expired during the period.

- *Options exercised*. If share options are exercised during the period, then note the share price on the exercise date; if exercised throughout the period, then disclose the weighted average share price during the period.

- *Options future details*. If share options are outstanding at the end of the reporting period, then note the range of possible exercise prices and the weighted average of the remaining contractual lives of those options.

4

INCOME TAXES

INTRODUCTION

This chapter contains the basic accounting transactions for income taxes, as well as the definitions of related terms used in international financial reporting standards (IFRS). However, income tax regulations vary considerably by government jurisdiction, as may local terminology, so the information noted below should be considered only general guidelines when dealing with local tax situations.

INCOME TAX TERMINOLOGY

There are a number of terms unique to income tax accounting under IFRS. Here are descriptions of the terms most commonly used in conjunction with income tax accounting, as well as explanatory examples:

- *Accounting profit*. The profit or loss *before* deducting the income tax expense.

- *Deferred tax assets and liabilities*. A deferred tax liability is income taxes payable in a future period, while a deferred tax asset is income taxes recoverable in a future period that is caused by a deductible temporary difference, and the carryforward of either unused tax losses or unused tax credits.

- *Tax base*. The amount of an asset that will be deductible for tax purposes against any taxable economic benefits generated by the asset. If the economic benefits are nontaxable, then an asset's tax base equals its carrying amount.

Example

City Tram has the following assets and liabilities at the end of its fiscal year (in millions):

	Carrying Amount	Tax Base	Temporary Difference
Cash	€3,500	€3,500	€ 0
Accounts receivable	8,000	8,500	(500)
Inventory	6,500	7,500	(1,000)
Plant and equipment	11,000	9,250	1,750
Accounts payable	2,000	2,000	0
			€ 250

In the table, the plant and equipment has a different valuation for tax purposes than for its carrying amount. City Tram has also made provisions for receivable bad debts of €500,000 and €1 million for inventory obsolescence, neither of which are allowed in the current year for tax purposes, but which can be used in the future. These issues result in a net difference between City Tram's carrying amounts and tax base of €250,000. Since the income tax rate is 35%, City Tram records a deferred tax provision of €87,500.

Example

Wilberforce Bakeries owns an automated baking oven that cost €100,000, it is depreciating the oven on a straight-line basis over ten years. After three years, it has depreciated €30,000 of the baking oven's cost. The remaining €70,000 cost will be deductible in future periods. The baked goods that Wilberforce produces with the baking oven generate taxable revenue. Consequently, the remaining €70,000 cost of the baking oven is the tax base of the asset, to be deducted against future revenues.

The tax base of a liability is its carrying amount minus any amount related to that liability that will be deductible for tax purposes in the future. If an entity receives revenue in advance, its tax base for the resulting liability will be its carrying amount, less any amount that will not be taxable in the future.

Example

The Aromas retail chain records accrued expenses of €5,000. Aromas reports its taxable results on a cash basis, so there is no tax base for the accrued expenses. If Aromas reported its taxable results on an accrual basis, the accrued expenses would have a tax base of €5,000.

- *Taxable profit*. The profit or loss upon which income taxes are payable. The composition of taxable profit varies by taxation authority, so it will vary depending on the rules of the taxation authorities within which an entity is located or does business.

- *Temporary difference*. The difference between the carrying amount of an asset or liability in the statement of financial position and its tax base. A temporary difference can be either of the following:

  ○ *Deductible*. A deductible temporary difference is a temporary difference that will yield amounts that can be deducted in the future to determine taxable profit or loss.

  ○ *Taxable*. A taxable temporary difference is a temporary difference that will yield taxable amounts in the future to determine taxable profit or loss.

In both cases, the differences are settled when the carrying amount of the asset or liability is recovered or settled.

Example

Brooklyn Pottery Company has a taxable temporary difference when it depreciates an automated glazing machine using accelerated depreciation for tax purposes, but uses straight-line depreciation to determine its accounting profit.

Brooklyn also has a taxable temporary difference when it deducts rent expenses on a cash payment basis to calculate its tax profit, but records it as a prepaid expense to calculate its accounting profit.

Example

Industrial Waste Management has a deductible temporary difference when it deducts retirement benefit costs to calculate its accounting profit, but does not deduct it for tax profit purposes until Industrial pays the benefits.

Similarly, Industrial has another deductible temporary difference when it recognizes research costs as an expense to determine its accounting profit, but cannot include it in the tax profit calculation until a later period.

Example

Cleaner Vacuum Company has an accounting profit of €500,000, as well as €60,000 of taxable temporary differences and €30,000 of deductible temporary differences. Its taxable income is:

(*continued*)

(continued)

Accounting profit	€500,000
Taxable temporary differences	(60,000)
Deductible temporary differences	30,000
Taxable profit	€470,000

Cleaner is subject to a 30% income tax rate. It records the following income tax entry:

Income tax expense - current	141,000	
Income tax expense - deferred	9,000	
Deferred tax asset	9,000	
Deferred tax liability		18,000
Payables – income taxes		141,000

Because of temporary differences, the tax expense that an entity incurs in a reporting period is usually comprised of both current tax expense or income, and deferred tax expense or income.

TAX PLANNING

A tax planning opportunity is an action an entity must take to create or increase taxable income in a period before the expiration of a tax loss or tax credit carryforward. Examples of tax planning are:

- *Asset swap*. Selling an asset that generates non-taxable income and using the funds to buy another asset that generates taxable income.

- *Asset sale*. Selling an asset that has appreciated, and for which the tax base has not been adjusted to reflect the appreciation. A variation on this approach is the sale and leaseback transaction (see the Leases chapter).

- *Deduction deferral*. Delay the recognition of some deductions from taxable profit that can be deferred.

- *Recognition basis*. Elect to recognize interest income for the calculation of taxable profit on either a received or receivable basis.

TAX ASSETS AND LIABILITIES

For both prior and current periods, you should measure tax liabilities and assets at the amount you expect to pay or be paid by a taxing authority. For future periods, you should measure deferred tax assets and liabilities at the tax rates that you expect to apply when the asset is realized or when the liability is settled.

In both cases, base the measurements on the tax rates that have been substantively enacted by the end of the reporting period.

When different tax rates apply to different amounts of taxable income, measure deferred assets and liabilities at the average rate that you expect to apply to the taxable profit or loss of the periods in which the differences should reverse.

When measuring deferred tax assets or liabilities, assume the tax consequences that will arise from the manner in which you expect to recover or settle the carrying amounts of the items under consideration.

Example

The Competition Kayak Company owns a baking oven in which it hardens polyethylene kayak molds. The oven has a carrying amount of £40,000 and a tax base of £30,000. Competition will incur a tax rate of 25% if it sells the oven, while a tax rate of 35% applies to other income.

Competition recognizes a deferred tax liability of £2,500 (£10,000 × 25% tax rate) if it expects to sell the oven without further use, or a deferred tax liability of £3,500 (£10,000 × 35% tax rate) if it expects to retain the oven and recover its carrying amount through continuing use.

Some tax jurisdictions require a different tax rate if the entity pays dividends, or may make some taxes refundable or payable in the event of a dividend payment. If so, measure current and deferred tax assets and liabilities at the tax rate that applies to undistributed profits.

Example

The Barstow Machining Company operates in a tax jurisdiction where income taxes are payable at a 40% rate on undistributed profits, with a 10% tax refund when profits are distributed. Thus, the tax rate on distributed profits is 30%. Taxable income for the year is €1 million. There is a net temporary tax difference for the year of €80,000.

Barstow recognizes a current tax liability and income tax expense of €400,000. Since there is no dividend declaration, Barstow does not recognize any tax that would be recoverable in the event of a future dividend. Barstow does recognize a deferred tax liability and deferred tax expense of €32,000 (€80,000 net temporary tax difference × 40% tax rate). This is the amount of income taxes that Barstow expects to pay when it settles the tax difference.

Two months later, Barstow's board of directors recognizes €250,000 of the prior year's taxable income as dividends payable, which triggers an income tax recovery of €25,000 (€250,000 × 10% tax rate reduction). Barstow records the income tax recovery as an income tax reduction and a current tax asset.

INITIAL CREATION OF A TEMPORARY DIFFERENCE

A temporary difference can arise upon the initial recognition of an asset or liability. A common reason is that some portion of an asset is not deductible for tax purposes; if so, an entity recognizes any deferred tax liability or asset, and recognizes the resulting deferred tax expense or income in profit or loss.

If the initial asset or liability recognition arises from a business combination, then the entity recognizes any deferred tax liability or asset, which in turn affects the amount of the goodwill or bargain purchase option that it recognizes as part of the business combination.

Finally, if the initial recognition of an asset or liability does not affect accounting profit or taxable profit, and is not caused by a business combination, then an entity cannot recognize any resulting deferred tax liability or asset at any time, nor can it recognize subsequent changes in the unrecognized deferred tax liability or asset as it depreciates.

Example

The AK-48 Pop-Gun Factory intends to acquire a conveyor belt which costs £40,000, use it for four years, and then dispose of it. AK-48's controller assumes there will be no residual value. The tax rate is 35%. In the tax jurisdiction in which AK-48 is located, depreciation of the conveyor belt is not deductible for tax purposes. When it disposes of the conveyor, any capital gain will not be taxable, nor will any capital loss be deductible.

After one year, AK-48 has depreciated £10,000 of the conveyor's cost, leaving a carrying value of £30,000. AK-48 earns taxable income of £30,000, and pays £10,500 in income taxes. AK-48 does not recognize the deferred tax liability of £10,500 because it results from the initial recognition of the conveyor.

TAXABLE TEMPORARY DIFFERENCES

You should recognize a deferred tax liability for all taxable temporary differences, except when the liability arises from the initial recognition of goodwill, or the recognition of an asset or liability that is not a business combination and affects neither accounting profit nor taxable profit or loss.

Example

Bailey Brick Company has an asset that costs £15,000, and has a carrying amount of £10,000. Cumulative tax depreciation on the asset is £9,000, and the tax rate is 35%.

Bailey's tax base in the asset is £6,000, which is the cost of £15,000 minus cumulative tax depreciation of £9,000. To recover the carrying amount of

(continued)

£10,000, Bailey must earn offsetting taxable income of £10,000; however, it can only deduct the remaining tax depreciation of £6,000. Thus, Bailey will pay income taxes of £1,400 (£4,000 × 35% tax rate) when it recovers the asset's carrying amount.

The difference between the carrying amount of £10,000 and the tax base of £6,000 is a taxable temporary difference of £4,000. Consequently, Bailey recognizes a deferred tax liability of £1,400 (£4,000 × 35% tax rate), which represents the income taxes it must pay when it recovers the asset's carrying amount.

A temporary difference may arise when an entity includes income or expense in accounting profit in one period, but in taxable profit in a different period. This results in a *timing difference*.

Example

Ram-Flow International incurs a large amount of development costs for its hypersonic ramjet engine. In the current year, it capitalized £28 million of development costs and will amortize it over future periods to determine its accounting profit. However, the tax jurisdiction in which Ram-Flow is located requires that all development costs be deducted as incurred to derive taxable profit.

The £28 million of development costs have no tax base, since Ram-Flow has already deducted them from its taxable profit. The temporary difference is the difference between the carrying amount of £28 million and their tax base of zero.

TAXABLE TEMPORARY DIFFERENCES RELATED TO GOODWILL

Many tax jurisdictions do not recognize a reduction in the carrying amount of goodwill as a deductible expense for calculating taxable profit. This results in a tax base of zero. Though there is a difference between the tax base and carrying amount of goodwill, the recognition of a deferred tax liability is not allowed. Similarly, you cannot recognize a reduction in a deferred tax liability resulting from a goodwill impairment loss.

However, it is possible to recognize a deferred tax liability for a *taxable* temporary difference relating to goodwill, if it does not arise from the initial recognition of goodwill.

Example

The Arrow Barley & Charlie consulting firm (ABC) recognizes €1,000,000 of goodwill as a result of a business combination. The tax jurisdiction in which it

(*continued*)

(*continued*)
is located allows it to deduct the goodwill for tax purposes at a rate of 10% per year. In the first year, this means the tax base of the goodwill is €1,000,000 immediately following the business combination and €900,000 at the end of the first year. If the carrying amount of ABC's goodwill at the end of the first year remains unchanged at €1,000,000, then a taxable temporary difference of €100,000 has arisen; this difference does not relate to the initial recognition of goodwill, so ABC can recognize the deferred tax liability.

DEDUCTIBLE TEMPORARY DIFFERENCES

An entity recognizes a deferred tax asset for all deductible temporary differences if it is probable that taxable profit will be available and against which the temporary difference can be utilized. However, this does not apply if the deferred tax asset arises from the initial recognition of an asset or liability in a transaction that affects neither accounting profit nor taxable profit or loss, or which is a business combination.

Example

The Plastic Toy Company recognizes a liability of €100,000 for accrued warranty costs on its children's toy products. The product warranty costs are not deductible for tax purposes until Plastic actually pays a warranty claim. The tax rate is 35%.

The tax base of the accrued liability is zero, while the carrying amount of the liability is €100,000. This results in a deductible temporary difference of €100,000. Thus, Plastic recognizes a deferred tax asset of €35,000 (€100,000 × 35% tax rate), provided that it is probable that Plastic will earn a sufficiently-large taxable profit in the future to benefit from this reduction in tax payments.

Here are other examples of deductible temporary differences resulting in deferred tax assets:

- *Business combination costs*. An entity recognizes identifiable assets and liabilities acquired in a business combination at their fair values. When an entity recognizes a liability at the acquisition date but does not deduct the related cost in the calculation of taxable profits until a later period, this creates a deferred tax asset. A deferred tax asset also arises when an entity recognizes the fair value of an acquired asset at less than its tax base.

- *Fair value situations*. An entity may revalue an asset to its fair value without making a corresponding adjustment for tax purposes. This creates a deductible temporary difference if the asset's tax base exceeds its carrying amount.

- *Research costs*. These costs are deducted for the purpose of calculating accounting profit as the entity incurs them, but it may only be deducted for tax profit calculations in a later period. Thus, the carrying amount of the research costs is zero, but the tax base (the amount that the taxing jurisdiction will allow as a future deduction) may be substantial. The difference is a deferred tax asset from which the entity will benefit whenever it is allowed to recognize the related expense.

- *Retirement benefit costs*. These costs are deducted for the purpose of calculating accounting profit as the entity provides service to the employee, but it may only be deducted for tax profit calculations when contributions are paid by the entity. Thus, the tax base of the liability is usually zero, which results in a deferred tax asset from which the entity will benefit when it eventually pays the contributions.

Deductible temporary differences should only be recorded if it is probable that there will be sufficient future taxable profits to offset them. This situation is probable when there are sufficient taxable temporary differences relating to the same tax jurisdiction and taxable entity which are expected to reverse in the same period as the expected reversal of the deductible temporary difference, or in periods into which a tax loss can be carried back or forward from the deferred tax asset. In these situations, recognize the deferred tax asset in the same period in which the deductible temporary difference also arises.

If there are insufficient taxable temporary differences relating to the same tax jurisdiction and taxable entity, then only recognize the deferred tax asset to the extent that it is probable that the entity will have sufficient taxable profit relating to the same tax jurisdiction in the same period as the reversal of the deductible temporary difference, or in periods into which a tax loss can be carried back or forward from the deferred tax asset. Alternatively, the entity can recognize the deferred tax asset to the extent that tax planning opportunities will create taxable profit in the appropriate periods.

UNUSED TAX LOSSES AND UNUSED TAX CREDITS

You should recognize a deferred tax asset for the carryforward of unused tax losses and unused tax credits to the extent that it is probable that future taxable profit will be available against which the unused tax losses and credits can be utilized.

The existence of unused tax losses is considered strong evidence that future taxable profit may not be available. Thus, when there is a history of recent losses, only recognize a deferred tax asset arising from unused tax losses or credits to the extent that the entity has sufficient taxable temporary differences, or if there is convincing evidence that sufficient taxable profit will be available to offset the unused tax losses or credits.

Consider the following criteria when assessing the probability of a future taxable profit against which to offset unused tax losses or credits:

- *Recurrence*. Do unused tax losses result from causes that are unlikely to recur?

- *Sufficient differences*. Are there sufficient taxable temporary differences that will result in taxable amounts against which unused tax losses or credits can be used prior to expiration?

- *Tax planning*. Are tax planning opportunities available that will create a taxable profit in the period when unused tax losses or credits can be utilized?

- *Timing*. Is it probable that the entity will have taxable profits before the unused tax losses or credits expire?

Do not recognize a deferred tax asset to the extent that it is not probable that taxable profit will be available for use against unused tax losses or credits.

THE TAX EFFECTS OF A BUSINESS COMBINATION

When an entity acquires assets and liabilities in a business combination, it recognizes them at their fair values as of the acquisition date. It will record temporary differences when the tax bases of the acquired assets and liabilities are either not affected by the business combination, or are affected differently.

Example

When Cleaner Vacuum Company acquired Big Suction Ltd., it increased the carrying amount of Big Suction's production equipment to fair value. However, the tax base of the production equipment remained at the previous owner's tax base. This creates a taxable temporary difference that results in a deferred tax liability.

If an entity is about to enter into a business combination as the acquirer, it should review its existing deferred tax assets to see if there is a changed probability of recovering the tax asset. For example, the acquiring entity may find that it can use previously unused tax losses against the future taxable profits of the acquiree. If so, the acquiring entity recognizes a change in the deferred tax asset in the same period as the business combination, but not as part of the accounting for the business combination. Thus, any such change has no impact on the acquiring entity's measurement of goodwill or bargain purchase gains associated with the business combination.

An acquiring entity can recognize acquired deferred tax benefits after a business combination, if it results from new information about facts and circumstances that existed at the acquisition date. The acquiring entity must apply these changes to the reduction of any goodwill relating to that acquisition. If the goodwill carrying amount is zero, then the acquiring entity shall recognize any remaining deferred tax benefits in profit or loss.

The acquiring entity shall recognize all other acquired deferred tax benefits that are realized in profit or loss.

THE TAX IMPACT OF INVESTMENTS IN OTHER ENTITIES

When there is a difference between the carrying amount and the tax base of an entity's investment in a subsidiary, branch, associate, or joint venture, this is a temporary difference. Examples of situations where this temporary difference can arise are:

- *Carrying amount*. When the entity reduces the carrying amount of its investment in an associate to what it estimates is the recoverable amount.

- *Exchange rates*. When there are changes in foreign exchange rates when the entities are based in different countries.

- *Profits*. When there are undistributed profits from a subsidiary, branch, associate, or joint venture.

A parent entity shall recognize a *deferred tax liability* for all taxable temporary differences involving its investments in subsidiaries, branches, associates, and joint ventures, unless the parent can control the timing of the reversal of a temporary difference *and* the temporary difference will probably not reverse in the foreseeable future. The parent entity can control the timing of the reversal of a temporary difference if it can control the dividend policy of the other entity.

A parent entity shall recognize a *deferred tax asset* for all deductible temporary differences involving its investments in subsidiaries, branches, associates, and joint ventures, but only to the extent that it is probable that the temporary difference will reverse in the foreseeable future and that a taxable profit will be available against which the temporary difference can be utilized.

If an entity's taxable profit or loss is determined in a different currency, then changes in the exchange rate create temporary differences. The entity should recognize this deferred tax liability or asset, and charge or credit the resulting deferred tax to profit or loss.

OTHER TAX ISSUES

This section describes the appropriate treatment under IFRS for a number of tax issues not large enough to justify separate discussion in their own sections:

- *Asset revaluation.* If you revalue an asset for tax purposes, and the revaluation is related to an accounting revaluation from another period, then recognize the tax effects of the asset revaluation and the tax base adjustment in other comprehensive income in the period in which they occur. If the revaluation for tax purposes is not related to an accounting revaluation from another period, then recognize the tax effects of the adjustment in profit and loss.

- *Carry back tax loss recognition.* If you record a tax loss that you can carry back to recover taxes paid in a previous period, you can recognize the eligible tax loss as an asset in the current period.

- *Carrying amount of deferred tax assets and liabilities.* You should alter the carrying amount of deferred tax assets and liabilities to match any changes in the amount of related temporary differences. In addition, change the carrying amounts when there is a change in tax rates, a change in the expected manner of asset recovery, or a reassessment of the recoverability of deferred tax assets. You should review the carrying amount of deferred tax assets at the end of each reporting period. Reduce the carrying amount of a deferred tax asset to the extent that it is no longer probable that sufficient taxable profit will be available for offset against the deferred tax asset. It is allowable to later reverse this reduction to the extent that it becomes probable that sufficient taxable profit will become available for offset.

- *Discounting of deferred tax assets and liabilities.* Discounting a deferred tax asset or liability requires a present value analysis that contains detailed payment and/or payout schedules. Given the uncertainty and complexity of future tax scenarios, it is difficult to create reliable discounted information, and so it is not required to report deferred tax assets or liabilities in this manner.

- *Goodwill less than its tax base.* If the carrying amount of goodwill from a business combination is less than its tax base, record a deferred tax asset. Recognize it to the extent that it is probable that taxable profit will be available against which the deductible temporary difference could be utilized.

- *Reassessment of unrecognized deferred tax assets.* Reassess unrecognized deferred tax assets at the end of each reporting period. You should recognize a previously unrecognized deferred tax asset to the extent that it has become probable that future taxable profit will allow for the recovery of the deferred tax asset.

- *Tax liability recognition.* You should record the current tax for current and prior periods as a liability, if not already paid. If you have paid more than the tax amount due in the current and prior periods, record the excess as an asset.

- *Tax recognition.* You should recognize current and deferred taxes as income or expense, except to the extent that the tax arises from a business combination or a transaction or event that is recognized outside profit or loss (e.g., in other comprehensive income or equity).

- *Tax withholdings on dividends.* If a tax jurisdiction requires that an entity remit a portion of any dividends on behalf of shareholders, then you should charge the amount remitted to the tax authorities to equity as part of the dividends.

- *Taxes on share-based payments.* Some tax jurisdictions grant to an entity a tax deduction for remuneration paid with various forms of equity, such as shares or share options. If so, there may be a timing difference between the receipt of services and equity grants, which results in a deductible temporary difference that the entity can record as a deferred tax asset. The amount of the tax deduction granted by the tax jurisdiction may not be ascertainable at once, since, for example, it may be based on the entity's share price on the date a share option is exercised. If so, the entity should estimate the amount of the deferred tax asset based on information available at the end of the period (such as the entity's share price at the end of the period).

OFFSETTING OF TAX ASSETS AND LIABILITIES

You can offset current tax assets and current tax liabilities in the balance sheet only when the entity has a legally enforceable right to do so, and intends to settle them on a net basis, or to settle both simultaneously.

You can offset deferred tax assets and deferred tax liabilities only when the entity has a legally enforceable right to do so, and these assets and liabilities relate to income taxes levied by the same tax jurisdiction on either the same taxable entity or different entities that intend to settle these assets and liabilities on a net basis or to settle both simultaneously.

DISCLOSURES

You should separately disclose the major components of tax income or expense. These components may include:

- Adjustments recognized in the period for current tax of prior periods
- Benefits arising from a previously unrecognized tax loss, tax credit, or temporary difference of a prior period used to reduce current tax expense
- Benefits from a previously unrecognized tax loss, tax credit, or temporary difference from a prior period that reduces deferred tax expense
- Changes in a pre-acquisition deferred tax asset caused by a business combination
- Current and deferred tax for items charged or credited to equity
- Current tax income or expense
- Deductible temporary differences, unused tax losses, and unused tax credits for which no deferred tax asset is recognized
- Deferred tax assets and the reason for recognizing them when utilizing them depends on future taxable profits exceeding those arising from the reversal of existing taxable temporary differences and the entity has recorded a recent loss
- Deferred tax benefits acquired in a business combination and recognized after the acquisition date, along with the description of the event causing the recognition
- Deferred tax expense from the write-down or reversal of a previous write-down of a deferred tax asset
- Deferred tax income or expense for changes in tax rates or new taxes
- Deferred tax income or expense relating to the origination and reversal of temporary differences
- Explanation of changes in the tax rate compared to the previous period
- For discontinued operations, the tax expense relating to the discontinuance gain or loss, and the profit or loss from the ordinary activities of the discontinued operation for all periods presented
- For each type of temporary difference, unused tax loss, unused tax credit, the amount of the deferred tax assets and liabilities recognized for each period presented, and the amount of deferred tax income or expense recognized in profit or loss

- Income tax consequences of proposed or declared dividends to shareholders, but not recognized as a liability

- Income tax for each component of other comprehensive income

- Potential income tax consequences resulting from the payment of dividends

- Reconciliation between tax income or expense and accounting profit

- Tax income or expense relating to changes in accounting policies or errors that are included in profit or loss

- Temporary differences for investments in subsidiaries and other entities for which deferred tax liabilities have not been recognized

PART TWO

ASSETS AND LIABILITIES

5

FINANCIAL INSTRUMENTS

INTRODUCTION

This chapter contains a discussion of two related topics–how to account for financial instruments, and for the hedges used to reduce their risk. There are a number of sub-topics as well that tie back to the main topic, such as how to use the effective interest method to record a financial asset, how to derive the fair value of a financial asset or liability, and how to qualify for a hedging relationship. The accounting for several different types of hedges is also noted, including fair value hedges, cash flow hedges, and the net investment hedge.

DEFINITIONS

The following definitions are useful for gaining an understanding of the concepts noted later in this chapter:

- *Available for sale investment*. A non-derivative asset that is designated as available for sale. It is not classified as held-to-maturity, or a loan, a receivable, or a financial asset at fair value through profit or loss.

- *Derecognition*. The removal of a financial asset or liability from an entity's statement of financial position that it had previously recognized. You should derecognize a financial asset if either the entity's contractual rights to the asset's cash flows have expired, or the asset has been transferred to a third party.

- *Derivative*. A financial instrument whose value changes in relation to changes in a variable, such as an interest rate, commodity price, credit rating, or foreign exchange rate. It also requires either a small or no initial investment, and it is settled at a future date. It allows an entity to speculate on or hedge against future changes in market factors at minimal initial cost. Examples of derivatives are call options, put options, forwards, futures, and swaps.

- *Hedge effectiveness*. The amount of changes in the fair value or cash flows of a hedged item that are offset by changes in the fair value or cash flows of a hedging instrument.

- *Hedged item*. An asset, liability, commitment, highly probable transaction, or investment in a foreign operation that exposes an entity to changes in fair value or cash flows, and is designated as being hedged.

- *Hedging instrument*. A designated financial instrument whose fair value or related cash flows should offset changes in the fair value or cash flows of a designated hedged item.

- *Hedging*. A risk reduction technique whereby an entity uses a derivative or similar instrument to offset future changes in the fair value or cash flows of an asset or liability.

- *Held-to-maturity investment*. A non-derivative financial asset having either fixed or determinable payments and a fixed maturity, and which an entity has both the ability and the intention to hold to maturity. It does not include financial assets that the entity designates as being at fair value through profit or loss, or as available for sale, or as loans, or receivables.

INITIAL ACCOUNTING FOR A FINANCIAL ASSET OR LIABILITY

An entity initially recognizes a financial asset or liability only when the entity becomes a party to the contractual provisions of the instrument. At that time, it recognizes the asset or liability at its fair value. Also, if the entity is not recognizing the asset or liability at its fair value through profit or loss, it should add to the fair value those transaction costs directly attributable to the acquisition or issuance of the asset or liability.

Example

The Micro Cell Phone Company acquires 10,000 shares of Scottish Cellular for £52 each, and incurs broker fees of £1 per share. Micro classifies the shares as available for sale, so that it does not recognize changes in fair value in profit or loss. Micro records the following entry, which includes the broker fee in the carrying amount of the available for sale asset:

Available for sale asset	530,000	
Cash		530,000

SUBSEQUENT ACCOUNTING FOR A FINANCIAL ASSET OR LIABILITY

After initial recognition, an entity classifies its financial assets into the following categories for measurement purposes:

- *Available-for-sale financial assets.* Measured at their fair value.

- *Financial assets at fair value through profit or loss.* Measured at their fair value.

- *Held-to maturity investments.* Measured at their amortized cost using the effective interest method.

- *Loans and receivables.* Measured at their amortized cost using the effective interest method.

If an entity invests in equity instruments that do not have a quoted market price in an active market, it should measure them at their cost.

After initial recognition, an entity measures all financial liabilities at their amortized cost using the effective interest method (see The Effective Interest Method section). However, it should not do so for financial liabilities designated at fair value through profit or loss.

DERECOGNITION OF A FINANCIAL ASSET OR LIABILITY

Follow these seven steps to derecognize a financial asset or liability:

1. *Segregate assets.* Segregate a part of a financial asset for derecognition purposes if it comprises of only specifically identified cash flows from a financial asset, it comprises of only a pro rata share of the cash flows from a financial asset, or it comprises of only a fully proportionate share of specifically identified cash flows from a financial asset.

2. *Identify asset expiration or transfer.* Apply the derecognition steps either to the financial asset in its entirety, or to the segregated parts of a financial asset that were segregated in the first step. Only apply derecognition steps when the entity's contractual rights to the cash flows from the financial asset expire, or it transfers the financial asset. A financial asset transfer only occurs when the entity transfers the contractual rights to receive cash flows from the financial asset, or it retains these rights but it assumes an obligation to pay the cash flows to a recipient (and shifts the risks and rewards of ownership, as well as control over the asset, to the recipient). To see if the risks and rewards of ownership have shifted, it may be necessary to compare the entity's exposure to variability in the present value of future net cash flows both before and after the transfer.

3. *Segregate servicing rights.* If the entity transfers the financial assets but retains the right to service the asset for a fee, then recognize a servicing asset or liability for the contract.

4. *Recognize new asset or liability.* If the entity transfers the asset or liability but obtains a new financial asset or liability as part of the transfer, then recognize it at its fair value.

5. *Derecognize.* Derecognition varies depending on the status of the transferred or canceled assets or liabilities, as follows:

    a. *Entire item.* If the entity derecognizes the entire financial asset or liability, it recognizes in profit or loss the difference between the carrying amount and the sum of any consideration received and any cumulative gain or loss that had been recognized in other comprehensive income.

    b. *Partial item.* If the entity derecognizes a portion of a financial asset or liability, it allocates the carrying amount of the total asset or liability between the parts to be recognized and derecognized, based on the fair values of the two parts on the transfer date. The amount it recognizes in profit or loss is based on the same calculation used if it had been for the entire financial asset or liability.

    c. *Some continuing involvement.* If the entity has some continuing involvement with an asset or liability, it measures the transferred amounts based on the rights and obligations that it has retained. In this calculation, the retained liability is either the amortized cost of the rights and obligations retained by the entity (if measured at amortized cost) or equal to their stand-alone fair value (if measured at fair value).

6. *Liability exchange.* If there is an exchange between an existing borrower and lender of debt instruments and the terms are substantially different, then the parties account for the original financial liability as a debt extinguishment, and recognize a new financial liability. The same accounting applies if there is a substantial modification of the terms of an existing financial liability. The difference between the carrying amount of the extinguished debt and the consideration paid for the replacement debt is recognized in profit or loss.

7. *Continuing income and expense recognition.* The entity continues to recognize any income earned or expense incurred on transferred assets and liabilities to the extent of its continuing involvement.

THE EFFECTIVE INTEREST METHOD

The effective interest method is a technique for calculating the amortized cost of a financial asset or liability, and which allocates interest income or expense over the relevant period. The calculation includes all fees and points paid or received, transaction costs, and all premiums and discounts. The *effective interest rate*, which is used in the calculation, exactly discounts estimated future cash payments or receipts over the expected life of the instrument.

Example

Toner Equipment Company, which makes fine chrome-plated weight lifting equipment, acquires a debt security having a stated principal amount of €100,000, which the issuer will repay in three years. The debt has a coupon interest rate of 5%, which it pays at the end of each year. Toner acquires the debt for €90,000, which is a discount of €10,000 to the principal amount of €100,000. Toner classifies the investment as held-to-maturity, and records this entry:

Held-to-maturity investments	90,000	
Cash		90,000

Based on a cash outflow of €90,000 to acquire the investment, three interest payments of €5,000 each, and a principal payment of €100,000 upon maturity, Toner calculates an effective interest rate of 8.95%. Using this interest rate, Toner calculates the following amortization table:

Year	(A) Beginning Amortized Cost	(B) Interest and Principal Payments	(C) Interest Income [A × 8.95%]	(D) Debt Discount Amortization [C − B]	Ending Amortized Cost [A + D]
1	90,000	5,000	8,055	3,055	93,055
2	93,055	5,000	8,328	3,328	96,383
3	96,383	105,000	8,617	3,617	100,000

Using the table, Toner makes the following entries at the end of each of the next three years:

YEAR 1:

Cash	5,000	
Held-to-maturity investment	3,055	
Interest income		8,055

YEAR 2:

Cash	5,000	
Held-to-maturity investment	3,328	
Interest income		8,328

(continued)

(continued)

YEAR 3:

Cash	105,000	
Held-to-maturity investment		96,383
Interest income		8,617

HOW TO DERIVE THE FAIR VALUE OF A FINANCIAL ASSET OR LIABILITY

The best evidence for fair value is a quoted price in an active market. If this source is not available, then the next best evidence is a valuation technique that assumes an arm's-length exchange. All of these valuation techniques are acceptable:

- Recent arm's-length market transactions between knowledgeable parties

- The current fair value of another instrument that is substantially the same

- Discounted cash flow analysis

- Option pricing models

If a valuation technique is currently being used by market participants to price the instrument, and that technique provides reliable pricing estimates, then that is the preferred technique.

It is better to use a valuation technique that uses market information as inputs, rather than entity-specific information.

Example

Lodestone Crystal, purveyors of fine crystal figurines, acquires 5,000 shares of Emerald Designs Ltd. for £15 per share, and classifies them as at fair value through profit or loss. At the end of the year, the quoted price of Emerald's shares declined to £13 per share. At the end of the following year, Lodestone sells the shares for £16 each. Lodestone records the following journal entries:

AT INITIAL STOCK PURCHASE:

Assets at fair value through profit or loss	75,000	
Cash		75,000

(continued)

AT THE END OF YEAR 1:

Profit or loss	10,000	
Assets at fair value through profit or loss		10,000

AT THE END OF YEAR 2:

Cash	80,000	
Assets at fair value through profit or loss		65,000
Gain		15,000

When measuring a financial liability that has a demand feature, its fair value must always be not less than the amount payable on demand, discounted from the first demand date.

ACCOUNTING FOR A CHANGE IN CARRYING COST

If it becomes appropriate to carry a financial asset or liability at its cost or amortized cost rather than its fair value, then the entity uses the fair value on the conversion date as its new carrying amount. If the entity had previously recognized any gains or losses in other comprehensive income, it recognizes the amounts under one of the following two methods:

- *Fixed maturity asset.* If the financial asset has a fixed maturity, then amortize the gain or loss to profit or loss over the remaining life of the investment, using the effective interest method.

- *No fixed maturity asset.* If the financial asset has no fixed maturity, recognize the gain or loss in profit or loss when the entity sells or disposes of the financial asset.

ACCOUNTING FOR A FAIR VALUE CHANGE IN A FINANCIAL ASSET

If there is a gain or loss in the fair value of a financial asset, and it is not part of a hedging relationship, then you account for it as follows:

- *Classified as at fair value through profit or loss.* If there is a gain or loss on a financial asset that is classified as at fair value through profit or loss, then recognize it in profit or loss.

- *Classified as available-for-sale.* If there is a gain or loss on a financial asset or liability that is classified as available-for-sale, then recognize it in other comprehensive income, and in profit or loss upon derecognition.

- *Carried at amortized cost.* If there is a gain or loss on a financial asset or liability that an entity carries at amortized cost, then recognize it in profit or loss upon derecognition, as well as through the amortization process.

ACCOUNTING FOR FINANCIAL ASSET IMPAIRMENT

At the end of each reporting period, assess whether there is any objective evidence of financial asset impairment. Such evidence arises from a *loss event* that impacts the estimated future cash flows of the asset. The loss event may actually be the cumulative effect of several events. The event must already have occurred; a loss expected from a future event does not cause a loss event. All of the following are loss events that can cause financial asset impairment or uncollectibility:

- The issuer or obligor is in significant financial difficulty.

- There has been a default or delinquency in interest or principal payments.

- The entity has granted the borrower a concession for legal or economic reasons.

- The borrower will likely enter bankruptcy or another form of reorganization.

- There is no active market for the financial asset, due to financial difficulties. However, a loss event does not arise just because an entity's financial instruments are no longer publicly traded.

- There is a measurable decline in estimated future cash flows from a group of financial assets since their initial recognition, caused by either declines in the payment status of borrowers or regional economic conditions correlating with asset defaults in the group.

- There is a significant or prolonged decline in the fair value of an equity investment below its cost.

Example

The Masterson Mortgage Company notes a decrease in property prices in the London district where it normally issues mortgages. This condition correlates strongly with mortgage defaults, so Masterson is experiencing a loss event.

The type of accounting for an impaired or uncollectible financial asset varies by the type of asset, which follows:

- *Available-for-sale assets.* If a fair value decline has already been recognized in other comprehensive income, reclassify the cumulative loss into profit or loss to the extent of the impairment. The amount so reclassified is the difference between the acquisition cost of the financial asset (net of principal repayments and amortization) and the current fair value, minus any previously recognized impairment loss.

- *Financial assets carried at cost.* Measure the amount of the loss as the difference between the asset's carrying amount and the present value of estimated future cash flows. For the discounting calculation, use the current market rate of return for similar assets.

- *Loans, receivables, held-to-maturity investments.* Measure the amount of the loss as the difference between the asset's carrying amount and the present value of estimated future cash flows. For the discounting calculation, use the effective interest rate used at initial recognition. Recognize the loss in profit or loss.

If an entity does not find that impairment is significant for an individual financial asset, it should include the asset in a group of assets having similar credit risk, and assess the group for impairment. If it recognizes an impairment loss for an individual asset, it does not include that asset in an impairment assessment of a group of assets.

It is allowable to reverse an impairment loss on a debt instrument classified as available-for-sale or a financial asset carried at amortized cost in a subsequent period. You can reverse the amount of an earlier impairment loss if the amount of the impairment subsequently declines, and the decline relates to an event occurring after the initial impairment recognition. You

---

Example

Smoke Alarm Company invests €50,000 in a debt security and classifies it as available-for-sale. The debt security decreases in value by €10,000, so Smoke has an unrealized holding loss of €10,000 that it charges to equity. The issuer of the debt security then has such significant financial difficulties that it appears unlikely that it can repay the debt security. Smoke's management decides that this constitutes objective evidence of impairment equaling the unrealized holding loss, and uses the following entry to recognize the loss:

Impairment loss	10,000	
Equity		10,000

should recognize the reversal in profit or loss, up to the amount of the original impairment.

An impairment loss on a financial asset carried at cost, or on an equity instrument classified as available for sale, is not reversible.

QUALIFYING FOR A HEDGING RELATIONSHIP

A hedging relationship only qualifies for hedge accounting if it meets all of the following criteria:

- *Documentation*. You must formally designate a hedge at its inception, as well as document the hedging relationship, the entity's risk management objective, and its strategy for undertaking the hedge. The documentation should identify the hedging instrument, the item being hedged, the nature of the risk to be hedged, and how the entity plans to assess the hedging instrument's effectiveness in offsetting fair value or cash flow changes in the hedged item.

- *Forecast probability*. If the hedge is a cash flow hedge, there must be a highly probable forecast transaction that is the subject of the hedge. Also, the forecast transaction must show an exposure to cash flow variations that could impact profit or loss.

- *Highly effective*. You expect the hedge to be highly effective in offsetting any changes in the fair value or cash flows attributable to the hedged risk.

- *Measurement reliability*. It is possible to reliably measure the effectiveness of the hedge.

- *Ongoing assessment*. You assess the hedge regularly, and determine that it was highly effective throughout the financial reporting periods for which you designated the hedge.

ACCOUNTING FOR A FAIR VALUE HEDGE

A fair value hedge is a hedge of an asset's or liability's exposure to changes in its fair value, which is attributable to a particular risk, and which could affect profit or loss.

You should record a gain or loss on re-measurement of the fair value hedge in profit or loss. Also, recognize in profit or loss the gain or loss on the hedged item that is attributable to the hedged risk, while also adjusting the carrying amount of the hedged item.

If there is an adjustment to the carrying amount of a hedged financial instrument for which you are using the effective interest method, then you

---

Example

Beta Investments buys a bond having a face value of £100,000 and paying interest of 4%, and records the purchase as an available-for-sale asset. The 4% rate paid by the bond matches the current market rate. If interest rates increase, the value of the bond will decline, so Beta enters into an interest rate swap, where it swaps the fixed interest payments it receives from the bond issuer for floating interest payments from a third party. Beta appropriately documents the interest rate swap as a hedge of the bond.

Market interest rates subsequently increase, reducing the fair value of the bond by £3,000, so Beta records the following entry:

Hedging loss (hedged item)	3,000	
Available-for-sale asset		3,000

Beta also records an increased value for the swap, which was positively impacted by the same increase in interest rates:

Swap asset	3,000	
Hedging gain (hedging instrument)		3,000

Since the changes in fair value of the bond and the interest rate swap exactly offset each other, there is no net gain or loss, and the hedge is 100% effective.

---

should amortize the adjustment to profit or loss, using a recalculated effective interest rate. However, if it is not practical to use a recalculated effective interest rate, then amortize the adjustment using the straight-line method. No matter what recognition method is used, any adjustment should be fully amortized as of the maturity date.

You should discontinue the hedge accounting if the hedging instrument expires or you sell, terminate, or exercise it. You should also discontinue the hedge accounting if the entity revokes the hedging designation, or the hedge no longer meets the hedge accounting criteria.

ACCOUNTING FOR A CASH FLOW HEDGE

A cash flow hedge is a hedge exposure to cash flow variability. This variability is attributable to either a specific risk on a recognized asset or liability, or a highly probable forecast transaction.

You should account for a cash flow hedge by recognizing the portion of the gain or loss on the hedging instrument in other comprehensive income, but only to the extent of the gain or loss that is effective. You should record the ineffective part of the gain or loss on the hedging instrument in profit or loss.

If you do not expect that a loss previously recognized in other comprehensive income will be recovered in the future, then reclassify the amount you do not expect to recover into profit or loss. Also, you should similarly reclassify a gain or loss previously recognized in other comprehensive income into profit or loss in the same period when the hedged forecast transaction affects profit or loss.

You should terminate cash flow hedge accounting in the following situations:

Termination Event	Resulting Accounting Action
Hedging instrument expires, is sold, terminated, or exercised	Retain cumulative gain or loss recognized in other comprehensive income until the forecast transaction occurs; then generally reclassify to profit or loss.
Hedging instrument no longer meets hedge accounting criteria	Retain cumulative gain or loss recognized in other comprehensive income until the forecast transaction occurs; then generally reclassify to profit or loss.
No longer expect forecasted transaction to occur	Reclassify any gains or losses recognized in other comprehensive income into profit or loss.
The entity revokes the hedging designation	Retain cumulative gain or loss recognized in other comprehensive income until the forecast transaction occurs; then generally reclassify to profit or loss. If the transaction is no longer expected to occur, reclassify to profit or loss.

Example

Puntagorda Hydroelectric orders a turbine from a supplier in the United States for $250,000, for delivery to its Canary Islands facility on November 30, which is 90 days in the future. Puntagorda's functional currency is the Euro. Currently, Puntagorda expects to pay €180,000 for the turbine, which reflects the current Euro/dollar exchange rate. However, if the dollar strengths against the Euro within the next 90 days, Puntagorda will have to pay more Euros for the purchase.

To avoid this exchange rate risk, Puntagorda enters into a forward contract to purchase $250,000 on November 30 for €180,000. Puntagorda appropriately designates the forward contract as a hedge of its exposure to increases in the dollar exchange rate.

After one month, the dollar has increased in value against the Euro, so that the $250,000 would require €185,000 on the open market, which represents a €5,000 increase in the value of the forward contract. Puntagorda records the change in value with this entry:

(continued)

| Forward asset | 5,000 | |
| Equity | | 5,000 |

Puntagorda settles the forward contract on November 30 with this entry:

| Cash | 5,000 | |
| Forward asset | | 5,000 |

Puntagorda then pays €185,000 for the turbine on November 30, and reduces the carrying amount of the machine with the following entry, which shifts the deferred gain from equity to the cost of the turbine:

| Equity | 5,000 | |
| Machinery | | 5,000 |

ACCOUNTING FOR A NET INVESTMENT HEDGE

A hedge of a net investment relates to an investment in a foreign operation. Hedge accounting can only be applied to the foreign exchange differences arising between the functional currencies of the foreign operation and the parent entity. The parent entity can hedge an amount equal to or less than the carrying amount of the net assets of the foreign operation.

You should account for it by recognizing the portion of the gain or loss on the hedging instrument in other comprehensive income, but only to the extent of the gain or loss that is effective. You should record the ineffective part of the gain or loss on the hedging instrument in profit or loss.

If the entity disposes of the foreign operation, then you should shift the related amount of the gain or loss previously recognized in other comprehensive income into profit or loss.

Example

Melbourne Motors invests 50 million Singapore dollars in an automobile production facility in Singapore, which it plans to sell in five years, likely at an amount that will recoup its original investment. To hedge the investment, Melbourne borrows 50 million Singapore dollars and designates the loan as a hedge of the net investment.

Over the next five years, there is a 500,000 Singapore dollar foreign currency gain on the loan. Melbourne defers the gain in equity, and then uses it to offset the 500,000 Singapore dollar foreign exchange loss when it sells the Singapore facility at the end of five years.

DESIGNATING A NON-FINANCIAL ITEM AS A HEDGED ITEM

If you want to designate a non-financial asset or liability as being hedged, you can only hedge it for either foreign currency risks or for all risks. The reason for this restricted treatment is that it is difficult to isolate and measure the various portions of cash flow or fair value changes attributable to the various types of risk.

DISCLOSURES IN THE STATEMENT OF FINANCIAL POSITION– FINANCIAL INSTRUMENTS

You should disclose the following information either within the statement of financial position or its attached notes:

- *Carrying amounts*. The carrying amounts of each of these categories of financial instruments:
  - Financial assets at fair value through profit or loss
  - Held-to-maturity investments
  - Loans and receivables
  - Available-for-sale financial assets
  - Financial liabilities at fair value through profit or loss
  - Financial liabilities measured at amortized cost
- *Loan or receivable at fair value through profit or loss*. If it designates either an individual or group of loans or receivables as at fair value through profit or loss, then disclose:
  - The maximum exposure to credit risk of the loan or receivable at the end of the period.
  - Amount of mitigation by related credit derivatives.
  - Amount of change in the fair value of the loan or receivable that is attributable to changes in credit risk, both during the period and cumulatively.
  - Changes in market conditions causing market risk, such as changes in a benchmark interest rate, commodity price, or foreign exchange rate.
  - Changes in the fair value of any related credit derivatives or similar, occurring both during the period and cumulatively since designation.

- *Financial liability at fair value through profit or loss.* If it designates a financial liability as at fair value through profit or loss, then disclose:

  ○ The amount of the change in the fair value of the liability attributable to changes in credit risk, both during the period and cumulatively

  ○ Changes in market conditions causing market risk, such as changes in a benchmark interest rate, commodity price, or foreign exchange rate

  ○ Difference between the liability carrying amount and the amount the entity is required to pay at maturity

- *Credit risk method.* The methods used to compile disclosure information about valuation changes caused by credit risk. If the entity does not believe that this disclosure faithfully represents the fair value change, then state the reasons for this conclusion.

- *Reclassification.* The amount reclassified into and out of each category and the reason for doing so, if the entity has reclassified a financial asset. If the entity has reclassified a financial asset out of either the fair value through profit or loss or the available-for-sale categories, then it should disclose:

  ○ The amount reclassified both into and out of each category.

  ○ The carrying amounts and fair values of all financial assets that were reclassified in the current and previous periods.

  ○ The fair value gain or loss on a financial asset recognized in profit or loss or other comprehensive income, both in that reporting period and the previous period.

  ○ The fair value gain or loss that would have been recognized in profit or loss or other comprehensive income in the absence of re-classification. Report this information for each period, starting with reclassification and continuing until derecognition.

  ○ The effective interest rate and estimated cash flows that the entity expects to recover, as of the reclassification date.

- *Derecognition.* If a financial asset is transferred but the entity cannot derecognize it, then disclose the following for each class of such assets:

  ○ The nature of the assets

  ○ The remaining risks and rewards of ownership to which the entity is still exposed

  ○ The carrying amounts of those assets and liabilities that it still recognizes

- ○ The total carrying amount of the original assets, the amount it continues to recognize, and the carrying amount of any related liabilities

- *Collateral.* The carrying amount of any financial assets that it has pledged as collateral, and the terms and conditions of such pledges. If the entity holds collateral and can sell or re-pledge it, then disclose the fair value of held collateral, the fair value of collateral sold or re-pledged, whether it has an obligation to return the collateral, and the terms and conditions linked to its use of the collateral.

- *Credit losses allowance.* Reconcile the changes in any allowance account for credit losses for each class of financial assets.

- *Compound instruments.* The existence of any compound financial instruments (containing both liability and equity components) that contain multiple embedded derivatives whose values are interdependent.

- *Defaults and breaches.* The details of any loan defaults during the period on any principal, interest, sinking fund, or redemption terms, as well as the carrying amount of loans payable in default at the end of the period. Also, discuss whether defaults were remedied, or the renegotiated terms of any loans before the financial statements were authorized for issuance.

DISCLOSURES IN THE STATEMENT OF COMPREHENSIVE INCOME–FINANCIAL INSTRUMENTS

You should disclose the following information either within the statement of comprehensive income or its attached notes:

- *Gains or losses.* The net gains or losses on financial assets or liabilities for the following categories:

  - ○ For at fair value through profit or loss financial assets and liabilities, separately show the gains or losses on financial assets and liabilities in profit or loss upon initial recognition, and for those classified as held for trading.

  - ○ For available-for-sale financial assets, separately disclose the amount recognized in other comprehensive income and the amount reclassified from equity to profit or loss.

  - ○ For held-to-maturity investments.

  - ○ For loans and receivables.

  - ○ For financial liabilities measured at amortized cost.

- *Interest income and expense.* Separately show total interest income and total interest expense, using the effective interest method, for financial assets and liabilities that are not at fair value through profit or loss.

- *Fee income and expense.* Separately show the fee income and expense arising from financial assets or liabilities not at fair value through profit or loss, and from fiduciary activities requiring the holding or investing of assets on behalf of others.

- *Impairment information.* Any interest income on impaired financial assets, and the amount of any impairment loss for each class of financial asset.

DISCLOSURES–HEDGING

You should disclose the following information separately for fair value hedges, cash flow hedges, and hedges of net investments in foreign operations:

- *Hedge description.* Each type of hedge, the financial instruments designated as hedging instruments, their fair values at the end of the reporting period, and the nature of the risks that the entity is hedging.

- *Cash-flow hedges.* Specifically for cash-flow hedges, the periods when cash flows are forecasted to occur and when they should affect profit or loss, any forecasted transactions for which hedging had previously been used but which is no longer expected, and the following amounts recognized during the reporting period:
  - The amount recognized in other comprehensive income
  - The amount reclassified from equity to profit or loss, showing the amounts in each line item in the statement of comprehensive income
  - The amount removed from equity and included in the initial cost of a non-financial asset or liability, which was a hedged highly probable forecast transaction
  - The amount of hedging ineffectiveness recognized in profit or loss

- *Fair value hedges.* Gains or losses on the hedging instrument, as well as on the hedged item attributable to the hedged risk.

- *Hedges of net investments in foreign operations.* The amount of hedging ineffectiveness recognized in profit or loss.

DISCLOSURES–FAIR VALUE

You should separately disclose, for each class of financial assets and financial liabilities, the following information:

- *Fair values*. The fair value of each class of financial assets and liabilities.

- *Methods and assumptions*. The methods and assumptions used to determine the fair value of each class of financial assets and liabilities. This may include, for example, assumptions about interest rates, credit losses, and prepayment rates.

- *Active market reliance*. Whether fair values are determined based on published price quotations from an active market, or whether they are estimated using a valuation technique.

- *Assumption changes*. If a valuation technique is used to determine fair value and altering a supporting assumption to a reasonably possible alternative causes a significant valuation change, then state this fact and note the resulting change.

- *Profit or loss impact*. If a valuation technique was used to determine fair value, disclose the total amount of the fair value change recognized in profit or loss during the period.

- *Initial valuation reconciliation*. If there is a difference between the fair value at initial recognition of a financial instrument and the transaction price, then describe the accounting policy for recognizing the difference in profit or loss, and a reconciliation of the aggregate difference not yet recognized from the beginning to the end of the period.

There is no need to disclose fair value information when the carrying amount of a financial instrument reasonably approximates its fair value, and when an equity instrument's fair value cannot be measured reliably. However, in the latter case, disclose the fact that fair value information has not been disclosed and why, describe the instruments, note their carrying values, describe the market for them, note how the entity intends to dispose of them, and, if derecognized, their carrying amounts at derecognition and the gain or loss recognized.

DISCLOSURES–FINANCIAL INSTRUMENT RISKS

In general, you should disclose enough information about the risks associated with financial instruments so that an entity's financial statement users can evaluate the type and size of these risks to which it is exposed. More specifically, disclose this information separately for each type of risk:

- *Qualitative*. The type of risk and how it occurs, any changes in it from the previous period, and the entity's risk-specific policies and procedures to manage and measure it.

- *Quantitative*. The summary-level quantitative exposure at the end of the period, based on information provided internally to key management personnel, as well as risk concentrations if not otherwise apparent.

Also disclose the following information by class of financial instrument:

- *Credit risk*. The maximum exposure to credit risk at the end of the period without accounting for any collateral held. Also describe the collateral held, state the credit quality of financial assets neither past due nor impaired, and the carrying amount of renegotiated financial assets that would otherwise be past due or impaired.

- *Non-current financial assets*. The age of those financial assets that are past due at the end of the period, those financial assets considered impaired and the factors the entity uses in making this assessment, and for both cases the collateral held as security (and their estimated fair value).

- *Collateral*. If the entity takes possession of any collateral or calls on guarantees during the period, state the nature and carrying amount of these assets, and if not readily convertible into cash, its collateral disposition or usage policies.

In addition, an entity should disclose a maturity analysis for any financial liabilities it holds, showing remaining contractual maturities, and describe how it manages this liquidity risk.

Further, disclose a sensitivity analysis for each type of market risk to which the entity has an exposure at the end of the period. This analysis should reveal how profit or loss and equity would have been altered by changes in specific risk variables that were reasonably possible at the end of the period. The disclosure should include the methods and assumptions used in making the analysis, as well as any changes in these methods and assumptions from the previous period, and why they were altered. If the sensitivity analysis is unrepresentative of the risk inherent in a financial instrument, then disclose that fact and the reason why; this situation can arise when year-end exposure levels vary from those during the year.

6

INTERESTS IN JOINT VENTURES

INTRODUCTION

An entity may enter into a variety of joint ventures with its business partners, and exercise different levels of control over each joint venture. This chapter discusses the types of joint venture, and how the accounting for each one may vary, depending upon the level of control.

SIGNIFICANT INFLUENCE

A key concept in joint venture accounting is *significant influence*, which is having the power to participate in the financial or operating policy decisions of an economic activity. However, it does not give an entity control or joint control over those policies.

TYPES OF JOINT VENTURES

There are three types of joint ventures, which are:

- *Jointly controlled operations*. There may not be a joint venture legal entity. Instead, the joint venture uses the assets and other resources of the venturers. Each venturer uses its own assets, incurs its own expenses, and raises its own financing. The joint venture agreement states how the revenues and expenses related to the joint venture shall be shared among the venturers.

Example

Blood Storage Devices enters into a joint venture agreement with Millennial Storage to offer plasma storage in Millennial's vaults. According to the agreement, Blood is paid 25% of all revenues in exchange for its sale of its thermally-efficient storage units to customers, while Millennial is paid the remaining 75% of revenues as part of an ongoing maintenance contract to store the plasma. Since there are jointly controlled operations to which each venturer contributes assets, this is a joint venture under the concept of jointly controlled operations.

Blood Storage Devices enters into another joint venture agreement, with Cardiac Transport Services, whereby the two entities jointly own a new joint venture entity called Plasma Collection Services, which pays donors to collect their plasma. Both Blood Storage and Cardiac Transport contribute assets to the new entity. This is a jointly controlled entity, and so qualifies as a joint venture.

- *Jointly controlled assets*. Venturers may jointly control or own the assets contributed to or acquired by a joint venture. Each venturer may receive a share of the assets' output, and accept a share of the expenses incurred. There may not be a joint venture legal entity.

- *Jointly controlled entities*. A jointly controlled venture involves a legal entity in which each venturer has an interest. This new legal entity controls the joint venture's assets and liabilities, as well as its revenues and expenses; it can enter into contracts and raise financing. Each venturer is entitled to a share of any output generated by the new entity. A jointly controlled entity maintains its own accounting records and prepares financial statements from those records. If a venturer contributes cash or other assets to a jointly controlled entity, the venturer records this transfer as an investment in the jointly controlled entity.

There may also be a variety of combinations of these concepts, such as when a venturer transfers its assets into a new joint venture entity.

In all three of these types of joint ventures, there are two or more venturers who are bound by a contractual agreement that established joint control over the entity.

ACCOUNTING FOR A JOINTLY CONTROLLED OPERATION

The venturer normally uses proportionate consolidation to recognize its interest in a jointly controlled entity. *Proportionate consolidation* is when a venturer combines its share of each of the assets, liabilities, income and expenses of a jointly controlled entity with similar items in its own financial statements, or reports them as separate line items in its own financial statements. The procedures you use for proportionate consolidation are similar to those used for consolidating investments in subsidiaries (See the Consolidated and Separate Financial Statements chapter for more information).

There are two proportionate consolidation reporting formats, which are:

- *Combined reporting.* The venturer combines its share of each of the assets, liabilities, revenues and expenses of the jointly controlled entity with similar line items in its financial statements.

- *Separate reporting.* The venturer reports each of its share of the assets, liabilities, revenues and expenses of the jointly controlled entity in separate line items in its financial statements.

Both approaches result in the same asset and liability totals, as well as net income or loss.

IFRS (international financial reporting standards) recommend using proportionate consolidation over the equity method, but allows the use of the equity method. The *equity method* is when a venturer initially records its interest in a jointly controlled entity at cost and later adjusts it for post-acquisition changes in the venturer's share of the jointly-controlled entity's net assets. The venturer includes in its profit or loss its share of the profit or loss of the jointly controlled entity. (See the Investments in Associates chapter for more information about the equity method).

ACCOUNTING FOR LOSS OF CONTROL IN A JOINT VENTURE

A venturer should stop using both the proportionate consolidation and equity methods as soon as it stops having joint control over a jointly-controlled entity. The accounting then changes to one of the following:

- *Associate.* If the entity becomes an associate, see the Investments in Associates chapter regarding how to account for the situation.

- *Subsidiary.* If the entity becomes a subsidiary, then see the Consolidated and Separate Financial Statements chapter regarding how to consolidate the results of the entity with those of the venturer.

- *Investment.* For the remaining situations, see the Financial Instruments chapter regarding how to account for the entity as an investment.

Example

Blood Collection Services is a jointly controlled entity which has €100,000 of available-for-sale securities. One of its controlling entities, Cardiac Transport Services, had previously recognized a gain of €10,000 in other comprehensive income on its share of those securities. Cardiac Transport loses joint control of Blood. On the date of its loss of control, Cardiac Transport should reclassify the €10,000 gain to profit or loss.

In all of these cases, on the date of loss of joint control, the venturer measures at fair value its investment in the entity that it formerly jointly controlled. The venturer then recognizes the following calculation in profit or loss:

Fair value of the investment and the proceeds from disposing of any interest in the jointly controlled entity	—	Carrying amount of the investment on the date when the venturer lost control of the jointly controlled entity

If a venturer loses control of a jointly controlled entity, it accounts for any amounts it had recognized in other comprehensive income related to that entity as though the jointly controlled entity had itself disposed of the related assets or liabilities. Thus, if a venturer had previously recognized a gain or loss in other comprehensive income, it reclassifies the entry to profit or loss when it loses joint control of the entity.

If a venturer's ownership interest in a jointly controlled entity is reduced but the venturer still has joint control, then the venturer only reclassifies to profit or loss a proportionate amount of any gain or loss that it previously recognized in other comprehensive income.

ACCOUNTING FOR A NON-MONETARY CONTRIBUTION TO A JOINT VENTURE

When a venturer contributes non-monetary assets to a joint venture entity in exchange for an equity interest, the accounting varies based on the terms of the transaction:

- *Full equity payment.* If the venturer receives payment fully in equity, then it recognizes in its profit or loss that portion of the gain or loss on the asset attributable to the equity interests of the other venturers. This does not apply when the venturer has not shifted the significant risks and rewards of ownership of the assets to the joint venture entity, or when it is not possible to reliably measure the gain or loss, or when the contribution lacks commercial substance. If any of these exceptions apply, the gain or loss remains unrealized.

- *Partial equity payment.* If the joint venture entity also pays the venturer with monetary or non-monetary assets in addition to some equity, then the venturer recognizes a corresponding portion of the gain or loss on the transaction in profit or loss.

If there are unrealized gains or losses on a non-monetary contribution, the venturer does not present them as deferred gains or losses. Instead, it eliminates them against the underlying assets when using either the proportionate consolidation or equity method.

ACCOUNTING FOR TRANSACTIONS BETWEEN A VENTURER AND A JOINT VENTURE

Any gain or loss from a transaction between a venturer and joint venture should reflect the substance of the transaction. The accounting is different if the transaction flows from the venturer to the joint venture entity, or vice versa:

- *Transactions from the venturer.* If the venturer has transferred the significant risks and rewards of ownership to the joint venture entity, then the venturer can only recognize that portion of the gain or loss attributable to the ownership interests of the other venturers. However, the venturer recognizes the full amount of any loss when the transfer transaction provides evidence that there was a reduction in the net realizable value of current assets, or that there was an impairment loss.

- *Transactions to the venturer.* If the venturer buys assets from the joint venture entity, it does not recognize its share of the joint venture's profit on the transaction until the venturer has resold the assets to an independent third party. If the joint venture entity realizes a loss on the transaction, the venturer recognizes its share of the joint venture's loss on the transaction, except that it recognizes losses at once when they arc a reduction in the asset's net realizable value, or represent an impairment loss (See the Asset Impairment chapter for more information about impairment losses).

ACCOUNTING FOR JOINTLY CONTROLLED ASSETS

The venturer should record its share of the jointly controlled assets, liabilities incurred, its share of liabilities jointly incurred with other venturers, and income and expenses generated or incurred by the joint venture. No other adjustments or consolidation activities are required.

The venturer should record assets involved in the joint venture as property, plant, and equipment, not as an investment.

DISCLOSURES

A venturer should separately disclose the following information regarding any joint ventures in which it is involved:

- *Accounting method*. The method it uses to recognize its interests in jointly controlled entities.

- *Commitments*. The aggregate amount of any capital commitments related to its joint ventures, its share of any jointly incurred commitments, and its share of the capital commitments of a joint venture entity.

- *Consolidated results*. If it accounts for a joint venture using proportionate consolidation or the equity method, disclose the aggregate amounts of the current assets, long-term assets, current liabilities, long-term liabilities, revenues and expenses related to the joint venture.

- *Contingent liabilities*. The aggregate amount of any contingent liabilities incurred in relation to its joint ventures, its share of any jointly incurred contingent liabilities, and its share of any contingent liabilities of the joint venture entity for which it is also liable, and those cases where it is contingently liable for the liabilities of the other venturers in the joint venture. This reporting is not needed if the probability of loss is remote.

- *Ownership interests*. Its interests in significant joint ventures, including the proportion of its ownership interests.

A venturer should disclose in its financial statements the amount of any assets it controls or liabilities it incurs that are related to a jointly controlled operation. It should also disclose the expenses it incurs and the share of income it earns from the operations of the joint venture.

A venturer should disclose in its financial statements its share of jointly controlled assets and liabilities incurred, and its share of liabilities incurred with other venturers, together with its share of any revenues and expenses generated or incurred by the joint venture.

7

INVESTMENTS
IN ASSOCIATES

INTRODUCTION

An entity may invest in another entity that is classified as an associate, for which the investment is usually recognized under the equity method of accounting. This chapter describes an associate, how to account for an investment in an associate, and how to disclose the investment.

QUALIFICATION AS AN INVESTMENT IN AN ASSOCIATE

An *associate* is an entity over which an investor has significant influence, and which is not a subsidiary or an interest in a joint venture. *Significant influence* is the power to participate in the operating and financial policy decisions of an entity; it is not control over those policies. *Control* is the power to govern the operating and financial policy decisions of an entity in order to obtain benefits from the entity.

If an investor holds at least 20% of the voting power of an investee, the investor is presumed to have significant influence. Conversely, the investor is presumed not to have significant influence if it holds less than 20% of the investee's voting power. In both cases, the assumption of influence can be reversed through a clear demonstration to the contrary.

It is possible for an investor to not have significant influence, even with majority ownership of an investee. It is possible to lose significant influence over an investee even in the absence of a change in ownership. For example, an investee may become subject to the control of a court, regulator, or government, or as the result of a contractual agreement. Any of the following items are considered to be evidence of significant influence:

- Board of directors representation

- Management personnel swapping or sharing

- Material transactions with the investee

- Policy-making participation

- Technical information exchanges

A parent entity and its subsidiaries may individually have holdings in an associate. If so, aggregate the holdings to determine the level of the group's influence over the associate. When doing so, ignore the holdings of the group's other associates or joint ventures.

ACCOUNTING FOR AN INVESTMENT IN AN ASSOCIATE

The normal method for recognizing an investment in an associate is to do so using the equity method. The equity method is an accounting methodology for initially recognizing an investment at cost and thereafter adjusting it for post-acquisition changes in the investor's share of the investee's net assets. The investor also recognizes a proportionate share of the profit or loss of the investee, and does so in its own profit or loss. If an investee issues a distribution to the investor, this is a reduction of the investor's carrying amount of the investment. An investor accounting for an investment in an associate records the investment as a non-current asset.

If the associate itself has subsidiaries, associates, or joint ventures, the investor should account for just those profits or losses and net assets recognized in the associate's financial statements; this will include the associate's share of any profits or losses and net assets of the entities just described.

Example

Gordon's Candy acquires 30% of the voting shares of Fire Bombs, Inc. for £5 million. Gordon's has significant influence over Fire Bombs. Fire Bombs' retained earnings were £2 million on the purchase date. At the end of Year 1, Fire Bombs' retained earnings were £4 million.

The carrying value of Gordon's investment in Fire Bombs at the end of Year 1 is calculated as follows:

Investment cost	£5,000,000
Share of post-investment reserves*	600,000
	£5,600,000

*£2 million net change in retained earnings × 30% ownership interest

---

The investor may also have to alter the carrying amount of its investment to reflect changes in the investee's other comprehensive income. These changes are typically caused by the revaluation of property, plant, and equipment, as well as from foreign exchange translation differences. The investor recognizes its share of these changes in its own other comprehensive income.

An associate may incur such substantial losses that an investor's share of them equals or exceeds its investment in the associate. If so, the investor immediately stops recognizing its share of any further losses. If the associate subsequently reports profits, then the investor resumes its recognition of the associate's profits, but only after its share of the profits equals the share of losses that it had not previously recognized. Once the investor's interest reaches zero, it may still provide for additional losses if it has incurred a legal or constructive obligation or made payments on behalf of the associate.

You should *not* use the equity method to account for an investment in an associate in the following cases:

- *Held for sale*. The investor has classified the investment as held for sale.

- *Subsidiary reporting*. The investor is itself a subsidiary and its owners do not object to the non-application of the equity method, in addition the investor's debt or equity is not publicly traded, and the investor is not filing with a regulatory organization to issue any financial instruments in a public market, and the investor's parent entity produces consolidated financial statements complying with IFRS (international financial reporting standards).

If an investor has classified its investment in an associate as held for sale and then changes this classification, it should start accounting for the investment under the equity method as of the change date, and also amend its financial statements for the periods since it classified the investment as held for sale.

RELATED REPORTING ISSUES

There are a number of ancillary issues related to the accounting for an investment in an associate, which may apply based on the circumstances of a specific investment. These issues are:

- *Different accounting policies*. If the associate uses different accounting policies than the investor to create its financial statements, then the investor should adjust the associate's financial statements as though they incorporate the accounting policies used by the investor. The investor should then use these adjusted financial statements when applying the equity method.

- *Different reporting periods.* If the associate uses a different reporting period from the one used by the investor, then the associate should prepare financial statements for the investor as of the same date as the financial statements used by the investor. The investor then uses these revised financial statements when applying the equity method. This approach is not required if it is impractical for the associate to provide such statements. If it is necessary to use the financial statements of an associate that have a different end date, then the investor must adjust for the effects of significant transactions or events occurring between the dates of the associate's and the investor's financial statements. It is never allowable for the difference between the end of the associate's and the investor's financial statements to be more than three months.

- *Preference shares.* If other parties than the investor have cumulative preference shares in an associate, and which are classified as equity, then the investor calculates its share of profits or losses after adjusting for the dividends on these shares, even if the dividends have not been declared.

WHEN TO STOP USING THE EQUITY METHOD

You should stop using the equity method when the investor no longer has significant influence over the investee. At that time, measure the investor's remaining investment in the investee at its fair value, and recognize in profit or loss the following amount:

Fair value of any retained investment in the associate, plus any proceeds from the disposal of a part interest in the associate	—	Carrying amount of the investor's investment on the date when it loses significant influence over the investee

If an investor loses significant influence over an associate, it accounts for any amounts it had recognized in other comprehensive income related to that entity as though the associate had itself disposed of the related assets or liabilities. Thus, if an investor had previously recognized a gain or loss in other comprehensive income, it reclassifies the entry to profit or loss when it loses significant influence over the associate.

If an investor's ownership interest in an associate is reduced but the investment continues to be that of an associate, then the investor only reclassifies to profit or loss a proportionate amount of any gain or loss that it previously recognized in other comprehensive income.

Example

Ambulance Transport Services is an investor in and has significant influence over Plasma Separation Services. Plasma Separation has €100,000 of available-for-sale securities, for which Ambulance Transport had previously recognized a gain of €10,000 in other comprehensive income on its share of those securities. Ambulance Transport loses significant influence over Plasma Separation. On the date of its loss of significant influence, Ambulance Transport should reclassify the €10,000 gain to profit or loss.

UPSTREAM AND DOWNSTREAM TRANSACTIONS WITH AN ASSOCIATE

An *upstream transaction* involves the movement of assets from the associate to the investor, such as a sale made by the associate to the investor. A *downstream transaction* involves the movement of assets from the investor to the associate, such as a sale made by the investor to the associate.

An investor recognizes in its financial statements the results of either transaction only to the extent of the proportional interests of unrelated investors in the associate. Thus, the investor does not recognize its own share in the associate's profits or losses resulting from upstream and downstream transactions.

DISCLOSURES

The investor should make the following disclosures regarding its investments in associates:

- *Contingent liabilities*. The investor's share of the contingent liabilities of an associate that it has jointly incurred with other investors, as well as contingent liabilities caused by the investor being severally liable for liabilities.

Example

Nursing Supplies Corporation sells €100,000 of first aid supplies to its 25% owned associate, Local First Response. The cost to Nursing of the inventory is €60,000.

Nursing initially records a profit of €40,000 on the sale to Local, but it must also reduce the profit by its 25% ownership of Local, resulting in a €30,000 profit. Nursing must defer recognition of the remaining profit until Local sells the inventory to an independent third party.

- *Equity method*. Whether or not the investor accounts for an associate using the equity method.

- *Fair values*. The fair value of investments in associates if there are published price quotations.

- *Financial information–non-equity method*. The amounts of total assets, total liabilities, revenues, and profits or losses for those associates not accounted for using the equity method.

- *Financial information*. Aggregated amounts of the assets, liabilities, revenues, and profits or losses of associates.

- *Reporting date*. The end of the reporting period of the associate's financial statements that are used in applying the equity method, if that date varies from the date used by the investor. Also disclose the reason for the difference in dates.

- *Share of associate results*. The investor's share of the profit or loss of its associates, as well as the carrying amount of those investments, and its share of any discontinued operations.

- *Significant influence presumption*. The reasons why the investor has significant influence over the associate despite having less than 20% voting power over it.

- *Transfer restrictions*. The nature and extent of any significant restrictions on the ability of any associates to transfer funds to the investor.

- *Unrecognized losses*. The investor's unrecognized share of losses in any associates, both for the current period and cumulatively. This applies only if the investor has stopped recognizing its share of the losses of associates.

8

INVENTORY

INTRODUCTION

Nearly any entity that sells goods has some inventory on hand, and so must know how to track its costs. This chapter describes which costs to include in inventory, how to allocate costs to inventory, and the allowable types of cost layering systems. It also addresses how and when to write down the value of inventory, and the methodology for assigning costs to by-products.

DEFINITIONS

The following terms are applicable to the discussion of inventory and how to account for it:

- *Fair value* is the amount for which inventory could be exchanged between knowledgeable and willing parties in a marketplace transaction. Fair value may not equal net realizable value.

- *Fixed production overhead costs* include those costs that remain stable regardless of production volume, such as equipment and building maintenance, depreciation, and factory administration and management.

- *Inventory* is an asset held for sale in the ordinary course of business, or which is in the process of being produced for sale, or the materials or supplies intended for consumption in the production process. This can include items purchased and held for resale. In the case of services, inventory can be the costs of a service for which related revenue has not yet been recognized.

- *Net realizable value* is the estimated selling price of inventory, minus its estimated cost of completion and any estimated cost to complete its sale. Thus, it is the net amount realized from the sale of inventory. Net realizable value may not equal fair value.

- *Variable production overhead costs* include those costs that vary approximately with production volume.

COSTS TO INCLUDE IN INVENTORY

Include in the cost of inventory all costs to purchase inventory, convert it to its final form, and any other costs incurred to bring the inventory to its present location and condition. Thus, the following costs can be included in the cost of inventory:

- Direct labor
- Freight
- Handling
- Import duties and related taxes
- Overhead for fixed and variable production costs
- Purchase price

It is acceptable to include in inventory the cost of designing a product for a specific customer, but the cost allocation must be to the inventory designed for that customer.

Deduct from the cost of inventory any import duties or other taxes that are subsequently recovered. Also, deduct any trade discounts or rebates related to the inventory.

Do not include in inventory any of the following items:

- Abnormal waste related to materials, labor, or other production costs
- Administrative costs
- Foreign exchange differences arising from the purchase of inventory
- Interest costs associated with deferred payment terms
- Selling costs
- Storage costs, unless they are needed in the production process

Any unbilled services can be charged to inventory at the cost of their production. Usually, these costs are comprised of the labor and related costs

Example

Edinburgh Industries produces Scottish plaid garments for export throughout Europe. Edinburgh has incurred the following expenses, which are itemized in the table as being included in the cost of inventory or charged to expense in the current period:

Category	Amount Incurred	Include in Inventory	Charge to Expense
Accounting department costs	£ 58,000		£ 58,000
Dye purchases	229,000	£ 229,000	
Equipment maintenance	142,000	142,000	
Equipment depreciation	93,000	93,000	
Fleece purchases	1,580,000	1,580,000	
Freight on purchases	42,000	42,000	
Import broker commission	10,000	10,000	
Import duties	19,000	19,000	
Insurance on purchases	12,000	12,000	
Longshoreman handling fees	11,000	11,000	
Sales commission	28,000		28,000
Trade discounts on purchases	−30,000	−30,000	
Warranty costs	21,000		21,000
Totals	£2,215,000	£2,108,000	£107,000

of those personnel engaged in providing a billable service. This can include the cost of supervisory personnel and overhead, as long as these costs are to eventually be billed. The cost of non-billable personnel must be charged to expense in the period incurred.

INVENTORY MEASUREMENT SYSTEMS

The default cost assignment methodology is either the *first-in, first-out* (FIFO) or *weighted average* method. The FIFO method assumes that those items purchased first are consumed first, thereby leaving the most recently purchased items still in stock at the end of the reporting period.

The weighted average method assigns costs based on the weighted average of the cost of similar items in stock at the beginning of or acquired during the reporting period.

It is acceptable to use the *standard cost* method to measure the cost of inventory, as long as the results approximate actual cost. Under this method, a standard cost is assigned to each inventory item for costing purposes; the standard cost is compared to actual costs periodically,

---

Example

Swiss Style, maker of stylish women's clothes, installs a FIFO inventory system. The following exhibit shows the FIFO cost calculations for a single inventory item, product number BK0043. The first row indicates the origination of the first layer of inventory, resulting in 50 units of inventory at a per-unit cost of €10.00. In the second row, the monthly inventory usage is 350 units. Under the FIFO system, Swiss uses the entire stock of 50 inventory units that were left over at the end of the preceding month, as well as 300 units that were purchased in the current month. This wipes out the first layer of inventory, leaving Swiss with a single new layer that is composed of 700 units at a cost of €9.58 per unit. In the third row, there are 400 units of usage, which again comes from the first inventory layer, shrinking it down to just 300 units. However, since extra stock was purchased in the same period, Swiss now has an extra inventory layer that comprises 250 units, at a cost of €10.65 per unit. The rest of the exhibit proceeds using the same FIFO layering assumptions.

---

and adjusted to match the actual cost; it is a simplified way to track costs with reduced effort. The standard costs assigned to an inventory item should assume normal usage levels for materials, supplies, labor, and facility utilization.

It is also acceptable to use the *retail method*, which is used in the retail industry for measuring large volumes of items having similar margins. Under this approach, reduce the sales value of the inventory by a percentage gross margin that is based on actual results to arrive at the estimated inventory cost. If the gross margin varies substantially by retail department, it is allowable to conduct a separate calculation for each department, using the gross margin that pertains to each one.

The assignment of specific costs to individual inventory items is required when goods are produced for specific projects. However, *specific identification* of costs is not appropriate when there are many interchangeable inventory items.

The *last-in, first out* (LIFO) method is specifically excluded from use in all situations.

A company should use the same cost assignment method for all inventories of a similar nature, and having a similar use to the company. If inventory does not have the same nature or use, then it is allowable to use a different cost assignment method. For example, a different method may be allowable for inventory located in different divisions, but not allowable merely because the inventory is located in different geographical regions.

Exhibit 8.1 The FIFO Calculation Spreadsheet

Column 1	Column 2	Column 3	Column 4	Column 5	Column 6	Column 7	Column 8
Date Purchased	Quantity Purchased	Cost per Unit	Monthly Usage	Net Inventory Remaining	Cost of 1st Inventory Layer	Cost of 2nd Inventory Layer	Extended Inventory Cost
05/03/10	500	€10.00	450	50	(50 × €10.00)	—	€ 500
06/04/10	1,000	€ 9.58	350	700	(700 × € 9.58)	—	€6,706
07/11/10	250	€10.65	400	550	(300 × € 9.58)	(250 × €10.65)	€5,537
08/01/10	475	€10.25	350	675	(200 × €10.65)	(475 × €10.25)	€6,999
08/30/10	375	€10.40	400	650	(275 × €10.25)	(375 × €10.40)	€6,719
09/09/10	850	€ 9.50	700	800	(800 × € 9.50)	—	€7,600
12/12/10	700	€ 9.75	900	600	(600 × € 9.75)	—	€5,850
05/07/11	200	€10.80	0	800	(600 × € 9.75)	(200 × €10.80)	€8,010

Example

Swiss Style considers switching to a weighted average inventory system. Swiss' controller elects to model the results of the system using the same transactions just noted for its FIFO costing system. The results appear in the following exhibit. The first row shows that Swiss had a remainder of 50 units in stock, at a cost of €10.00. Since there has only been one purchase so far, the controller can easily calculate that the total inventory valuation is €500 by multiplying the unit cost of €10.00 in column 3 by the number of units remaining in stock, as shown in column 6.

In the second row, Swiss has purchased another 1,000 units at a cost of €9.58 per unit. After monthly usage, there are 700 units in stock, of which 650 were added from the most recent purchase. To determine the new weighted average cost of the inventory, the controller first determines the extended cost of this newest inventory addition. As shown in column 7, he arrives at a cost of €6,227 by multiplying the value in column 3 by the value in column 6. The controller then adds this amount to the existing total inventory valuation (€6,227 + €500) to arrive at the new extended inventory cost of €6,727, as shown in column 8. Finally, the controller divides the new extended cost in column 8 by the total number of units now in stock, as shown in column 5, to arrive at the new per-unit cost of €9.61. The rest of the exhibit proceeds using the same weighted average calculations.

ALLOCATION OF OVERHEAD COSTS TO INVENTORY

Allocate fixed overhead costs to inventory based on the *normal capacity* of the production facilities. Normal capacity is the average level of production to be expected over multiple time periods and under normal circumstances, incorporating a normal amount of planned maintenance. It is acceptable to use the actual production level as the basis for this calculation, as long as actual production approximates normal production.

It is not acceptable to alter the amount of the fixed overhead allocation if actual production activity is unusually low. This holds true even if the plant is idle; the normal amount of fixed overhead costs should still be charged to expense during that time. However, an unusually high production period calls for a reduction of the fixed overhead allocation in order to avoid allocating more cost to inventory than actually exists in the cost pool. Without making this adjustment, inventory would be recorded above cost.

The formula for allocating variable overhead costs is much simpler–just allocate it to each unit of production based on actual production volumes.

If overhead costs cannot be allocated, then charge them to expense in the period incurred.

Exhibit 8.2 The Weighted Average Spreadsheet

Column 1	Column 2	Column 3	Column 4	Column 5	Column 6	Column 7	Column 8	Column 9
Date Purchased	Quantity Purchased	Cost per Unit	Monthly Usage	Net Inventory Remaining	Net Change in Inventory During Period	Extended Cost of New Inventory Layer	Extended Inventory Cost	Average Inventory Cost/Unit
05/03/10	500	€10.00	450	50	50	€ 500.00	€ 500.00	€10.00
06/04/10	1,000	€ 9.58	350	700	650	€6,227.00	€6,727.00	€ 9.61
07/11/10	250	€10.65	400	550	−150	€ 0.00	€5,285.50	€ 9.61
08/01/10	475	€10.25	350	675	125	€1,281.25	€6,566.75	€ 9.73
08/30/10	375	€10.40	400	650	−25	€ 0.00	€6,323.54	€ 9.73
09/09/10	850	€ 9.50	700	800	150	€1,425.00	€7,748.54	€ 9.69
12/12/10	700	€ 9.75	900	600	−200	€ 0.00	€5,811.40	€ 9.69
05/07/11	200	€10.80	0	800	200	€2,160.00	€7,971.40	€ 9.96

WRITING DOWN THE VALUE OF INVENTORY

Always measure inventory at the *lower* of its cost or its net realizable value. *Net realizable value* is the estimated selling price of the inventory, minus its estimated cost of completion and any estimated cost to complete the sale. A write-down to net realizable value may be necessary in the following situations:

- Inventory is damaged

- Inventory is obsolete

- The cost of completion has increased

- The selling price has declined

- The cost to complete the sale has increased

Do not write down the value of raw materials if the finished goods into which they are incorporated are expected to sell at or above cost. However, if a subsequent raw materials price decline indicates that the cost of those finished goods exceeds their net realizable value, then write down the raw materials to their net realizable value (which is likely to be their replacement cost).

The write-down to net realizable value is normally on an individual item basis, but can apply to a group of related items that cannot be practicably evaluated individually. However, it is not appropriate to write down the value of an entire class of inventory, such as work-in-progress or finished goods.

Example

Crevasse Designs is a German manufacturer of climbing equipment. It has five major product lines, which are noted in the following table. At its fiscal year-end, Crevasse calculates the lower of its cost or net realizable value (NRV) in the following table:

Product Line	Quantity on Hand	Unit Cost	Inventory at Cost	NRV per Unit	Lower of Cost or NRV
Footwear	2,000	€190	€380,000	€230	€380,000
Ice tools	500	140	70,000	170	70,000
Outerwear	950	135	128,250	120	114,000
Ropes	1,250	180	225,000	140	175,000
Tents	780	270	210,600	350	210,600

Based on the table, the net realizable value is lower than cost on the outerwear and rope product lines. Accordingly, Crevasse should recognize a loss on the outerwear product line of €14,250 (€128,250 − €114,000) and a loss on the rope product line of €50,000 (€225,000 − €175,000).

Conduct the write-down assessment when circumstances arise that indicate that the net realizable value has declined below the product cost, and charge any write down to expense at that time. Continue to assess the situation in each subsequent period until circumstances causing the write-down have abated.

You can reverse a write-down to the extent of the original write-down. Recognize it as a reduction in the amount of inventories recognized as an expense in the period when the valuation reversal occurs.

ALLOCATING PRODUCTION COSTS TO BYPRODUCTS

If a production process produces multiple products and the cost of producing each one is not separately identifiable, then allocate production costs to each one on a rational and consistent basis. This means that a variety of systems may be used, as long as they are defensible and are used consistently over time. For example, the allocation can be based on the sales value of each of the produced items. Alternatively, if there is a main product and a byproduct, measure the net realizable value of the byproduct and deduct it from the cost of the main product.

Example

Shelled Pistachio is a pistachio nut processor that is based in Greece. Its staff hand-picks pistachio nuts, peels the shells, and processes the nuts for shipment. It sells the shells as a byproduct. Shelled incurred €80,000 to pick and process a recent batch of pistachio nuts. Of this amount, it incurred €60,000 through the point when the shells were peeled from the nuts. Shelled assigns this cost to the nut and shell products based on their relative sales value at the split-off point.

At the split-off point, Shelled can sell the nuts for €130,000 and the shells for €5,000, for a total sales value of €135,000. Thus, Shelled assigns €57,778 of the cost to the nuts and €2,222 of the cost to the shells based on the following formula:

Item	Calculation		Result
Nuts	(€130,000 sales value ÷ €135,000 total sales value) × €60,000	=	€57,778
Shells	(€5,000 sales value ÷ €135,000 total sales value) × €60,000	=	€ 2,222
	Total		€60,000

In addition, Shelled assigns the remaining €20,000 of subsequent processing costs solely to the pistachio nuts, since this processing no longer involves the shells. Thus, the total cost assigned to the nuts is €77,778 and €2,222 to the shells.

DISCLOSURES

Disclose the following information related to inventory:

- The accounting policies used when measuring inventory.
- The total carrying amount of inventory, by classification. Sample classifications are raw materials, work-in-progress, finished goods, supplies, and merchandise. A services provider can categorize its services inventory as work-in-progress.
- The total carrying amount of inventory at its fair value, less costs to sell.
- The amount of inventory charged to expense during the period.
- The amount of any inventory write-down during the period.
- The amount of any write-down reversal during the period.
- The reason for the write-down reversal.
- The carrying amount of inventories pledged as collateral.

9

PROPERTY, PLANT, AND EQUIPMENT

INTRODUCTION

An entity may have invested a significant proportion of its funds in expensive assets that it plans to use for an extended period of time, such as production equipment. If so, read this chapter to learn about the types of costs to capitalize, how to calculate related borrowing costs, the methods for depreciating such assets, exchanging them, and periodically revaluing them.

DEFINITIONS

Property, plant, and equipment (PP&E) are tangible items that are expected to be used in more than one period, and which are used in production, for rental, or for administration. This can include items acquired for safety or environmental reasons, since they may be necessary for deriving future economic benefits from other assets.

A PP&E *class* is a group of assets having a similar nature and use. Most PP&E items should belong to a single class, which impacts the type of depreciation used and whether the items are to be periodically revalued. Sample classes are:

Aircraft	Machinery
Buildings	Motor vehicles
Furniture and fixtures	Office equipment
Land	Ships

COSTS TO INCLUDE IN PP&E

In general, the costs to include in PP&E are an item's purchase cost and any costs incurred to bring the asset to the location and condition needed for it to operate in the manner intended by management. More specifically, include the following costs in PP&E:

- Purchase price of the item and related taxes

- Construction cost of the item, which can include labor and employee benefits

- Import duties

- Inbound freight and handling

- Site preparation

- Installation and assembly

- Asset startup testing

- Professional fees

- Estimated cost to subsequently dismantle and remove the item, if this is an obligation

- Less: trade discounts and rebates

- Less: net proceeds from the sale of any items produced during initial testing

---

Example

Shelled Pistachio is building a new pistachio nut processing facility in Preveza, Greece. The following table shows the costs it incurs for the Preveza facility, and whether they can be capitalized or charged to expense as incurred:

Cost Type	Expenditure	Capitalized	Expensed
Accounting charges	€ 65,000		€ 65,000
Architect's fees	280,000	€ 280,000	
Borrowing costs	185,000	185,000	
Construction cost	4,095,000	4,095,000	
Estimated dismantling cost	320,000	320,000	
Operating losses	150,000		150,000
Sale of tested items	−25,000	−25,000	
Shipping and handling	410,000	410,000	
Site preparation	500,000	500,000	
Startup testing	100,000	100,000	
Totals	€6,080,000	€5,865,000	€215,000

Example

Bergen Defense & Aerospace, operator of the Andoya Rocket Range in northern Norway, uses a €175,000 tractor to haul sounding rockets to its launch towers. Seven years after it purchased the tractor, the tractor engine fails and must be replaced. A new engine costs €75,000. A new engine provides economic benefits and its cost can be measured, so Bergen should recognize it as an asset.

The original invoice for the tractor did not separately specify the cost of the engine, so Bergen can use the cost of the replacement engine as the basis for determining the cost of the original engine. To do so, it uses its 6% cost of capital to discount the €75,000 engine for seven years, yielding a discounted cost of €49,880 (€75,000 × 0.66506).

Bergen then eliminates the €49,880 cost of the original engine from the asset record, and adds the new engine, resulting in a total new tractor cost of €200,120 (€175,000 − €49,880 + €75,000).

Also, include in PP&E the cost of major periodic replacements. For example, an aircraft requires new engines and a building requires a new roof after a certain usage interval or time period. Upon replacement, the new items are recorded in PP&E, and the carrying amounts of any replaced items are derecognized.

It may be necessary to perform periodic major inspections of an asset for faults, even if parts will not require replacement. This is a common requirement for airplanes, boilers, and elevators. The cost of each such inspection is included in the cost of the PP&E item, and any remaining carrying amount of the preceding inspection is derecognized.

COSTS *NOT* TO INCLUDE IN PP&E

Do *not* include the following costs in PP&E:

- Administration and general overhead costs
- Costs incurred after an asset is ready for use, but has not yet been used or is not yet operating at full capacity
- Costs incurred that are not necessary to bring the asset to the location and condition necessary for it to operate
- Initial operating losses
- New customer acquisition costs
- New facility opening costs

- New product or service introduction costs
- Relocation or reorganization costs

Do not recognize in PP&E the ongoing costs of servicing a PP&E item, which typically includes maintenance labor, consumables, and minor maintenance parts; these costs should instead be charged to expense as incurred.

If a PP&E item is self-constructed, the cost of any abnormal waste related to materials, labor, or other resources cannot be included in the asset cost.

THE INCLUSION OF BORROWING COSTS IN PP&E

You can include borrowing costs only for those assets that take a substantial period of time to prepare for use. This does not include assets that are ready for their intended use when acquired. Within this restriction, you can capitalize borrowing costs that are directly attributable to a PP&E item as part of its cost, if the borrowing costs can be reliably measured and will result in future economic benefits.

There are two ways to determine the borrowing costs to include in PP&E:

- *Directly attributable borrowing costs.* If borrowings specifically occurred to obtain the asset, then the borrowing cost to capitalize is the actual borrowing cost incurred, minus any investment income earned from the interim investment of those borrowings.

- *Borrowing costs from a general fund.* Borrowings may be handled centrally for general corporate needs, and may be obtained through a variety of debt instruments. In this case, derive an interest rate from the weighted average of the entity's borrowing costs during the period applicable to the asset. The amount of allowable borrowing costs using this method is capped at the entity's total borrowing costs during the applicable period.

You can begin capitalizing the borrowing costs associated with an asset when the entity begins incurring expenditures and borrowing costs for the asset, and begins preparing the asset for its intended use. This does not include the period when an asset is being held without any activities that change the asset's condition.

Also, if you suspend active development of an asset for an extended period, you cannot capitalize borrowing costs during that time. This restriction does not apply if the entity continues to engage in substantial technical and administrative work related to the asset, or if a temporary delay is a necessary part of the asset preparation process.

Example

Omnipresent Security is building a new world headquarters in Westminster, near New Scotland Yard. Omnipresent made payments of £25,000,000 on January 1 and £40,000,000 on July 1; the building was completed on December 31.

For the construction period, Omnipresent can capitalize the full £25,000,000 of the first payment and half of the second payment, as noted in the following table:

Date	Payment	Capitalization Period[*]	Average Payment
1/1	£25,000,000	12/12	£25,000,000
7/1	40,000,000	6/12	20,000,000
			£45,000,000

[*]The number of months between the payment date and the date when interest capitalization ends.

During this time, Omnipresent has a loan outstanding on which it pays 7.5% interest. The amount of interest cost it can capitalize as part of the construction project is £3,375,000 (£45,000,000 × 7.5% interest).

Capitalization of borrowing costs terminates when the entity has substantially completed all activities needed to prepare the asset for its intended use. Substantial completion is assumed to have occurred when physical construction is complete; work on minor modifications will not extend the capitalization period. If the entity is constructing multiple parts of a project and it can use some parts while construction continues on other parts, then it should stop capitalization of borrowing costs on those parts that it completes.

Example

Crevasse Designs is constructing a new facility in Niedernach, Germany, near the Austrian border. The facility is located in the middle of a roe deer migration path, so the town council requires Crevasse to shut down construction activities during the April through May migration period. Since this delay is a necessary part of construction, Crevasse can continue to capitalize borrowing costs during the shutdown period.

Example

Swedish Energy is constructing a wind farm. It can begin using each of the wind turbines as they are completed, so it stops capitalizing the borrowing costs related to each one as soon as it becomes usable.

Calculate the borrowing costs in any period by multiplying the interest rate by the average carrying amount of the asset during the period.

THE RESIDUAL VALUE OF AN ASSET

An asset's residual value is the estimated amount that the owner would currently obtain by disposing of the asset, less any disposal cost, assuming that the asset is at the age and condition to be expected at the end of its useful life.

Review the residual value of an asset at least at the end of each fiscal year. If the estimate changes, then account for it as a change in accounting estimate (see the Changes in Accounting Estimates and Errors chapter).

ACCOUNTING FOR AN ASSET EXCHANGE

When a PP&E item is acquired in exchange for another non-monetary asset, measure the acquired asset at its fair value. However, do not measure it at fair value if the exchange lacks commercial substance or it is not possible to reliably measure the asset received or the asset given up. If it is not possible to measure at fair value, then measure the acquired asset at the carrying amount of the asset given up. If the fair values of both the acquired asset and the asset given up are available, then use the fair value of the asset given up to measure the cost of the acquired asset.

An asset exchange has commercial substance if:

- The risk, timing, and amount of the post-tax cash flows of the acquired asset vary from those of the transferred asset, and the difference is significant relative to the fair value of the asset exchanged.

- The acquiring entity's value is affected by the exchange, and the difference is significant relative to the fair value of the assets exchanged.

It is possible to reliably measure the fair value of an acquired asset if there is not a significant variability in the range of fair value estimates, or it is possible to assess the probabilities associated with each estimate.

SUBSEQUENT PP&E MEASUREMENTS

You can either carry an asset at its cost or periodically revalue it to its fair value. In either case, subsequent measurement must include reductions for any accumulated depreciation and impairment losses. If you choose to revalue a single asset, then you must also revalue the entire class of PP&E in which it belongs, in order to avoid selective revaluation. It is acceptable to revalue a class of assets on a rolling basis, as long as the revaluation is completed within a short period of time.

If you choose periodic revaluation, then conduct revaluations with sufficient regularity to ensure that the carrying amount does not vary significantly from its fair value. For those PP&E items having significant and volatile changes in fair value, it may be necessary to revalue annually. When there are insignificant changes in fair value, a revaluation once every three to five years is sufficient.

Revaluations are normally conducted by the following means:

Asset Type	Source
Buildings	Professionally qualified valuers
Equipment	Market value determined by appraisal
Land	Professionally qualified valuers

In all of the above cases, if there is no market-based evidence of fair value, it is allowable to estimate fair value using either the income or depreciated replacement cost methods.

ACCOUNTING FOR ASSET REVALUATIONS

Use the following table to determine the proper accounting for an asset that has been revalued:

Asset value increases	Recognize in other comprehensive income and as "revaluation surplus" in equity
Asset value increases, but reverses a prior revaluation decrease	Recognize as profit to the extent that it reverses a revaluation decrease previously recognized in profit or loss
Asset value decreases	Recognize as a loss
Asset value decreases, but credit balance exists in the revaluation surplus for the asset	Recognize in other comprehensive income to the extent of any revaluation surplus for the asset, with any excess recognized as a loss

When an asset is retired or disposed of, transfer any revaluation surplus for that item to retained earnings. You can also transfer that portion of

Example

Catholic Designs creates elaborate church pews. It owns a three-dimensional CNC router that automatically carves six pews at once. Catholic bought the router for £600,000. It elects to revalue the router at three-year intervals. At the first revaluation, the router has accumulated £150,000 of depreciation, and an appraiser assigns a fair value of £475,000 to the router. Catholic's controller creates the following entry to eliminate the existing accumulated depreciation:

	Debit	Credit
Accumulated depreciation	150,000	
Equipment		150,000

In addition, Catholic's controller creates the following entry to increase the net asset value of the router to its fair value:

	Debit	Credit
Equipment	25,000	
Other comprehensive income – gain on revaluation		25,000

Three years later, the next revaluation reveals a fair value decline of £30,000. The following entry records the transaction:

	Debit	Credit
Other comprehensive income – gain on revaluation	25,000	
Loss on revaluation – Equipment	5,000	
Equipment		30,000

a revaluation surplus to retained earnings that is the difference between the depreciation on the original and revalued asset costs.

ASSETS NOT SUBJECT TO DEPRECIATION

Land is not depreciated, since it has an unlimited useful life. If land has a limited useful life, as is the case with a quarry, then it is acceptable to depreciate it over its useful life. If the cost of land includes any costs incurred for site dismantlement and/or restoration, then depreciate these costs over the period over which any resulting benefits are obtained.

If an entity acquires a parcel of land, which includes a building, then separate the two assets and depreciate the building.

THE DEPRECIATION TIME PERIOD

Begin depreciating an asset when it is available for use, even if it is not actually in use at that time. Spread the depreciation on a systematic basis over the asset's useful life. Consider the following factors when determining an asset's useful life:

- *Expected usage*. Refers to the expected volume of production output.

- *Expected wear*. Can be impacted by such factors as the level of maintenance and the number of shifts over which the asset is used.

- *Legal limits*. Caused by government-mandated usage levels or lease expiration dates, for example.

- *Obsolescence*. Can be caused by changes in technology or market demand, for example.

Review the useful life of each asset at least at the end of every fiscal year. If the estimate changes, then account for it as a change in accounting estimate (see the Changes in Accounting Estimates and Errors chapter).

Stop depreciating the asset at the earlier of the date when it is classified as being held for sale, the date when it is derecognized, or when it is fully depreciated. Thus, do not stop depreciating an asset simply because it is currently idle or retired from active use. However, if the asset is being depreciated based on some method of asset usage, then there may be no depreciation while the asset is not being used.

Example

Brutus' Brewery, maker of the famous Brutus' Premium Bitter, built a brewery in the village of Once Brewed, near Hadrian's Wall. Part of its brewing equipment is a large mash tun (for mashing), which has an original cost of £250,000. At the time of acquisition, management estimated that the mash tun would have a useful life of ten years, with a residual value of £50,000. Thus, the depreciable asset value was £200,000 (£250,000 − £50,000).

At the end of year seven, management reviews both the useful life and residual value of the mash tun; it concludes that the useful life can be extended to 13 years, due to its use of a spray ball for periodic deep cleaning. Given the longer useful life and greater usage, however, the mash tun's residual value will likely decline to £25,000.

At the end of year seven, Brutus' Brewery had accumulated £140,000 of depreciation on the mash tun. The original depreciable asset value of £200,000 has declined to £60,000 because of the ongoing depreciation, but is now increased by the £25,000 reduction in the mash tun's residual value, for a remaining depreciable asset value of £85,000. With the change in useful life, the mash tun can now be depreciated for six more years. Consequently, the future annual depreciation rate should be £14,167 (£85,000 ÷ 6 years).

Charge all periodic depreciation to the accounting period in which it is incurred, except when the asset is used to produce other assets. In that case, charge the depreciation to the other assets. For example, depreciation on production equipment can be included in an overhead cost pool that is then allocated to the cost of inventory.

TYPES OF DEPRECIATION METHODS

Select a depreciation method that reflects the pattern in which an entity expects to consume an asset's future economic benefits.

Review the depreciation method applied to an asset at least at the end of each fiscal year, and revise the method if there has been a significant change in the pattern of consumption. This is a change in accounting estimate (see the Changes in Accounting Estimates and Errors chapter).

The following depreciation methods are acceptable:

- *Diminishing balance method*. Charges depreciation at a decreasing rate over the useful life of the asset.

- *Straight-line method*. Charges depreciation at a constant rate over the useful life of the asset.

- *Units of production method*. Charges depreciation based on expected usage.

Example

The Forest Products Company (FPC) harvests timber in northern Finland, and maintains a sawmill on the outskirts of Kittila.

Straight-line method. FPC separately depreciates the building that houses its sawmill equipment. This structure cost €3,000,000 to construct, and should be usable for 30 years, with no residual value. Given the steady usage pattern likely to occur, FPC uses the straight-line depreciation method to depreciate it. The annual depreciation is €100,000 (€3,000,000 cost ÷ 30 years).

Diminishing balance method. FPC finds that the band saws it uses in the sawmill wear out fast, and so uses double-declining balance depreciation to reflect their rapid decline in value. Each band saw costs €40,000 and should be fully depreciated, with no residual value, after four years. The diminishing balance method requires use of twice the straight-line rate, multiplied by the book value at the beginning of the year. Any remaining asset value is fully depreciated in the final year. The calculation appears in the following table:

(*continued*)

Beginning Balance	Straight Line Rate		Rate Doubler		Annual Depreciation	Remaining Balance
€40,000	× 25%	×	2	=	€20,000	€20,000
20,000	× 25%	×	2	=	10,000	10,000
10,000	× 25%	×	2	=	5,000	5,000
5,000	× Remaining value			=	5,000	0

Units of production method. FPC owns a grapple-skidder, for collecting downed timber. Its wear pattern is closely tied to the number of trees that it collects, so the units of production method is the most appropriate form of depreciation. The grapple-skidder cost €120,000 and has an estimated residual value of €20,000. Management estimates it can lift 200,000 trees during its estimated useful life, which results in per-unit depreciation of €0.5 (€100,000 depreciable value ÷ 200,000 units of production). In June, the grapple-skidder lifts 2,500 trees, so depreciation during that month is €1,250 (2,500 trees × €0.5/unit).

DEPRECIATING REVALUED ITEMS

When a PP&E item is revalued to its fair value, you have two available means for dealing with any accumulated depreciation, which are:

- Eliminate the accumulated depreciation against the gross carrying amount of the item, and restate its net amount to the revalued amount.

- Make the carrying amount of the asset equal the revalued amount by restating the accumulated depreciation proportionately with the change in the gross carrying amount.

ACCOUNTING FOR A DERECOGNIZED ASSET

An asset is derecognized upon its disposal, or when no future economic benefits can be expected from its use or disposal. Derecognition can arise from a variety of events, such as an asset's sale, scrapping, or donation.

You can recognize a gain or loss from an asset's derecognition, though a gain on derecognition cannot be recorded as revenue. The gain or loss on derecognition is calculated as the net disposal proceeds, minus the asset's carrying value.

If an entity replaces part of an asset, then that part is derecognized, even if the replaced part had not been depreciated separately. If the entity cannot determine the carrying amount of the part that has been replaced, it can use the cost of the replacement part as a reasonable estimate of the cost of the part when the asset was acquired or built.

However, an entity may be in the business of routinely selling assets that it had previously held for rental; if so, it transfers the assets to inventory, which then become held for sale; it can then recognize revenue upon their sale to a third party.

DISCLOSURES

Disclose the following information related to PP&E:

- *PP&E summary.* The following information for each class of PP&E:
  - Carrying amount reconciliation during the period, showing additions, assets held for sale, acquisitions from business combinations, revaluation changes, impairment losses, depreciation, and net exchange differences caused by currency translation
  - Depreciation methods used
  - Gross carrying amount and accumulated depreciation at the beginning and end of the period
  - Measurement bases used
  - Useful lives used
- *Borrowing costs.* The amount of any borrowing costs capitalized during the period, and the capitalization rate used.
- *Change in estimate.* Any changes in accounting estimate for residual values, useful lives, depreciation methods, or estimated costs to dismantle, remove, or restore PP&E items.
- *Commitments.* The amount of any contractual commitments to acquire PP&E.
- *Construction-in-progress.* The carrying amount of any PP&E items while under construction.
- *Dispositions.* The amount received from asset dispositions.
- *Restrictions.* Any restrictions on title to PP&E items, or PP&E pledged as collateral.
- *Revalued items.* For any revalued items, the date of the revaluation, whether an independent appraiser was used, the methods applied to estimate fair values, and the extent to which fair values were derived from market transactions. Also, state for each class of revalued items the carrying amount that would have been recognized without a

revaluation. Finally, note the revaluation surplus, any changes in it, and shareholder distribution restrictions for the surplus.

- *Other*. The following items are recommended for disclosure, but not required:

  ◦ Carrying amount of temporary PP&E

  ◦ Gross carrying amount of any fully depreciated PP&E still in use

  ◦ Carrying amount of any retired PP&E that is not held for sale

  ◦ When recording PP&E at cost, any asset fair values that are materially different from the carrying amounts

10

INTANGIBLE ASSETS

INTRODUCTION

Some intangible assets are formally recognized on an entity's balance sheet, while others effectively add value to a business, but are not formally recognized. There are many types of intangible items, which generally fall into the following categories:

- Intellectual property

- Licenses

- Market knowledge

- Process or system implementation

- Scientific or technical knowledge

- Trademarks

All of the following are examples of intangible items:

Copyrights	Franchises	Mortgage servicing rights
Customer lists	Import quotas	Motion pictures
Customer loyalty	Market share	Patents
Customer relationships	Marketing rights	Software
Fishing licenses		

If an intangible item meets the criteria of identifiability, control over the resource, and the existence of future economic benefits, then you can record it as an asset. The criteria are:

- *Control*. The entity has the power to obtain the future economic benefits generated by the item, and can restrict the access of other entities to those benefits. This is normally demonstrated by having legal rights to the item, such as a copyright, patent, or restraint of trade agreement.

- *Future economic benefits*. The item creates revenues, cost savings, or other benefits. For example, an entity has intellectual property that allows it to double the efficiency of a production line, thereby generating cost savings.

- *Identifiability*. The item must be capable of being separated from the entity and exchanged, licensed, rented, sold, or transferred. Alternatively, the item must arise from contractual or other legal rights, even if those rights are not transferable.

If an intangible asset does not meet all of these criteria, then recognize any expenses incurred to acquire or generate it when incurred.

RECOGNITION OF INTANGIBLE ASSETS

You can only recognize an intangible asset when you can reliably measure the cost of the asset, and it is probable that expected future economic benefits attributable to the asset will flow to the entity. You should assess the probability of expected future economic benefits using reasonable and supportable assumptions.

If an item meets the definition of an intangible item and meets the criteria for an intangible asset, then you can record the expenditures associated with the item as an asset. These expenditures can include the costs incurred to acquire or create the item. Expenditures incurred to subsequently add to, replace part of, or maintain an intangible asset are almost always charged to expense in the period incurred, on the grounds that they cannot be distinguished from expenditures to develop the entire business.

Example

Pull Door Handle Corporation has created a unique door handle design. It spends £25,000 in legal fees and £15,000 of in-house labor costs to register the patent. Later, it spends £50,000 in legal fees to defend the patent.

Pull can record the initial £40,000 registration cost as an intangible asset, as long as it can identify future economic benefits to associate with the patent. It must charge the defense costs to expense. Further, if it loses the lawsuit, this calls into question the viability of the asset, which may require Pull to write down the asset's carrying value.

Example

Pounce Ltd., purveyor of the Pounce energy drink, expends 20% of its revenues on brand enhancement through such methods as triathlon and adventure athlete sponsorships as well as advertising at extreme sports events. These expenditures clearly support Pounce's brand, but cannot be recorded as an intangible asset, because they cannot be distinguished from general business development expenditures.

Expenditures that cannot be included in the cost of an intangible asset are the costs of introducing a new product or service, adding a new location or class of customer, and general overhead costs.

RECOGNITION OF ACQUIRED INTANGIBLE ASSETS

If the entity acquires an intangible asset, then you can assume that all of the previously-noted recognition criteria have been satisfied. The following costs are included in the total cost of an acquired intangible asset:

- Purchase price

- Import duties

- Nonrefundable purchase taxes

- Directly attributable cost of preparing the asset for use (such as professional fees, labor, and testing). This does not include the cost of incidental operations not necessary to prepare the asset for use.

- Less: trade discounts and rebates

You must stop accumulating costs to be recorded as part of the intangible asset once it can be operated in the manner intended by management, in addition you cannot include the cost of initial operating losses.

If you defer payment for an intangible asset beyond normal credit terms, then record its purchase price as the cash price equivalent; record any cost above this amount as interest expense over the credit period.

RECOGNITION OF INTANGIBLE ASSETS ACQUIRED IN A BUSINESS COMBINATION

If you acquire an intangible asset in a business combination, then record its fair value on the acquisition date as its cost. Use the four following valuation methods, which are presented in declining order of preference:

Example

Voltaic Power Company acquires Sulphur Solutions, which manufactures sodium-sulphur batteries to store the electricity generated by wind farms. Sulphur Solutions has a major in-process research and development project to create lower-cost sodium-sulphur batteries. It is conducting the work under a €20,000,000 contract with Swedish Energy, from which it expects discounted cash flows of €4,500,000. Voltaic can use the discounted cash flows as the fair value of the research work, and records €4,500,000 as the cost of the intangible asset.

1. *Bid price.* The asset's bid price in an active market.

2. *Most recent transaction.* If there are no current bid prices but there is an active market, then use the price of the most recent similar transaction, unless there has been a significant change in economic circumstances since the transaction date.

3. *Arm's-length transaction.* If there is no active market, then use the amount that the entity would pay for the asset in an arm's-length transaction between knowledgeable parties. You should consider the outcome of recent similar transactions when deriving this amount.

4. *Multiples or cash flows.* Apply a multiple, such as a revenue or profit multiple, to the asset's cash flows that reflects current market transactions. Alternatively, calculate its discounted estimated future cash flows.

WEBSITE DEVELOPMENT COSTS

You can record the development expenditures associated with the development stages of a web site as an intangible asset, but only if they meet the preceding control, future economic benefits, and identifiability criteria. If the website only promotes the entity's own products and so cannot clearly show a stream of future economic benefits, then charge all expenditures related to its development to expense in the period in which they are incurred.

The following table shows the proper accounting treatment of the various expenditures incurred to develop a web site:

Expenditure Type	Charged to Expense	Capitalized
Feasibility study	√	
Define specifications	√	
Evaluate alternatives	√	
Final system selection	√	

Domain name procurement		√
Computer hardware		√
Software development		√
Application installation		√
Web page design		√
Stress testing		√
Overhead allocations	√	
System backups	√	
System maintenance	√	
General and administrative	√	

Expenditures related to the advertising and promotion of an entity's own products and services should always be charged to expense.

RESEARCH AND DEVELOPMENT EXPENDITURES

If an entity incurs expenditures on a research and development project, then recognize it as an expense if it is a research-related expenditure. You can record a development-related expenditure as an intangible asset only if it meets all of the following criteria:

- *Completion intent.* The entity intends to complete the asset, and to either use or sell it.

- *Feasibility.* It is technically feasible to make the asset available for use or sale.

- *Future benefits.* There is a demonstrated ability to generate future economic benefits, such as the existence of a market for the asset or its output.

- *Measurement.* The entity can reliably measure development-related expenditures for the asset.

- *Resources.* There are adequate resources to complete the development process and use or sell the asset, as can be detailed in a business plan and supported by the entity's demonstrated ability to procure the necessary resources.

- *Use intent.* The entity is able to use or sell the asset.

If an entity cannot meet all of these requirements for a development project, then charge the expenditures to expense in the period incurred.

Examples of research activities include obtaining new knowledge, searching for research findings, in addition to searching for and selecting alternatives to current materials, products, and systems. Examples of development activities include the design, construction and testing of prototypes,

Example

Sulphur Solutions is developing a new, lighter version of its sodium-sulphur battery that is to be used to store electricity from residential wind turbines. During Year 1, it expends €290,000 on basic research to create greater storage capacity. During Year 2, it incurs €200,000 per fiscal quarter to incorporate the new battery into its existing production process. At the beginning of the fourth quarter of Year 2, Sulphur Solutions demonstrates that the improved production process meets the criteria for recognition as an intangible asset. Sulphur also incurs €450,000 of expenditures in Year 3 to complete the development process.

Sulphur Solutions can recognize €650,000 as an intangible asset. This is the expenditure it incurred since the date when Sulphur met the recognition criteria. Sulphur charges all of the expenditures it incurred prior to this date to expense.

tools, molds, dies, pilot plants, and alternatives to existing materials, products, and systems.

SUBSEQUENT RECOGNITION OF INTANGIBLE ASSETS

You can measure an intangible asset after its initial recognition using one of the following methods:

- *Cost model*. Carry the asset at its cost, minus any accumulated amortization and impairment losses.

- *Revaluation model*. Carry the asset at its periodically revalued fair value, minus any subsequent accumulated amortization and subsequent impairment losses. Revaluations should be sufficiently frequent to ensure that the asset's carrying amount does not differ materially from its fair value; with frequency being dictated by the volatility of fair values. This method can be used to revalue an intangible asset that was received as part of a government grant and initially recorded at a nominal amount.

  If you use this method, then you must also measure all other intangible assets in its class simultaneously and using the same model, unless there is no active market for those assets. A class of intangible assets is a group of assets having a similar nature and use.

  It can be difficult to obtain a fair value for an intangible asset, since many assets, such as trademarks and patents are by their nature unique. However, there is an active market for many types of licenses and quotas, and which can provide fair market information for a periodic revaluation.

Example

Nova Taxi owns a taxi operator's license, which it acquired for €30,000. The license term is five years, after which the city government will auction it again to the highest bidder. Nova can also sell its rights to the license at any time, and there is an active market for doing so.

    Nova has been amortizing the cost of the license using the straight-line method for the past year, so that €6,000 of the acquisition price has now been amortized. At the end of that year, the city government reduces 20% of the outstanding taxi operator licenses by retiring them upon their renewal dates. This immediately increases the price of the remaining taxi operator licenses to €40,000, as evidenced by multiple license re-sales on the open market.

    Nova revalues the license based on these new prices by using the elimination method to eliminate the accumulated amortization and increase the net book value of the license asset. The entries are:

Accumulated amortization	€ 6,000	
Intangible assets		€ 6,000
Intangible assets	€16,000	
Revaluation reserve		€16,000

    Nova now has four years in which to amortize the €40,000 carrying amount of the license, so it will amortize €10,000 in each of the next four years.

If it is impossible to revalue an intangible asset, then carry it at its cost, minus any accumulated amortization and impairment losses.

If you revalue an intangible asset, there are two ways to treat any accumulated amortization outstanding as of the revaluation date:

- *Proportional restatement*. Restate the accumulated depreciation so that it remains in the same proportion to the gross carrying amount, such that the carrying amount after revaluation matches its revalued amount.

- *Elimination*. Eliminate the accumulated depreciation, so that the carrying amount of the asset matches its revalued amount.

RECOGNITION OF INTANGIBLE ASSET REVALUATIONS

If you use the revaluation model to adjust the carrying amount of an intangible asset, use the following table to record changes in value:

Result	Treatment
Increased valuation and there was no prior valuation decrease	Increase in other comprehensive income and in equity as a revaluation surplus.
Increased valuation and there was a prior valuation decrease	Increase in profit or loss to offset any earlier revaluation decrease of the same asset. Any remainder is an increase in comprehensive income.
Decreased valuation and there was no prior valuation increase	Decrease in profit or loss.
Decreased valuation and there was a prior valuation decrease	Decrease in other comprehensive income to offset any earlier revaluation increase of the same asset; also decrease the revaluation surplus in equity. Any remainder is a decrease in profit or loss.

When the revaluation surplus is realized, as upon the retirement or disposal of an asset, transfer the surplus to the retained earnings account.

DETERMINING THE USEFUL LIFE OF AN INTANGIBLE ASSET

An intangible asset can have either a finite or indefinite life. You assign an asset an indefinite life when there is no foreseeable limit to the period over which the asset is expected to generate net cash flows for the entity. Consider the following factors when determining the useful life of an intangible asset:

- *Competition*. Projected actions by current and potential competitors.

- *Control period*. The time period over which the entity has control of the asset.

- *Dependencies*. Whether the asset's useful life is dependent upon the useful life of other assets.

- *Life cycle*. The typical product life cycle of this type of asset, including public information about similar products.

- *Maintenance*. The amount of maintenance expenditures needed to obtain future economic benefits, and the entity's willingness to make those expenditures.

- *Market stability*. Changes in market demand for the asset, and the stability of the industry in which the asset is used.

- *Obsolescence*. Any type of obsolescence that may impact the asset.

- *Usage*. The expected usage of the asset.

Example

The Sprained Back Chair Company acquires the mailing list of the Chiropractor Today magazine, with the intent of sending direct mail pieces to everyone on the list. Sprained Back's marketing manager believes the mailing list will have a useful life of between six and 18 months, and so adopts a useful life of 12 months for the purpose of amortizing the acquisition cost of the mailing list.

An indefinite useful life is not necessarily an infinite useful life. If the useful life span is uncertain, then estimate it on a prudent basis, given full consideration to the impact of obsolescence that is affected by rapid changes in technology.

If these rights are renewable, then only extend the useful life into the renewal periods if there is evidence that the entity can renew without significant cost. This evidence should indicate that the renewal will occur, that required renewal conditions will be satisfied, and that the renewal cost is not significant in relation to the future economic benefits arising from renewal.

If the entity acquires an intangible asset through a business combination that is a reacquired right, then set its useful life at the remaining contractual period of the contract in which the right was granted. Do not extend the right for any contractual renewal periods.

You should review an intangible asset with an indefinite useful life once a year, and whenever there is an indication that the asset may be impaired. This review will assess whether there is any asset impairment, and if the indefinite useful life is still warranted. If the useful life is no longer indefinite, then determine a useful life and begin amortization over that period.

Example

Emerald Fire Candy acquires the Red Hot Loving candy line from a competitor, along with the trademark for the Red Hot Loving name. Emerald initially considered the Red Hot Loving name to have an indefinite useful life, along with continuing cash flows at the current level. However, management estimates that recent competition from the Smooches candy line will reduce future cash inflows by 25%.

Based on this information, there is no need for Emerald to assign a useful life to the Red Hot Loving trademark, but it should determine if the estimated recoverable amount is now less than its carrying amount. If so, Emerald should record an impairment charge to reduce the carrying amount to the recoverable amount.

Example

Square Tile Company buys the rights to a patented production process that allows it to fuse custom-designed images to tile substrate in high temperature kilns. Square pays €100,000 to use the process, and elects to amortize it under the units of production method, whereby it amortizes €1 for every tile produced. It then includes the €1/unit amortization in the bill of materials for each tile. When Square completes a tile, it transfers the standard cost of the tile (including the amortization charge) to inventory. It charges the inventoried cost of the tile to the cost of goods sold every time it sells a tile.

INTANGIBLE ASSET AMORTIZATION

Amortization of an intangible asset having a finite useful life begins when the asset is available for use, and stops on the earlier of being classified as held for sale or when it is derecognized. The most appropriate amortization method is the one that most closely matches the expected pattern of consumption of the asset's expected future economic benefits. If there is no way to determine the pattern of consumption, then use the straight-line method for amortization. Alternative methods to consider are the diminishing balance method and the unit of production method. Do not change the amortization method unless there is a change in the expected pattern of consumption of future economic benefits.

You normally recognize amortization expense in profit or loss. However, there are situations where the future economic benefits of an intangible asset are used in the production of other assets. If so, include the amortization expense in the cost of the other assets. Any amortization expense treated in this fashion will then be charged to expense when the economic benefits of the other assets are realized.

You should review the amortization period and amortization method at least at the end of each fiscal year for all intangible assets having finite lives. If the expected useful life of the asset is different from the period you currently use, then change the amortization period to the new estimate. If there has been a change in the pattern of consumption of the asset's future economic benefits, then change the amortization method to reflect the new pattern. These are changes in accounting estimates, and so require no retrospective application.

DISCLOSURES

Disclose the following information for each class of intangible assets:

- *Amortization methods*. The amortization methods used for those assets having finite useful lives.

- *Carrying amounts.* The gross carrying amounts, accumulated amortization, and accumulated impairment losses at the beginning and end of the period.

- *Line items.* The line items in the statement of comprehensive income where amortization is included.

- *Reconciliation.* A reconciliation for the carrying amounts at the beginning and end of the period. It should include additions, assets classified as held for sale, revaluation changes and impairment changes impacting other comprehensive income, impairment losses and reversals impacting profit or loss, amortization, net foreign exchange differences resulting from translation into the presentation currency, and any other changes in the carrying amount.

- *Useful lives.* State whether the useful lives are indefinite or finite. If finite, state either the useful lives or the amortization rates being used.

When disclosing the preceding information, distinguish between internally generated and other intangible assets.

It may also be necessary to disclose the following information:

- *Accounting estimate.* Any changes in accounting estimate, such as modifications of an asset's useful life, amortization method or residual value, whether or not either has a material effect on the current period or is expected to have a material effect in subsequent periods.

- *Commitments.* The amounts of any contractual commitments to acquire intangible assets.

- *Government grants.* If intangible assets were acquired through government grants and initially recognized at their fair value, disclose the fair value initially recognized, their carrying amount, and whether they are measured under the cost or revaluation models.

- *Indefinite useful life.* If an intangible asset has an indefinite useful life, then disclose its carrying amount and the reasons why it is assessed as having an indefinite useful life.

- *Material assets.* A description of any individual intangible asset that is material to the entity's financial statements, as well as its carrying amount and remaining amortization period.

- *Research and development.* The aggregate amount of research and development expenditures recognized as expense during the period.

- *Restricted assets.* The carrying amounts of any intangible assets whose title is restricted or which are pledged as security for other liabilities.

- *Revaluation*. If intangible assets have been revalued, then disclose (for each class of assets) the date of the revaluation, the revalued carrying amounts, and the carrying amount that would have been recognized under the cost model. Also disclose the amount of the revaluation surplus relating to intangible assets at the beginning and end of the period, changes during the period, and any restrictions on distributing the surplus to shareholders. Also describe the methods and assumptions used in estimating the assets' fair values.

11

ASSET IMPAIRMENT

INTRODUCTION

Asset impairment happens when the carrying amount of an asset is greater than the amount recoverable either through using or selling an asset. If such is the case, the asset is impaired, and you must recognize an impairment loss to reduce the carrying amount. This chapter includes definitions applicable to asset impairment testing, notes which assets to test, how to conduct the tests, and subsequently record any impairment.

DEFINITIONS

The following definitions are useful for understanding asset impairment concepts:

- *Carrying amount.* The recorded amount of an asset, net of any accumulated depreciation or accumulated impairment losses.

- *Cash-generating unit.* The smallest group of assets that independently generate cash flow, and which is largely independent of the cash flows generated by other assets.

- *Goodwill.* The difference between the purchase price in an acquisition and the amount of the price not assigned to assets acquired in the acquisition that are specifically identified. Goodwill does not independently generate cash flows, and it may not be possible to allocate goodwill on a non-arbitrary basis to individual cash-generating units.

- *Recoverable amount.* The greater of an asset's fair value less costs to sell, and its value in use.

- *Value in use*. The present value of future cash flows expected to be derived from an asset.

APPLICABLE ASSETS

Impairment testing applies to all assets *other than* the following:

Agricultural assets measured at fair value	Financial instruments
Assets arising from construction contracts	Held for sale assets
Assets arising from employee benefits	Inventory
Deferred acquisition costs of insurance contracts	Investment property measured at fair value
Deferred tax assets	

THE IMPAIRMENT TEST

In general, an entity must carry out an asset impairment assessment at the end of every reporting period when there is any indication of asset impairment. If so, it must estimate the recoverable amount of the asset as of the end of that period. Also, use the following table to determine the frequency of impairment testing:

Asset Type	Impairment Test Frequency*
Intangible, with indefinite useful life	Annual
Intangible, not yet available for use	Annual
Goodwill acquired in business combination	Annual

*To be conducted even if there is no indication of impairment, and to be completed for each item at the same time every year. It is acceptable to measure different intangible assets at different times of the year.

At a minimum, consider the following factors when assessing asset impairment:

- *Asset use*. The asset is or will become idle or discontinued.

- *Damage*. The asset is damaged.

- *Dividend*. The dividend from a subsidiary or jointly controlled entity exceeds the total comprehensive income of that entity when the dividend was declared.

- *Environmental changes.* There have been or will be significant negative changes to the entity related to the legal, economic, technological, or market environment.

- *Interest rate changes.* The market interest rate has increased, affecting the entity's discount rate used for calculating asset valuations. This does not apply for changes in short-term interest rates that do not impact the discount rate for assets having a long remaining life.

- *Life.* The asset is reclassified from having an indefinite life to having a finite life.

- *Market value.* The asset's market value has significantly declined more than expected through normal use or the passage of time.

- *Obsolescence.* The asset is obsolete.

- *Performance.* The economic performance of the asset either is or will be worse than expected. This may include increased usage costs.

If a previous analysis showed that an asset's recoverable amount was not sensitive to some of the above items, then those factors do not need to be considered again.

If the preceding calculation of an asset's valuation reveals a recoverable amount much greater than its carrying amount, and there have been no events that would alter the difference, then there is no need to re-estimate the recoverable amount.

If a detailed assessment was performed in a previous period for an intangible asset, then the calculation used for that assessment may be used for the current-period impairment assessment, provided that the last such calculation revealed a substantial excess of the recoverable amount over the carrying amount, and subsequent events reveal that a decline of the recoverable amount to a level below the carrying amount is remote.

You should reduce the carrying amount of an asset to its recoverable amount if the recoverable amount is less than the carrying amount. This reduction is an asset impairment loss. Recognize this loss in the current period.

If it is not possible to estimate the recoverable amount for an individual asset, then determine it for the cash-generating unit of which the asset is a part. This situation arises when the cash flow linked to an asset is negligible.

Identify cash-generating units consistently over time for the same asset or groups of assets. Do not alter the composition of cash-generating units without justification.

The cash flows from a cash-generating unit shall be based on management's best estimate of future prices that could be achieved in an arm's length transaction, even if most or all of the output from that unit is used

---

Example

Magnetic Tram operates an articulated tram system in London. It does so under a contract with the city government to provide a minimum amount of system-wide service. It is possible to identify cash flows by tram line, and one of the tram lines clearly operates at a loss. The service contract is for the entire city area, and Magnetic Tram is not allowed to modify or terminate any tram line. Consequently, the lowest level of identifiable cash flows is for the entire tram network.

---

internally. These estimated cash flows shall override any internal transfer pricing used by the entity.

Following recognition of an impairment loss, adjust future depreciation charges to allocate an asset's revised carrying amount over its remaining useful life.

IMPAIRMENT TEST SOURCE INFORMATION: FAIR VALUE LESS COSTS TO SELL

There are a variety of information sources for determining the fair value of an asset less costs to sell. Here are three sources, presented in declining order of information quality:

1. *Sales agreement*. The price noted in a binding arm's length sales agreement.

2. *Price in an active market*. The asset's price in an active market, which is usually the current bid price, less disposal costs. In the absence of a current bid, the next best information is the price of the most recent transaction.

3. *Disposal cost*. The asset's price in an arm's length disposal transaction between knowledgeable, willing parties. This can be based on recent transactions involving similar assets in the same industry. This should not be a forced sale, unless management must sell immediately.

The costs to sell noted in these transactions include taxes and the costs of legal services, asset removal, and asset preparation for sale.

IMPAIRMENT TEST SOURCE INFORMATION: RECOVERABLE VALUE

If either an asset's fair value less costs to sell, or its value in use (present value of future cash flows) is greater than the asset's carrying amount, then

---

Example

Swedish Energy owns a wind farm in the Gulf of Bothnia. The gross cost of the facility is €80,000,000, less €15,000,000 of accumulated depreciation. The company has received a signed letter of intent to buy the facility for €68,000,000; the offer includes a requirement that Swedish Energy complete €1,000,000-worth of maintenance prior to the sale. Swedish Energy has also determined that the facility's value-in-use is €52,000,000. Is the wind farm's value impaired?

No. The carrying amount of the facility (gross cost less depreciation) is €65,000,000, and the fair value less costs to sell is €67,000,000, so the recoverable value exceeds its carrying amount. The value in use is not relevant, as long as the fair value less costs to sell exceeds the carrying amount.

---

it is not impaired. If it is not possible to measure fair value less costs to sell, then use the value in use instead.

If an asset is being held for disposal, then its value in use can be ignored (since future cash flows will be negligible) in favor of its fair value less costs to sell.

The recoverable amount is normally determined by individual asset. However, if a single asset generates cash flows only as part of a group of assets, then conduct the assessment for the group of assets.

IMPAIRMENT TEST SOURCE INFORMATION: CASH FLOW PROJECTIONS

When calculating an asset's value in use (present value of future cash flows), consider the future cash flows specifically derived from it, as modified by future cash flow variations, the current risk-free interest rate, and other factors influencing cash flows. These other factors can modify either the interest rate or the future cash flows. If there are multiple estimates of cash flows, then compile a weighted average of the various estimates.

Base the cash flow projections on reasonable and supportable assumptions comprising of the range of economic conditions most likely to exist over the remaining useful life of the asset. The projections should be founded upon the most recent budget or forecast, but such projections should *not* cover a period of more than five years, unless there is a justifiable reason for using a longer period, you are confident that these projections are reliable, and you have a demonstrated ability to forecast cash flows accurately over a longer period. When extrapolating cash flows beyond the term of a budget or forecast, incorporate a steady or declining growth rate for later years, unless there is a justifiable reason for increasing the growth rate. This growth rate should not exceed the long-term average growth rate for the product, industry, or country without justification.

Example

Magnetic Tram is reviewing its Czech subsidiary for impairment. There is no active market for the sale of this type of business, so no market-based fair value can be obtained. The subsidiary's carrying amount is €42,000,000. Management creates two computations of the subsidiary's value in use. The first computation of €38,000,000 excludes the cost reductions expected from a future employee layoff, while the second computation of €43,000,000 includes it.

Magnetic Tram should not take into account the benefit of the future layoff when calculating value in use. Consequently, there is an impairment of €4,000,000 because the value in use from the first computation is lower than the carrying amount of €42,000,000.

Cash flow projections should extend as far as the end of an asset's useful life. Since the useful life may extend well beyond the five-year budget limitation, it is acceptable to extrapolate cash flow projections based on the shorter-term budget, using a growth rate for subsequent years that is usually steady or declining.

Do not include in future cash flows any estimated changes arising from future restructurings or the projected enhancement of an asset's performance. Thus, cash flows are based on the asset remaining in its current condition.

Do not include in future cash flows any inflows or outflows from financing activities, because the discounting of future cash flows to their present value already incorporate financing costs. Also, do not include any inflows or outflows from income taxes, since the discount rate is determined on a pre-tax basis.

You should also assess the reasonableness of any differences between historical and projected cash flows, including a review of how the assumptions used for current projections have changed from the past.

REUSE OF PRIOR PERIOD IMPAIRMENT CALCULATIONS

It is allowable to use the detailed impairment calculations from a preceding period to determine the recoverable amount of a cash-generating unit to which goodwill has been allocated. This is allowable only if:

- The most recent impairment test revealed that the recoverable amount substantially exceeded the carrying amount.

- The assets and liabilities comprising the unit have not changed significantly since the last test.

- The circumstances since the last test have not changed sufficiently to indicate the presence of impairment.

REVERSAL OF AN IMPAIRMENT LOSS

At the end of each reporting period, assess whether there is any indication that a previously recognized impairment loss (not including goodwill) may have either declined or no longer exists. Use the following indicators to make the determination:

- *Favorable effects*. There are favorable effects involving the entity's business environment, or will be.

- *Interest rates*. Market interest rates have declined, and will affect the discount rate used to determine the present value of cash flows associated with the asset.

- *Internal improvements*. The asset's usage or expectations for its use have changed, such as through efficiency improvements.

- *Market value*. The asset's market value has increased.

- *Usage period*. The entity expects a longer performance period for the asset.

Estimate the recoverable amount of the asset if one or more of these indicators have changed. It is *only* allowable to reverse an impairment loss if there is a change in the estimates used to determine the asset's recoverable amount. If so, increase the carrying amount of the asset to its recoverable amount. The amount of the reversal cannot exceed the asset's carrying amount (net of depreciation) had no impairment originally been recognized.

At the time of the impairment loss reversal, recognize the change in the current reporting period in the income statement.

Once the impairment reversal is complete, adjust the asset's depreciation or amortization charge in future periods to allocate the newly-revised carrying amount, less any residual value, for the remainder of its estimated useful life.

Whether or not this review reveals a change in the impairment loss, the entity should consider whether any of the indicators warrant alterations to the asset's useful life, depreciation method, or residual value.

GOODWILL IMPAIRMENT TESTING

If goodwill has been allocated to a cash-generating unit, test it for impairment annually. In addition, test it whenever there is an indication of impairment.

The annual test can be performed at any time of the year, as long as you test it consistently at the same time every year. There is no requirement to test all cash-generating units at the same time; each unit may be scheduled for a test at a different time of the year. If goodwill is allocated to a unit in the current fiscal year, then conduct an impairment test before the end of the current fiscal year.

To test for impairment, compare the recoverable amount of a cash-generating unit to its carrying amount (including any allocated goodwill). If the carrying amount exceeds the recoverable amount, then recognize the difference between the two values as an impairment loss.

If there is an indication of impairment of an asset within a cash-generating unit to which goodwill has been allocated, follow these two impairment assessment steps:

1. Test the specific asset for impairment, and recognize any impairment loss on the asset.

2. Then test the cash-generating unit of which the asset is a part, and recognize any impairment loss on the unit.

Corporate assets should be allocated to a cash-generating unit before conducting an impairment test. If it is not possible to allocate corporate assets on a reasonable and consistent basis, then follow these two steps:

1. Test for and recognize any impairment without an allocation of corporate assets.

2. Move up from the cash-generating unit under examination to the next-largest cash generating unit to which corporate assets can be allocated on a reasonable and consistent basis; test for and recognize any impairment at that level.

If an impairment assessment reveals an impairment loss, then allocate the loss to reduce the carrying amount of the assets in the cash-generating unit in the following two-step sequence:

1. Reduce the carrying amount of goodwill allocated to the unit.

2. Allocate the loss to the other assets in the unit. Do this based on the carrying amount of each asset in the unit.

It is not allowable to reduce the carrying amount of an asset below the higher of the asset's value in use (present value of future cash flows), fair value less costs to sell, or zero. If this means that the allocated amount of an impairment loss cannot be fully charged against that asset, then allocate that excess portion of the impairment loss to the other assets in the unit on a pro rata basis.

Example

White Light Corporation has conducted an asset impairment test for its LED light cash-generating unit. Prior to the assessment, it had assets with the following carrying amounts:

Production facility	€28,000,000
Property	16,000,000
Goodwill	12,000,000
	€56,000,000

White Light now determines that the recoverable amount of the cash-generating unit is €40,000,000. The following table shows its allocation of the impairment loss to the net assets of the unit:

	Production Facility	Property	Goodwill	Total
Carrying amount	€28,000,000	€16,000,000	€12,000,000	€56,000,000
Proportion of carrying amount*	64%	36%	—	100%
Impairment loss	(2,560,000)	(1,440,000)	(12,000,000)	(16,000,000)
Carrying amount after impairment	€25,440,000	€14,560,000	€ 0	€40,000,000

*Not including the goodwill asset

If it is not practicable to estimate the recoverable amount of each asset in a unit, then it is allowable to arbitrarily allocate an impairment loss among the assets of a unit.

Example

A large batch sugar boiler on one of Harper Candy's production lines sustains permanent damage that reduces its safe production volume by 25%. There are several other sugar boilers in the production line, so management shifts work to the other boilers, resulting in no net change in the production line's total output. The smallest cash-generating unit is the entire production line, since no smaller aggregation of assets produces cash flow.

Management does not intend to replace the damaged boiler, but rather will continue to use it. Since the boiler is generating cash flow as part of the greater cash-generating unit, the recoverable amount can only be estimated as part of the unit, so it is not possible to recognize impairment for the boiler.

(continued)

(continued)

The boiler's condition deteriorates further. Management now commits to sell it, and removes it from the production line. It now has no discernible cash flows, so its recoverable value is solely based on its fair value less costs to sell of £15,000. This value is less than the boiler's carrying amount of £25,000, so Harper recognizes an impairment loss on the boiler of £10,000.

REVERSAL OF A GOODWILL IMPAIRMENT LOSS

If an impairment loss has already been recognized for goodwill, you cannot reverse it in a subsequent period. You also cannot reverse an impairment loss recognized in a previous interim period. This would constitute the recognition of internally generated goodwill, which is not allowed.

Example

White Light Corporation previously recognized a €16,000,000 impairment loss on its LED light cash-generating unit. The original loss calculation follows:

	Production Facility	Property	Goodwill	Total
Carrying amount	€28,000,000	€16,000,000	€12,000,000	€56,000,000
Proportion of carrying amount*	64%	36%	—	100%
Impairment loss	(2,560,000)	(1,440,000)	(12,000,000)	(16,000,000)
Carrying amount after impairment	€25,440,000	€14,560,000	€ 0	€40,000,000

*Not including the goodwill asset

After a three-year interval, White Light conducts another impairment assessment, which reveals that the value in use of the cash-generating unit has increased by €10,000,000. Since the last assessment, White Light has incurred deprecation of €2,000,000 on its production facility and €500,000 on its property. It allocates the valuation increase based on the current carrying amount of the production facility and property, but does not allocate it to the goodwill asset. The result appears in the following table:

(continued)

	Production Facility	Property	Goodwill	Total
Prior carrying amount	€25,440,000	€14,560,000	€0	€40,000,000
Less: subsequent depreciation	2,000,000	500,000	0	2,500,000
Current carrying amount	23,440,000	14,060,000	0	37,500,000
Proportion of carrying amount	63%	37%	—	100%
Impairment loss reversal	6,300,000	3,700,000	—	10,000,000
Carrying amount after impairment	€29,740,000	€17,760,000	€0	€47,500,000

DISCLOSURES FOR ASSET CLASSES

For each class of assets, disclose the following information:

- *Impairment losses.* The amount of impairment losses recognized during the period and the line items where they are located.

- *Impairment reversals.* The amount of impairment reversals recognized during the period and the line items where they are located.

- *Revalued asset impairment.* The amount of impairment losses on revalued assets during the period.

- *Revalued asset reversals.* The amount of impairment reversals on revalued assets recognized during the period.

DISCLOSURES FOR RECOGNIZED OR REVERSED IMPAIRMENT LOSSES

If you recognize a material impairment loss or loss reversal for an asset or a cash-generating unit, then disclose the following information for that reporting period:

- *Asset classes.* The main asset classes affected by the impairment losses and reversals, and the events and circumstances leading to those losses and reversals.

- *Asset information.* For an individual asset, the nature of the asset.

- *Circumstances.* The events and circumstances causing the impairment or reversal.

- *Quantification*. The impairment or reversal amount.

- *Type of valuation*. Whether the recoverable amount of the asset or cash-generating unit was derived from its fair value less costs to sell, or its value in use (present value of cash flows). If the former, state how the fair value was derived. If the latter, state the discount rate used in the current and previous derivations of value in use.

- *Unallocated goodwill*. If any goodwill acquired in a business combination has not been allocated to a cash-generating unit by the end of the reporting period, state the unallocated amount and the reason for non-allocation.

- *Unit information*. For a cash-generating unit, a description of the unit, the amount of loss or reversal by class of assets, any changes in the composition of the unit and the reason for altering the composition.

DISCLOSURES FOR ESTIMATIONS OF RECOVERABLE AMOUNTS

Disclose the following information for each cash-generating unit where there is a significant amount of allocated goodwill or intangible assets with indefinite useful lives:

- *Goodwill allocation*. The carrying amount of allocated goodwill.

- *Intangible assets*. The carrying amount of intangible assets with indefinite useful lives.

- *Basis*. Whether the recoverable amount of the unit is based on fair value less costs to sell or value in use (present value of cash flows).

- *Value in use information*. If the recoverable amount is based on the unit's value in use, describe the key assumptions used to create the cash flow projections, whether those assumptions are consistent with past experience or external information (or why they differ from such information), the duration of projections (and why any duration longer than five years is justified), the discount rates used for the projections, and the growth rate used to extrapolate cash flow projections (and the reason for using a growth rate above the norm).

- *Fair value information*. If the recoverable amount is based on the unit's fair value less costs to sell, then state the valuation methodology; if this does not involve an observable market price, describe the key assumptions used to derive the fair value and whether those assumptions are consistent with past experience or external information (or why they differ from such information). If the fair value is based on discounted cash flow projections, describe the period of the projections, the growth rate used to extrapolate projections, and the discount rate applied to them.

- *Sensitivity analysis.* If a reasonably possible change in a key assumption would cause a cash-generating unit's recoverable amount to drop below its carrying amount, then describe the amount by which the unit's recoverable amount currently exceeds its carrying amount, the value assigned to this key assumption, and the amount by which this value must change for the recoverable amount to equal its carrying amount.

DISCLOSURES FOR ALLOCATED GOODWILL OR INTANGIBLE ASSETS

If any portion of the carrying amount of goodwill or intangible assets with indefinite lives is allocated amongst more than one cash-generating unit, and the amount allocated to each unit is *not* significant, then disclose the following information:

- *Significance.* State that the allocation amount is not significant.
- *Carrying amount.* State the aggregate carrying amount of goodwill or intangible assets with indefinite useful lives allocated to the units.

If the recoverable amounts of the cash-generating units are derived from the same key assumptions and the aggregate carrying amount of goodwill or intangible assets with indefinite useful lives allocated to them *is* significant, then disclose that fact, along with the following:

- *Carrying amount.* The aggregate carrying amount of goodwill and/or intangible assets with indefinite useful lives allocated to the units.
- *Assumptions.* A description of the key assumptions.
- *Value determination.* A description of how management determines the values assigned to key assumptions, whether those values either reflect past experience or external information sources, and if not, why they differ.
- *Sensitivity analysis.* If a reasonably possible assumption change causes the unit's carrying amounts to exceed their recoverable amounts, then describe the values assigned to the key assumptions, the amount by which the recoverable amounts exceed carrying amounts, and the amount by which the assumption values must change for the recoverable amounts to equal the carrying amounts.

12

PROVISIONS AND CONTINGENCIES

INTRODUCTION

Any entity will periodically have provisions and contingencies, and must decide whether to recognize and disclose them. This chapter describes contingencies and provisions, and the rules under which they may be recognized.

DEFINITIONS

A *provision* is a liability that has an uncertain timing or amount. A *contingent liability* is either a possible obligation arising from past events and depending on future events not under the entity's control, or a present obligation not recognized because either the entity cannot measure the obligation or settlement is not probable.

ACCOUNTING FOR A CONTINGENT LIABILITY

Do not recognize a contingent liability. Instead, disclose the existence of the contingent liability, unless the possibility of payment is remote.

Assess contingent liabilities continually to determine whether payment has become probable. If a payment becomes probable for an item previously disclosed as a contingent liability, then create a provision in the period in which the change in probability occurs (unless you cannot create a reliable estimate of the amount of the payment).

ACCOUNTING FOR A PROVISION

You can recognize a provision when there is a *present obligation* resulting from a *past event*, there is a *probable payment* required to settle the obligation, and you can *reliably estimate* the amount of the obligation. If the provision does not meet these conditions, then do not recognize a provision. Here is additional discussion of the conditions creating a provision:

- *Present obligation.* If it is not clear whether there is a present obligation, then assume there is an obligation if it is more likely than not that a present obligation exists at the end of the reporting period, taking into account all available evidence. This assessment can include any additional evidence arising after the reporting period has ended. If an obligation does exist, then recognize a provision. If it is more likely that no obligation exists at the end of the reporting period, then disclose a contingent liability, unless there is a remote possibility of payment.

- *Past event.* A past event creates an obligation for payment if there is no reasonable alternative to settling the obligation. This is the case only when the settlement can be enforced by law or if there is a constructive obligation. A constructive obligation is an obligation derived from an entity's prior indications that it will accept certain responsibilities, which creates an expectation that it will fulfill those obligations. Do not recognize a provision for costs to be incurred in the future.

- *Probable payment.* There must be a probability of payment to settle the obligation. Probability of payment arises when the event is more likely than not to occur. When payment is not probable, then instead disclose a contingent liability, unless the probability of payment is remote.

- *Reliable estimate.* You should be able to determine a range of possible outcomes, thereby allowing you to make an estimate of the obligation amount that is reliable enough to recognize a provision. If it is not possible to create a reliable estimate, then instead disclose the liability as a contingent liability.

It is not necessary to know to whom an obligation is owed at the time of recognizing a provision. The obligation may even be to the public at large, as would be the case with a prospective penalty to be paid to the government.

Do not recognize a provision for prospective repair and maintenance expenditures, since there is no obligation to incur these costs independently of an entity's future actions; an entity could instead sell the assets prior to their repair.

Example

Sifters Gravel operates a gravel pit on the shore of the Oder River. Environmentalists have protested that Sifters is destroying the soil on its property. There is no local legislation requiring Sifters to restore the site once its operations have been completed, but the president of Sifters has stated in numerous televised interviews that the company is very conscious of its environmental responsibilities; it also has a history of restoring its other properties.

The company's actions and statements create a constructive obligation. Sifters also knows how much it cost to restore other properties, so it knows there will be a quantifiable outflow of resources. Therefore, it should create a provision related to the site restoration.

If the effect of the time value of money is material, then record a provision at the present value of the expenditure you expect is needed to settle the obligation. Thus, recording the present value of an obligation that will likely be settled in a few months is not necessary.

Use a discount rate for the present value calculation that reflects current market assessments of the time value of money and the risks specific to the liability.

MEASUREMENT OF A PROVISION

The amount that you recognize as a provision is your best estimate of the expenditure required to settle the present obligation at the end of the reporting period. This is the amount that the entity would rationally pay to settle the obligation or transfer it to a third party. This may require the input of management and outside experts, supplemented by experience with similar transactions, and includes information obtained from events occurring after the reporting period.

Example

The management of a nuclear power plant expects to decommission it in 20 years. Management has already identified €55 million of environmental damage caused by the plant, and which must be rectified during decommissioning. Management uses a discount rate of 5%, which results in a present value of the provision of €20,729,000 (€55,000,000 × 0.376889). Accordingly, the facility records a provision of €20,729,000, which it gradually increases over the succeeding 20 years, until it reaches a total provision of €55,000,000.

Example

Youth Swing Company makes the Baby Care Swing product, for which it provides a one-year full warranty for all manufacturing defects. Youth sells 100,000 Baby Care Swings in the current year. If consumers find minor repair issues in all 100,000 swings, Youth will incur a cost of €2,000,000 for repairs. If consumers detect major problems, then Youth will incur a cost of €50,000,000 to replace all of the swings.

The swing product has been in the marketplace for three years, so there is a history of having 5% of the swings returned for minor repairs, and 0.5% for major repairs. Management believes that the same proportions can be expected in the future. Based on this information, Youth creates a warranty provision in the following amount:

$$€350,000 = (€2,000,000 \times 5\%) + (€50,000,000 \times 0.5\%)$$

If there are a number of possible outcomes of a provision, then estimate the obligation by weighting all possible outcomes by their associated probabilities to derive an expected value. If there is an equal probability of multiple outcomes occurring, then use the mid-point of the range.

Even if a single outcome to an obligation appears to be the most likely estimate of a liability, you should consider other possible outcomes. If other outcomes are mostly higher or mostly lower than the most likely outcome, then you should record either a higher or lower amount, respectively.

If there is a significant amount of risk or uncertainty regarding a provision, this likely increases the amount of the provision. This does not justify creating a deliberate overstatement of a liability; you should create prudent estimates when factoring high-risk levels into your estimates.

Example

Universal Wind Power has sold a wind turbine to Swedish Energy for a wind farm. Swedish calls in Universal Wind to fix a turbine that is malfunctioning. Universal Wind is liable for any repairs during the first year of operation. Universal Wind believes the most likely problem is worn bearings, which is a simple replacement costing €500. However, all other potential problems with the turbine are more expensive to repair, costing anywhere from €10,000 to €80,000. Universal Wind should record a provision for a higher amount than €500 until it has more complete information about the exact nature of the required repair.

ACCOUNTING FOR A PROVISION REIMBURSEMENT

If you expect to be reimbursed for any expenditure under a provision, then recognize the reimbursement when it is virtually certain that the entity will receive reimbursement. If so, treat it as a separate asset. Do not record a reimbursement asset that exceeds the amount of the provision. It is allowable to present the provision net of the projected reimbursement.

PROVISIONS FOR ONEROUS CONTRACTS

An onerous contract is a contract requiring expenditures or net exit costs that exceed any economic benefits to be expected from it. You should recognize the present obligation under such a contract as a provision.

THE IMPACT OF FUTURE EVENTS ON A PROVISION

You should factor any future events affecting the amount needed to settle an obligation into a provision. This is only necessary if there is sufficient

---

Example

Dominican Shipping loses an entire shipload of cargo to a rogue wave off the coast of Patagonia. The value of the cargo is €15 million. The cargo was insured, less a 20% deductible, and the insurer has stated in writing that it will not contest Dominican's claim.

Dominican can recognize a contingent reimbursement (asset) of €12 million, which is the net amount its insurance company has committed to pay it.

Example

General Software operates its software development group from a facility in Edinburgh under a lease having a five-year term. At the end of Year 1, General buys a company in nearby Queensferry, and shifts its Edinburgh staff into the Queensferry location. General is still required to make monthly lease payments on the old facility for the next four years, it cannot cancel the lease, and the landlord refuses to allow subtenants.

There are no economic benefits that General can realize from the Edinburgh facility, and all lease payments are probable, so General should recognize a provision for the present value of the remaining lease payments.

Example

Loften Petrochemicals has operated a small refinery at Junglinster for more than 30 years. There has been increasing evidence that leaks from the Junglinster facility have penetrated the water table, causing problems with the local drinking water. Consequently, it is virtually certain that the Luxembourg Chamber of Deputies will pass legislation shortly after year-end, requiring that all refineries implement groundwater remediation activities. The company has already engaged a consulting firm to determine the monetary impact of the new legislation, and accordingly creates a €35 million provision, based on the most likely estimates in the consulting report.

---

objective evidence that the future events will occur. For example, a future event can be possible new legislation that is virtually certain to be enacted, or expected cost reductions associated with increased experience in applying existing technology.

RESTRUCTURING PROVISIONS

It is acceptable to create a provision for a restructuring only when it meets the general criteria for a provision. In addition, there is only an obligation to restructure when an entity has a formal restructuring plan that identifies the business, location, and employees to be terminated, the expenditures to be undertaken, when this will happen, and has raised a valid expectation of implementation (such as through a detailed public announcement). If there is a long delay prior to the restructuring, or if the restructuring will take a long time, then this does not raise a valid expectation of implementation, and a provision is not needed. If the board of directors has approved a restructuring, that is not sufficient grounds to recognize a provision; it must be accompanied by actual implementation or the entity must have announced a detailed restructuring plan. If a restructuring is based on the sale of an operation, do not record a provision until there is a binding sale agreement.

Only include in a restructuring provision those expenditures necessarily entailed by the event, and not associated with any ongoing activities of the entity. Thus, you cannot include in the provision expenditures for retraining or relocating continuing staff, or marketing, or investments in new systems and distribution networks, or future operating losses, or gains on future asset disposals.

Examples of restructuring events are the sale or termination of a business, the closure or relocation of business locations, changes in the management structure, or events having a material effect on operations.

Example

Blood Storage Devices maintains low-temperature storage facilities for fresh frozen plasma, with multiple power redundancies to avoid temperature increases. Blood's board of directors concludes that its Italian facility is unprofitable, and approves a detailed plan to close it. In addition, the company sends letters to its Italian hospital customers, notifying them of the shutdown and advising them regarding alternative storage facilities. It also notifies the staff of the Italian facility that they will be terminated. The cost associated with the restructuring is €15 million. Since the company has created a valid expectation of closure and payments are probable, Blood should record a €15 million restructuring provision.

PROVISION ADJUSTMENTS

Review all provisions at the end of each reporting period and adjust them to reflect the current best estimate. As time passes, increase the amount of any provisions for which discounting has been used, in order to reflect the passage of time. This incremental increase is a borrowing cost.

ACCOUNTING FOR A CONTINGENT ASSET

A contingent asset is a possible asset arising from past events and which will only be confirmed by future events not under the entity's control. Do not recognize a contingent asset, only disclose it when an incoming payment is probable. However, if the realization of income is virtually certain, then the related asset is no longer a contingent asset, and you can recognize it in the period when the change occurs.

You should continually assess contingent assets to ensure that they are properly disclosed in the financial statements.

Example

South African Salvage (SAS) rescues the passengers and crew of the *Southern Star* passenger ship after it hits an iceberg in the Weddell Sea, and also refloats the ship. SAS files suit against the owner of the *Southern Star*, claiming that the *Southern Star*'s captain agreed to a "no cure–no pay" contract, under which SAS is entitled to 20% of the hull value only if it can salvage the ship. The *Southern Star*'s owners claim that the contract was actually only for time and materials, which would result in a much smaller settlement.

(continued)

> (*continued*)
>
> In Year 1, the outcome of the lawsuit is uncertain throughout the legal proceedings, so SAS cannot recognize a contingent asset. At the beginning of Year 2, a court ruling requires that the *Southern Star*'s owner must pay SAS the full amount of its claim within 90 days. During that 90-day period, SAS can record a contingent asset for the payment amount.

DISCLOSURES

For each class of provision, you should disclose the following:

- *Balances and activity*. The carrying amount at the beginning and end of the period, changes during the period, unused amounts reversed during the period, and any increases caused by discounted amounts arising from either the passage of time or changes in the discount rate.

- *Description*. A description of the nature of the obligation, payment timing, any uncertainties about payment timing, expected reimbursements, and major assumptions made regarding future events.

For each class of contingent liability, you should disclose the following unless there is only a remote possibility of payment:

- *Description*. The nature of the contingent liability.

- *Quantification*. Estimate its financial effect.

- *Reimbursements*. The possibility of any reimbursement.

- *Uncertainties*. Indicate the uncertainties relating to the amount or timing of payments.

If there is a probable inflow of economic benefits, describe the nature of the contingent asset and estimate its financial effect.

Examples of classes of provisions or contingencies are warranties and amounts subject to legal proceedings, which you should aggregate into separate classes.

If the same set of circumstances creates both a provision and a contingent liability, disclose the link between the provision and the contingent liability.

If any of the preceding disclosures may seriously prejudice an entity's position in a dispute with another party, then do not disclose the information. Instead, disclose the general nature of the dispute, as well as the reason why additional information has not been disclosed.

PART THREE

THE FINANCIAL STATEMENTS

13

FINANCIAL STATEMENTS PRESENTATION

INTRODUCTION

An entity is supposed to report the results of its activities and its financial position in accordance with a strict set of rules mandated by the international financial reporting standards (IFRS). This chapter describes the layout and contents of the various financial statements, as well as a discussion of the disclosures that should accompany the financial statements.

DEFINITIONS

Profit or loss is the total of an entity's revenues and expenses, not including any components of other comprehensive income. It is also known as *net income*.

Total comprehensive income is the combination of profit or loss and other comprehensive income.

Other comprehensive income includes financial items that are not permitted in profit or loss. Items that you should insert into other comprehensive income include:

- *Actuarial gains and losses on defined benefit plans* (see the Employee Benefits chapter).

- *Available-for-sale gains and losses caused by re-measurement* (see the Financial Instruments chapter).

- *Cash flow hedge gains and losses, effective portion only* (see the Financial Instruments chapter).

- *Changes in the revaluation surplus* (see the Property, Plant, and Equipment chapter).

- *Foreign currency translation gains and losses* (see the Effects of Foreign Exchange Rate Changes chapter).

Reclassification adjustments are amounts reclassified into profit or loss in the current period that had been recognized in other comprehensive income in either the current or previous periods.

CONTENTS OF THE FINANCIAL STATEMENTS

All of the following financial reports should be included in a complete set of financial statements for a reporting period:

Statement	Description
Statement of financial position	Contains all asset, liability, and equity items
Statement of comprehensive income	Contains all income and expense items
Statement of changes in equity	Reconciles changes in equity for the presented periods
Statement of cash flows	Displays all cash inflows and outflows from operating, financing, and investing activities
Notes	Summarizes accounting policies and explanatory information

You should clearly identify these financial statements and distinguish them from other information presented in the same report. It is important to do this, because international financial reporting standards only apply to financial statements; thus, users will be more likely to understand which documents within the report adhere to specific accounting standards.

You should include in the financial statements a prominent display of the name of the reporting entity (and note any change in it from the preceding reporting period), whether the statements are for a single entity or group of entities, the period covered by the statements, the presentation currency, and the level of rounding used to present amounts. This information is usually most easily presented in column and page headers.

CONTENTS OF THE STATEMENT OF FINANCIAL POSITION

You should include the following line items, at a minimum, in the statement of financial position:

Assets:

- Cash and cash equivalents
- Trade and other receivables
- Investments accounted for using the equity method
- Other financial assets
- Current tax assets
- Investment property
- Inventories
- Biological assets
- Property, plant, and equipment
- Intangible assets
- Assets held for sale
- Deferred tax assets (do not classify as a current asset)

Liabilities:

- Trade and other payables
- Provisions
- Current tax liabilities
- Other financial liabilities
- Deferred tax liabilities (do not classify as a current liability)
- Liabilities held for sale

Equity:

- Non-controlling interests
- Issued capital and reserves attributable to owners of the parent company

You should add headings and subtotals to this minimum set of information if it will improve a user's understanding of the financial statements. You should add other line items when their size, nature, or function makes separate presentation relevant to the user.

You should provide additional sub-classifications of the primary line items required for the statement of financial position, if needed to clarify an entity's operations, or to be in accordance with the various IFRSs. Examples of these additional classifications are:

Example

Ninja Cutlery presents its statement of financial position in the following format:

NINJA CUTLERY
STATEMENT OF FINANCIAL POSITION

(000s)	as at 12/31/x2	as at 12/31/x1
ASSETS		
Non-current assets		
Property, plant, and equipment	€ 551,000	€ 529,000
Goodwill	82,000	82,000
Other intangible assets	143,000	143,000
Investments in associates	71,000	93,000
Available-for-sale financial assets	121,000	108,000
	968,000	955,000
Current assets		
Inventories	139,000	128,000
Trade receivables	147,000	139,000
Other current assets	15,000	27,000
Cash and cash equivalents	270,000	215,000
	571,000	509,000
Total assets	€1,539,000	€1,464,000
EQUITY AND LIABILITIES		
Equity attributable to owners of the parent company		
Share capital	€ 500,000	€500,000
Retained earnings	425,000	350,000
Other components of equity	25,000	19,000
	950,000	869,000
Non-controlling interests	57,000	38,000
Total equity	1,007,000	907,000
Non-current liabilities		
Long-term borrowings	85,000	65,000
Deferred tax	19,000	17,000
Long-term provisions	38,000	34,000
Total non-current liabilities	142,000	116,000

(continued)

Current liabilities		
Trade and other payables	217,000	198,000
Short-term borrowings	133,000	202,000
Current portion of long-term borrowings	5,000	5,000
Current tax payable	26,000	23,000
Short-term provisions	9,000	13,000
Total current liabilities	390,000	441,000
Total liabilities	532,000	557,000
Total equity and liabilities	€1,539,000	€1,464,000

- Separate property, plant, and equipment into different asset classifications

- Separate accounts receivable into amounts receivable from trade customers, related parties, and prepayments

- Separate inventories into merchandise, supplies, raw materials, work in process, and finished goods

- Separate equity into paid-in capital, share premiums, and reserves

For each class of share capital, you disclose the following:

- *Internal holdings.* Any shares held by the entity or its subsidiaries or associates.

- *Par value.* The par value per share. If there is no par value, state this fact.

- *Reclassifications.* Any reclassifications of financial instruments between liabilities and equity, and the timing and reasons for the reclassifications.

- *Reconciliation.* Reconcile the share totals at the beginning and end of the reporting period.

- *Reserved shares.* Any outstanding share options or other contracts for the sale of shares, as well as the terms of these agreements.

- *Reserves.* The nature of any equity reserves.

- *Rights and restrictions.* Restrictions on dividend distribution and capital repayment, as well as any other rights, preferences, and restrictions.

- *Shares.* The number of shares authorized, issued and fully paid, and issued but not fully paid.

You should classify an asset as current when an entity expects to sell or consume it during its normal operating cycle or within 12 months after the reporting period, or if it holds the asset in order to trade it, or if it is a cash or cash equivalent (unless it is restricted from use). Current assets always include cash, inventories, and assets held for trading. You should classify all other assets as non-current.

You should classify a liability as current when the entity expects to settle it during its normal operating cycle or within 12 months after the reporting period, if it holds the liability in order to trade it, if it is scheduled for settlement within 12 months, or if the entity does not have the right to defer its settlement for at least 12 months. You should classify financial liabilities as current when they are scheduled for settlement within 12 months, even if the original term was for a longer period. Current liabilities always include trade payables and accruals for employee and other operating costs. You should classify all other liabilities as non-current.

If an entity reaches an agreement after the reporting period but before the financial statements are authorized for issuance, to reschedule payments or refinance so that payments are due *after* the 12-month period, you should still categorize them as current liabilities. If an entity expects and has the ability to refinance or roll over an obligation so that it is due more than 12 months after the reporting period, then you should classify the obligation as non-current.

If an entity breaches a provision of a long-term debt agreement during a reporting period that effectively makes the agreement payable on demand, you should categorize it as a current liability, even if the lender agrees, before the financial statements are authorized for issuance, not to demand payment. However, if the lender agrees, by the end of the reporting period, to provide at least a 12-month grace period, then you can classify the debt as non-current.

CONTENTS OF THE STATEMENT OF COMPREHENSIVE INCOME

You should present all items of income and expense for the reporting period in a statement of comprehensive income. Alternatively, you can split this information into an income statement and a statement of comprehensive income.

You should include the following line items, at a minimum, in the statement of comprehensive income:

- Revenue

- Finance costs

- Share of associates' and joint ventures' profit or loss recorded with the equity method

- Tax expense

- Post-tax profit or loss for discontinued operations and for the disposal of these operations

- Profit or loss

- Other comprehensive income, subdivided into each component thereof

- Share of associates' and joint ventures' other comprehensive income recorded with the equity method

- Total comprehensive income

A key additional item is to present an analysis of the expenses in profit or loss, using a classification based on their nature or functional area, maximizing the relevance and reliability of presented information. If you elect to present expenses by their nature, the format looks similar to the following:

Revenue		XXX
Expenses:		
Change in finished goods inventories	XXX	
Raw materials used	XXX	
Employee benefits expense	XXX	
Depreciation expense	XXX	
Telephone expense	XXX	
Other expenses	XXX	
Total expenses		XXX
Profit before tax		XXX

Alternatively, if you present expenses by their functional area, the format looks similar to the following:

Revenue	XXX
Cost of sales	XXX
Gross profit	XXX
Administrative expenses	XXX
Distribution expenses	XXX
Research and development expenses	XXX
Other expenses	XXX
Total expenses	XXX
Profit before tax	XXX

Of the two methods, presenting expenses by their nature is easier, since it requires no allocation of expenses between functional areas.

Conversely, the functional area presentation may be more relevant to users of the information, who can more easily see where resources are being consumed. If you elect to use a functional area presentation, you must also disclose information about the nature of the expenses, at least including separate presentation of depreciation expense, amortization expense, and employee benefits expense.

In addition, you should disclose the profit or loss and total comprehensive income attributable to any non-controlling interests, and the owners of the parent entity.

Taxes require additional disclosure to the line items noted above. You should disclose the amount of tax related to each component of other comprehensive income. This information can be included in the statement itself or in the associated notes. You should not present any components of other comprehensive income net of related taxes.

You should add additional headings, subtotals, and line items to the items noted above if doing so will increase a user's understanding of the entity's financial performance.

Example

Blood Storage Devices presents its statement of financial position in two statements by their nature, resulting in the following format, beginning with the income statement:

BLOOD STORAGE DEVICES INCOME STATEMENT
FOR THE YEARS ENDED DECEMBER 31

(000s)	20x2	20x1
Revenue	€900,000	€850,000
Other income	25,000	20,000
Changes in finished goods inventories	(270,000)	(255,000)
Raw materials used	(90,000)	(85,000)
Employee benefits expense	(180,000)	(170,000)
Depreciation and amortization expense	(135,000)	(125,000)
Impairment of property, plant, and equipment	0	(50,000)
Other expenses	(75,000)	(72,000)
Finance costs	(29,000)	(23,000)
Share of profit of associates	21,000	30,000
Profit before tax	167,000	120,000
Income tax expense	(58,000)	(42,000)

(continued)

Profit for the year from continuing operations	109,000	78,000
Loss for the year from discontinued operations	(42,000)	0
PROFIT FOR THE YEAR	€67,000	€78,000
Profit attributable to:		
Owners of the parent	60,000	70,000
Non-controlling interests	7,000	8,000
	€67,000	€78,000
Earnings per share:		
Basic	€ 0.13	€ 0.16
Diluted	0.09	0.10

Blood Storage Devices then continues with the following statement of comprehensive income:

BLOOD STORAGE DEVICES STATEMENT OF COMPREHENSIVE INCOME

(000s)	20x2	20x1
Profit for the year	€67,000	€78,000
Other comprehensive income:		
Exchange differences on translating foreign operations	5,000	9,000
Available-for-sale financial assets	10,000	(2,000)
Cash flow hedges	(1,000)	(3,000)
Gains on property revaluation	7,000	11,000
Actuarial losses on defined benefit pension plan	(2,000)	(2,000)
Share of other comprehensive income of associates	1,000	4,000
Other comprehensive income, net of tax	20,000	17,000
TOTAL COMPREHENSIVE INCOME	€87,000	€95,000
Total comprehensive income attributable to:		
Owners of the parent	78,000	86,000
Non-controlling interests	9,000	9,000
	€87,000	€95,000

You should ensure that the following information is included in either the statement of comprehensive income or its associated notes:

- *Reclassification adjustments.* Any reclassification adjustments related to components of other comprehensive income (arises when items previously recognized in other comprehensive income are shifted into profit or loss).

- *Material items.* If an income or expense item is material, separately disclose its nature and amount. Examples of items that may require separate disclosure are inventory write-downs, restructurings, asset disposals, discontinued operations, provision reversals, and the settlement of litigation.

CONTENTS OF THE STATEMENT OF CHANGES IN EQUITY

You should include the following line items in the statement of changes in equity:

- Total comprehensive income (with separate presentation of the amounts attributable to the owners of the parent entity and to non-controlling interests)

- Effects of retrospective applications or restatements on each component of equity (which are usually adjustments to the opening balance of retained earnings)

- Reconciliation of changes during the period for each component of equity resulting from profit or loss, each item of other comprehensive income, and transactions with owners (including contributions by and distributions to them)

- Dividends recognized, and the related amount per share (this item can alternatively be presented in the associated notes)

Example

Ancestral Heritage Company presents its statement of changes in equity as follows to reflect changes in its equity over a two-year period:

	Share Capital	Retained Earnings	Total	Non-Controlling Interests	Total Equity
Balance at Jan. 01, 20x1	€350,000	€50,000	€400,000	€40,000	€440,000
Accounting policy change	–	(3,000)	(3,000)	–	(3,000)
Restated balance	350,000	47,000	397,000	40,000	437,000
Changes in equity for 20x1					
Dividends	–	(25,000)	(25,000)	–	(25,000)
Total comprehensive income	–	42,000	42,000	4,000	46,000
Balance at Dec. 31, 20x1	€350,000	€64,000	€414,000	€44,000	€458,000
Changes in equity for 20x2					
Dividends	–	(18,000)	(18,000)	–	(18,000)
Issue of share capital	125,000	–	125,000	–	125,000
Total comprehensive income	–	37,000	37,000	4,000	41,000
Balance at Dec. 31, 20x2	€475,000	€83,000	€558,000	€48,000	€606,000

CONTENTS OF THE STATEMENT OF CASH FLOWS

The statement of cash flows contains information about activities that generate and use cash. You can use the *direct method* or the *indirect method* to present the statement of cash flows. The direct method presents the specific cash flows associated with items that affect cash flow. Items typically affecting cash flow include:

- Cash collected from customers

- Interest and dividends received

- Cash paid to employees

- Cash paid to suppliers

- Interest paid

- Income taxes paid

Under the indirect method, the presentation begins with net income or loss, with subsequent additions to or deductions from that amount for non-cash revenue and expense items, resulting in net cash provided by operating activities.

The primary activities shown in the statement of cash flows are:

- *Operating activities* are an entity's primary revenue-producing activities. Examples of operating activities are cash receipts from the sale of goods, as well as from royalties and commissions, and payments to employees and suppliers.

- *Investing activities* involve the acquisition and disposal of long-term assets. Examples of investing activities are cash receipts from the sale of property, the sale of debt or equity instruments of other entities, repayment of loans made to other entities, as well as from futures contracts, swap contracts, and forward contracts. Examples of cash payments that are investment activities include capitalized development costs, the acquisition of property, plant, and equipment, purchases of the debt or equity of other entities, and payments for futures contracts, swap contracts, and forward contracts.

- *Financing activities* are those activities resulting in alterations to the amount of contributed equity and the entity's borrowings. Examples of financing activities include cash receipts from the sale of the entity's own equity instruments or from issuing debt, as well as cash payments to buy back shares and to pay off outstanding debt.

The information you should include in these activities is as follows:

- *Operating activities.* Use either the direct method (disclosing major classes of gross cash receipts and payments) or the indirect method (adjusting profit or loss for changes in inventories, receivables, payables, and a variety of non-cash items). The IFRS-recommended approach is to use the direct method.

- *Investing activities.* Separately report the major classes of gross cash receipts and payments caused by investing activities.

- *Financing activities.* Separately report the major classes of gross cash receipts and payments caused by financing activities.

The statement of cash flows also incorporates the concept of *cash and cash equivalents*. A cash equivalent is a short-term (usually maturing in three months or less), very liquid investment that is easily convertible into cash, and which is at minimal risk of a change in value.

Example

Norwegian Defense and Aerospace constructs the following statement of cash flows using the direct method:

NORWEGIAN DEFENSE AND AEROSPACE STATEMENT OF CASH FLOWS FOR THE YEAR 12/31/x1

Cash flows from operating activities		
Cash receipts from customers	€45,800,000	
Cash paid to suppliers	(29,800,000)	
Cash paid to employees	(11,200,000)	
Cash generated from operations	4,800,000	
Interest paid	(310,000)	
Income taxes paid	(1,700,000)	
Net cash from operating activities		€2,790,000
Cash flows from investing activities		
Purchase of property, plant, and equipment	(580,000)	
Proceeds from sale of equipment	110,000	
Interest received	12,000	
Dividends received	5,000	
Net cash used in investing activities		€ (453,000)
Cash flows from financing activities		
Proceeds from issuance of share capital	1,000,000	
Proceeds from borrowings	500,000	
Dividends paid	(450,000)	
Net cash used in financing activities		€1,050,000
Net increase in cash and cash equivalents		3,387,000
Cash and cash equivalents at beginning of period		1,613,000
Cash and cash equivalents at end of period		€5,000,000

Example

Corn Syrup Candy constructs the following statement of cash flows using the indirect method:

**CORN SYRUP CANDY STATEMENT OF CASH FLOWS
FOR THE YEAR ENDED 12/31x1**

Cash flows from operating activities		
Profit before taxation		£3,000,000
Adjustments for:		
Depreciation	£125,000	
Foreign exchange loss	20,000	
Investment income	(80,000)	
Interest expense	40,000	
		£105,000
Increase in trade receivables	(250,000)	
Decrease in inventories	325,000	
Decrease in trade payables	(50,000)	
		25,000
Cash generated from operations		£3,130,000
Interest paid		(12,000)
Income taxes paid		(870,000)
Net cash from operating activities		2,248,000
Cash flows from investing activities		
Purchase of property, plant, and equipment	(500,000)	
Proceeds from sale of equipment	35,000	
Interest received	10,000	
Dividends received	8,000	
Net cash used in investing activities		(447,000)
Cash flows from financing activities		
Proceeds from issue of share capital	150,000	
Proceeds from borrowings	175,000	
Payment of finance lease liabilities	(45,000)	
Net cash used in financing activities		280,000
Net increase in cash and cash equivalents		2,081,000
Cash and cash equivalents at beginning of period		2,919,000
Cash and cash equivalents at end of period		£5,000,000

DISCLOSURES–GENERAL

You should present financial statement notes in the following sequence:

   i. Statement of compliance with IFRS

  ii. Summary of the entity's significant accounting policies

iii. Supporting information for line items in the financial statements, in the order in which the various statements are presented

iv. Other disclosures, such as for non-financial information

You should include the following information in the notes accompanying the financial statements:

- *Assumptions.* Information about major assumptions regarding the future.

- *Basis of preparation.* The measurement basis used to prepare the statements (e.g., historical cost, current cost, net realizable value, fair value, or recoverable amount), and other accounting policies used that are relevant to understanding the statements. If you use more than one measurement basis, then indicate which basis is used for general categories of assets and liabilities. It is especially important to disclose an accounting policy when an IFRS allows alternative treatment.

- *Capital management.* Description of capital that the entity manages, how it meets its capital management objectives, the nature of any externally imposed capital requirements, and a summary of what it manages as capital and how capital levels have changed during the period. Also note whether the entity has complied with any externally imposed capital requirements; if not, describe the consequences of non-compliance.

- *Dividends.* The amount of dividends not recognized as a distribution, but proposed or declared before the financial statements were authorized for issuance. Also, note the unrecognized amount of any cumulative preference dividends.

- *Domicile.* The domicile of the entity, its country of incorporation, and the address of its registered office.

- *Estimation uncertainty.* Major sources of estimation uncertainty that may result in a significant material adjustment of the carrying amount of the entity's assets and liabilities within the next fiscal year. Note the nature and carrying amount of the potentially impacted assets and liabilities. For example, there may be estimation uncertainty about the future recoverable amounts of assets, the impact of technological obsolescence on inventories, and the requirements of defined benefit plans. This disclosure is not needed for those assets and liabilities already being measured at their fair values based on recent market prices.

- *IFRS requirements.* Disclosures required by other IFRS that are not already included in the financial statements.

- *Legal form.* The legal form of the entity.

- *Life.* If the entity has a limited duration, note the length of its life.

- *Management judgments.* The judgments that management has made when applying accounting policies, and which have a significant effect on financial results. Examples are the decision to classify an asset as held-to-maturity, whether sales are actually financing arrangements, and whether the entity exercises control over another entity.

- *Name.* The name of the entity's parent company and of the ultimate parent company of the group.

- *Operations.* The nature of the entity's operations.

- *Puttable financial instruments.* For puttable financial instruments, note the amount classified as equity, the objectives, policies, and processes for redeeming these instruments, the cash outflow caused by the expected redemption, and information about how you determined the redemption amount.

- *Other information.* Other information not presented elsewhere in the financial statements, but which is relevant to understanding them.

You should cross-reference items in the various financial statements with these notes.

DISCLOSURES–COMPARATIVE INFORMATION

You should disclose comparative information for the previous period(s) for all amounts that an entity is reporting in its current-period financial statements. This may include narrative information if it improves user's understanding of the financial statements. The following table reveals the extent of comparative information requirements for different situations:

Report Name	Minimum Scenario	For Retrospective Policy Change, Restatement, Reclassification
Statement of financial position	End of current period and preceding period	End of current period, end of preceding period, and beginning of the earliest comparable period

(continued)

(*continued*)

Statement of comprehensive income	Current period and preceding period	Current period and preceding period
Statement of changes in equity	Current period and preceding period	Current period and preceding period
Statement of cash flows	Current period and preceding period	Current period and preceding period
Notes	Current period and preceding period	Current period and preceding period

14

CONSOLIDATED AND SEPARATE FINANCIAL STATEMENTS

INTRODUCTION

An entity may have to consolidate the results of any number of subsidiaries or investees in its own financial statements, depending upon the level of control that it exercises over the other entities. This chapter describes the rules under which you should use consolidation, how to complete a consolidation, and what to do if the results of an entity should no longer be consolidated into the results of the parent entity.

DEFINITIONS

Consolidated financial statements are the financial statements of a group of entities that are presented as being those of a single economic entity. A *group* is a parent entity and all of its subsidiaries. A *subsidiary* is an entity that is controlled by a parent entity.

WHEN TO USE CONSOLIDATION

A parent entity presents consolidated financial statements in which it consolidates the investments it has made in its subsidiaries.

An entity does not present consolidated financial statements if it is itself a subsidiary of another entity, the parent's financial instruments are not publicly traded, the parent has not and is not filing with a regulatory organization to issue any financial instruments in a public market, and the ultimate parent entity produces consolidated financial statements that comply with IFRS (international financial reporting standards).

Consolidated financial statements must include all of the subsidiaries of the parent entity. These subsidiaries are entities over which the parent entity has:

- More than half of the voting power of the entity (unless such ownership does not constitute control)

- Indirect voting power over more than half of the voting rights of the entity through an agreement with other investors

- The power to govern the entity's financial and operating policies

- The power to appoint or remove a majority of the entity's board of directors

- The power to cast the majority of votes at the entity's board meetings

---

Example

The Avuncular, Bitter, and Cheery Companies each own 30% of the voting shares of Domino Company. In addition, Bitter owns call options that it can exercise at any time at a fixed price; if it does so, Bitter will own a majority of the voting rights in Domino. Even though Bitter's management does not intend to exercise the call options, the existence of the call options gives Bitter control over Domino for consolidation purposes.

A parent entity must include a subsidiary in its consolidated financial statements even if the subsidiary's business activities are not similar to those of the other subsidiaries whose results are included in the consolidated financial statements.

A parent entity must still consolidate the financial results of its subsidiaries as defined here, even if the parent is a venture capital organization, unit trust, mutual fund, or some similar type of entity.

THE FINANCIAL STATEMENT CONSOLIDATION PROCESS

The general process for consolidating the financial statements of a parent entity and its subsidiaries is to combine the statements line by line. More specifically shown in the following nine steps:

1. Adjust the financial statements of any member of the group to conform to the accounting policies used by the parent entity for consolidating the financial statements.

2. Make adjustments for the effects of significant transactions or events occurring between the dates of the financial statements of the subsidiaries and the parent, if they differ.

3. Eliminate all intra-group balances, transactions, income and expenses. This includes the elimination of profits and losses resulting from intra-group transactions.

4. Eliminate the carrying amount of the parent's investment in each subsidiary and the parent's portion of equity of each subsidiary.

5. Identify non-controlling interests in the profit or loss of consolidated subsidiaries.

6. Separately identify the non-controlling interests in the net assets of the consolidated subsidiaries. These non-controlling interests include the amount of non-controlling interests at the date of the original combination and the non-controlling interests' share of any changes in equity since the date of combination.

7. Present non-controlling interests in the consolidated statement of financial position within equity, separately from the equity of the parent entity's owners.

8. If there are outstanding cumulative preference shares at the subsidiary level that are held by non-controlling interests, then the parent entity computes its share of profits or losses after adjusting for the dividends on these shares, irrespective of a dividend declaration.

9. Attribute profit or loss and each component of other comprehensive income to the owners of the parent entity and to non-controlling interests, even if the result is a deficit balance for the non-controlling interests.

If the financial statements prepared by a subsidiary for inclusion in consolidated statements are of a different date than the date used for the statements of the parent, then the subsidiary shall prepare additional financial statements that are of the same date as those of the parent, unless it is impracticable to do so. It is not allowable to ever have a difference between the dates of the financial statements of the parent and its subsidiaries of more than three months.

You should include the revenues and expenses of a newly-acquired subsidiary in the consolidated financial statements of the parent entity beginning on the acquisition date.

CONSOLIDATING A SPECIAL PURPOSE ENTITY

A special purpose entity (SPE) is created to accomplish a specific objective, such as research and development activities, or the securitization of accounts receivable. The entity on whose behalf the SPE was created typically shifts assets to the SPE, may have the right to use the output of the SPE, and so may be considered to have control over it. A parent entity should consolidate an SPE when the substance of the relationship indicates a control situation, using the indicators noted in the answer to the last question.

The following situations may indicate a control situation that would require consolidation:

- The parent entity obtains benefits from the SPE's operations.

- The parent entity has the power to obtain most of the benefits of the SPE, or originally set up the SPE to do so.

- The parent entity retains a majority of the ownership and operational risks of the SPE.

Example

Barbados Exploratory Consortium helps to create an SPE that researches new methods for deep-water mineral exploration. Part of the operating agreement of the SPE allows Barbados to acquire any patents filed by the SPE in exchange for a minimum payment. Since Barbados has the power to obtain the benefits of the SPE, it should include the results of the SPE in its consolidated financial statements.

REPORTING CHANGES IF THERE IS A LOSS OF CONTROL

If the parent entity loses control of a subsidiary, it takes the following five steps as of the date of loss of control:

1. Derecognize the assets and liabilities of the subsidiary at their carrying amounts. This includes the derecognition of goodwill.

2. Derecognize the carrying amount of any non-controlling interests in the former subsidiary. This includes any items of other comprehensive income attributable to the non-controlling interests.

3. Recognize the fair value of any consideration received from the event resulting in the loss of control. This includes the fair value of any distribution of the subsidiary's shares to the owners.

4. Recognize any investment still retained in the former subsidiary at its fair value.

5. Account for all amounts recognized in other comprehensive income for the subsidiary as though the parent had disposed of the related assets or liabilities. For example, if a revaluation surplus recognized in other comprehensive income would have been transferred to retained earnings upon asset disposal, then do so when the parent loses control of the subsidiary.

Example

Cardiac Transport Services is an investor in and has significant influence over Blood Collection Services. Blood Collection has €100,000 of available-for-sale securities, for which Cardiac Transport had previously recognized a gain of €10,000 in other comprehensive income on its share of those securities. Cardiac Transport loses significant influence over Blood. On the date of its loss of significant influence, Cardiac Transport should reclassify the €10,000 gain to profit or loss.

DISCLOSURES

The parent entity should disclose the following information in its consolidated financial statements:

- *Cash restrictions*. Any significant restrictions on the ability of subsidiaries to transfer funds to the parent entity.

- *Control reasoning*. The reasons why the parent does not have control over an entity, despite having more than half of the voting power.

- *Date differentials*. The date of the financial statements of a subsidiary if they vary from those of the parent entity, and the reason for allowing this different date.

- *Joint control or associate investments*. If the parent entity has an interest in a jointly controlled entity or an associate and prepares separate financial statements, then disclose that the statements are reported separately, and why these statements are prepared. Also, list the parent entity's significant investments in subsidiaries, jointly controlled entities and associates, its ownership interest in each one, their locations, and the method used to account for these investments.

- *Loss of control*. The gain or loss recognized upon loss of control in a subsidiary, the portion of that amount attributable to recognizing investments retained in the subsidiary at its fair value, and where the gain or loss is recognized in the statement of comprehensive income.

- *Non-consolidation disclosures*. If the parent prepares non-consolidated financial statements, then disclose that the statements are reported separately under an exemption from consolidation, and the name, address, and country of the parent entity that has made its IFRS-compliant consolidated financial statements available. Also, list the parent entity's significant investments in subsidiaries, jointly controlled entities and associates, its ownership interest in each one, their locations, and the method used to account for these investments.

- *Ownership changes*. A schedule revealing the effects of ownership changes in a subsidiary.

- *Partial voting power*. The nature of the parent's relationship with a subsidiary when the parent does not own more than half of the voting power.

15

RELATED PARTY DISCLOSURES

INTRODUCTION

A related party transaction is a transfer of obligations, resources, or services between related parties. It is possible that a price will not be charged in exchange for these transfers.

If an entity does business with a related party, it must disclose certain information about the transaction. This chapter defines a related party and itemizes the various types of required disclosures.

DEFINITION OF A RELATED PARTY

A party is related to an entity if any of the following situations apply to it:

- *Associate.* The party is an associate of the entity (see the Investments in Associates chapter).

- *Common control.* The party is, directly or indirectly, either under common control with the entity, or has significant or joint control over the entity.

- *Family member.* The party is a close family member of a person who is part of key management personnel, or which controls the entity. A close family member is the individual's domestic partner and children, children of the domestic partner, and dependents of the individual or the individual's domestic partner.

- *Individual control.* The party is controlled or significantly influenced by a member of key management personnel, or which controls the entity.

- *Joint venture*. The party is a joint venture in which the entity is a venture partner (see the Interests in Joint Ventures chapter).

- *Key management*. The party is a member of an entity's or its parent's key management personnel.

- *Post-employment plan*. The party is a post-employment benefit plan for the entity's employees.

The determination of related party status depends on the substance of the relationship, not just its legal form.

The following are not necessarily related parties:

- A business partner with whom the entity transacts a significant volume of business

- Funding providers

- Governments

- Public utilities

- Trade unions

- Two entities that share key management personnel

- Two venturers that share joint control of a joint venture

The term *key management personnel* includes those people having authority and responsibility for planning, directing, and controlling the activities of an entity, either directly or indirectly. This includes the entity's directors.

Significant influence occurs when an individual or entity has the power to participate in the financial and operating policy decisions of an entity, but does not have direct control over those policies.

DISCLOSURES

You should disclose the following related party information:

- *Compensation*. Total compensation for key management personnel, and separately for these personnel short-term benefits, post-employment benefits, other long-term benefits, termination benefits, and share-based payments.

- *Relationships*. The relationships between parent and subsidiary entities, even if there have been no transactions between the parties. An entity should disclose the name of its parent, as well as the name of the ultimate controlling party (if different from the parent). If the financial statements of neither the parent nor the ultimate controlling party are available for public use, then also disclose the name of the next most senior parent above the immediate parent that produces consolidated financial statements that are available for public use.

- *Transactions*. If there have been related party transactions, then the nature of the relationship, a description of the transactions, any outstanding balances (as well as related terms, conditions, and guarantees), the amount of the transactions, provisions for doubtful debts, and the related bad debt recognized during the period. Separately disclose all of these items for related party transactions with the parent, entities with joint or significant control over the entity, subsidiaries, associates, joint ventures, key management personnel, and other related parties.

Examples of possible related party transactions, depending upon the substance of the relationship, are:

- Financing arrangements

- Leases

- Provision of guarantees or collateral

- Purchase or sale of goods, assets (or property), or services

- Risk-sharing in a defined benefit plan

- Settlement of liabilities on behalf of the other entity

- Transfers of research and development, or under license agreements

---

Example

Dutch Machining Company leases storage trailers from an entity owned by the chief executive officer's son. In addition, it is the beneficiary of a low-interest loan from one its directors. Finally, it obtains half of its primary raw materials from the Avignon Steel Foundry; there is no ownership arrangement between Dutch and Avignon.

Dutch must disclose a related party relationship for the storage trailer lease, since it involves a family member. It must also disclose the low-interest loan, since it involves a member of key management. However, it does not have to disclose the supplier relationship, since there is no indication of a related party relationship.

16

EVENTS AFTER THE REPORTING PERIOD

INTRODUCTION

An event after the reporting period is one that occurs between the end of the reporting period and the date when the financial statements are authorized for issuance. These events either provide evidence of conditions existing at (an *adjusting event*) or after (a *non-adjusting event*) the end of the reporting period. If financial statements are approved by shareholders (such as at an annual meeting) or a supervisory board, then you should consider the statements to be authorized for issuance on the date of issuance; this may be substantially sooner than the meetings of the shareholders or the supervisory board.

An event still qualifies as an event after the reporting period even if it occurs after the public announcement of selected financial information, as long as it occurs before the financial statements are authorized for issuance.

This chapter describes how to account for events occurring after the reporting period, as well as how to disclose the information.

ACCOUNTING FOR ADJUSTING EVENTS AFTER THE REPORTING PERIOD

You should adjust the amounts that an entity recognizes in its financial statements to reflect any adjusting events after the reporting period, but only until the date when the financial statements are authorized for issuance.

Example

The Industrial Bagel Company reaches a settlement with a government entity, regarding charges that it provided stale bagels for soldier's combat meals. The settlement confirms that Industrial had an obligation at the end of its reporting period of £250,000. Industrial had previously recognized a provision of £50,000, so it now increases the provision by £200,000.

Industrial Bagel receives a report from an independent appraiser, stating that the carrying amount of its bagel shrink-wrapping machine was impaired by £25,000 at the end of the reporting period. Accordingly, Industrial writes down the asset value within the reporting period.

Industrial Bagel discovers that a major retail chain customer filed for bankruptcy two weeks after the end of the reporting period. Industrial has no reserve for bad debts, and so must write down the entire amount of the related £50,000 account receivable in the preceding reporting period.

Industrial Bagel's internal audit staff discovers that the company's warehouse manager has been giving large quantities of bagels to the local police department in exchange for free security, and covered up the inventory shortfall at the end of the reporting period. The amount of the fraud is £10,000, which Industrial records within the reporting period.

In all of the above cases, Industrial Bagel should only adjust the financial statements of the reporting period if the events occur prior to authorization of the financial statements for issuance.

ACCOUNTING FOR NON-ADJUSTING EVENTS AFTER THE REPORTING PERIOD

You do not adjust the financial statements of a reporting period for non-adjusting events that occur after the reporting period.

Example

The market value of the investments held by United Power Supply Company decline precipitously following the end of a reporting period. This decline in value does not relate to the marketability of the investments at the end of the reporting period, so United does not adjust its financial statements.

ACCOUNTING FOR DIVIDENDS DECLARED AFTER THE REPORTING PERIOD

If an entity declares dividends after the reporting period, do not recognize the dividends as a liability at the end of the reporting period. This is because there was no obligation at the end of the reporting period.

ACCOUNTING FOR A GOING CONCERN ISSUE THAT ARISES AFTER PERIOD-END

You shall not prepare an entity's financial statements on a going concern basis if management determines after the reporting period that it has no realistic alternative other than to liquidate the entity or cease trading. This only applies if the financial statements have not yet been authorized for issuance.

DISCLOSURE

You should disclose the following information related to events arising after the reporting date:

- *Authorization date.* The date when an entity's financial statements were authorized for issuance, and who gave the authorization. If anyone can amend the financial statements after their issuance, disclose this fact.

- *Non-adjusting events.* If there are material non-adjusting events after the reporting period, you should disclose the nature of the event and either estimate its financial effect or state that you cannot make such an estimate.

- *Period-end conditions.* If you receive subsequent information about conditions existing at the end of the reporting period, then update the disclosures to reflect this information.

Example

Following its year-end reporting period, Grand Cayman Shipping issues several press releases in which it announces the divestiture of its Indonesian subsidiary, the acquisition of a cruise line operating off the coast of Norway, the classification of a group of oil tankers as held for sale, the restructuring of its corporate headquarters staff, a reverse share split, and the issuance of a significant loan guarantee for its African subsidiary.

In all cases, these are non-adjusting events. Grand Cayman should not adjust its financial statements for the previous period, but it should disclose the events.

17

FINANCIAL REPORTING IN HYPERINFLATIONARY ECONOMIES

INTRODUCTION

Since international financial reporting standards (IFRS) are designed to be applied to any country, it is possible that an entity using them will have as its functional currency the currency of a country having a hyperinflationary economy. This chapter shows to restate the financial statements of an entity that finds itself in a hyperinflationary environment.

DESIGNATING AN ECONOMY AS HYPERINFLATIONARY

There is no fixed standard for determining whether an economy is hyper-inflationary. It is indicated by a combination of the following characteristics:

- *Cumulative inflation rate*. The cumulative inflation rate over three years is near to or more than 100%.

- *Price indexing*. Interest rates, wages, and prices are commonly linked to and increased based on a price index.

- *Price quotes*. Prices are quoted in a foreign currency.

- *Prices increased for credit*. If a customer intends to buy on credit terms, then prices are higher to reflect the expected loss of purchasing power during the credit period.

- *Wealth stored elsewhere.* The general population prefers to store its wealth in a stable foreign currency or in non-monetary assets.

When an economy is no longer hyperinflationary, an entity stops using the restatements required for a hyperinflationary economy. Also, it uses the amounts expressed in the measuring unit at the end of the previous reporting period as the carrying amounts in its subsequent financial statements.

HOW TO RESTATE FINANCIAL RESULTS

If an entity's functional currency is the currency of a hyperinflationary economy, the entity should present its financial statements in terms of the measuring unit current at the end of the reporting period. The entity should also restate the results of any presented financial information from earlier periods in terms of the measuring unit current at the end of the reporting period.

The entity should include any gain or loss on its net monetary position in profit or loss, and disclose this amount separately.

You should follow these rules when restating financial statements that used historical costs:

- *General.* Apply a general price index to amounts in the statement of financial position that are not already expressed in the measuring unit current at the end of the reporting period.

- *Cash.* Do not restate cash.

- *Deferred payment items.* If an entity has delayed payment terms on an asset purchase, it may not be practical to impute the amount of related interest expense. Instead, restate the assets from the payment date, rather than the purchase date.

- *Equity method investments.* If an investor accounts for an investment in an investee under the equity method, the investee should restate its financial results based on a general price index; the investor should use the restated results when calculating its share of the investee's net assets and profit or loss.

- *Gain or loss on net monetary position.* During a period of hyperinflation, an entity holding more assets than liabilities will lose purchasing power (since their assets are worth less), while the reverse is true for those entities holding more liabilities than assets (since their liabilities are worth less). An entity should record this gain or loss on its net monetary position in profit or loss. Calculate the gain or loss on net monetary position by multiplying the change in the general price index by the weighted average for the period of the difference between the entity's monetary assets and monetary liabilities, and then subtract any changes to index-linked items (see next bullet point).

- *Index-linked items.* Do not restate items that are already linked to price indexes through contractual agreements. These items will require separate adjustment in accordance with the contractual agreements to which they are linked.

- *Non-monetary assets and liabilities.* If an item is already carried at its fair value, then do not restate it. You should restate all other non-monetary assets and liabilities. If a non-monetary item is carried at cost (or cost minus depreciation), then apply the change in the general price index from the item's acquisition date to the end of the reporting period. Examples of items carried at cost that require restatement are property, plant, and equipment, inventories, goodwill, and intangible assets. However, the restatement amount of an asset should not exceed its recoverable amount, and the restatement amount of inventory should not exceed its net realizable value.

- *Owners' equity.* When first restating an entity's financial statements, you should restate owners' equity as of the beginning of the first period, except for retained earnings and any revaluation surplus. Also, eliminate any revaluation surplus from previous periods. At the end of the first period and thereafter, restate all components of owners' equity using a price index from the beginning of the period or the date of contribution (if later).

- *Statement of comprehensive income.* Restate all items in the statement of comprehensive income, using the change in the general price index from the dates when the income and expense items were originally recorded.

If there is no evidence of the acquisition date of an asset whose cost must be restated, then obtain a professional assessment of its value; this becomes the basis from which future restatements are calculated.

Example

Milton Minerals has operated several platinum mines within Zimbabwe for one year, and purchased all of its assets at the beginning of the year. Its functional currency is the Zimbabwe dollar, which is currently experiencing hyperinflation. It converts its year-end balance sheet based on the following table, and a general price index that increased from 100 to 200 in the past year. Milton has three months' inventory in stock.

(continued)

(*continued*)

(000,000,000s)	Pre-Adjusted Balance Sheet	Calculation	Post-Adjusted Balance Sheet
Cash	250	Monetary item, so no change	250
Inventory	600	600 × (200 ÷ 175)	685
Fixed assets	3,000	3,000 × (200 ÷ 100)	6,000
Assets	3,850		6,935
Loan	1,050	Monetary item, so no change	1,050
Share capital	2,500	2,500 × (200 ÷ 100)	5,000
Retained earnings	300	Remaining balance	885
Liabilities/Equity	3,850		6,935

Do not restate financial statement items that are already stated at their current costs. If any items are not stated at their current cost, then use the restatements already noted for financial statements that use historical costs.

A current cost statement of comprehensive income uses costs as of the date of incurrence or consumption, so use a general price index to restate all of the amounts listed in the statement of comprehensive income into the measuring unit that was current at the end of the reporting period.

SELECTING A GENERAL PRICE INDEX

You should pick a general price index that reflects changes in general purchasing power. Also, for reporting consistency, all entities reporting in the same currency should use the same general price index for restatement purposes.

If there is no general price index available to use for restatements, then you must use an estimated price index. For example, an estimated price index could be based on movements in the functional currency's exchange rate and the exchange rate of a relatively stable foreign currency.

DISCLOSURES

An entity whose functional currency is the currency of a hyperinflationary economy should disclose the following information:

- *Basis*. Whether its financial statements are based on a historical or current cost approach.

- *Price index*. The price index used, and its level at the end of the reporting period, as well as the index's movement during the current period and the previous reporting period.

- *Restatement*. The fact that its financial statements have been restated in terms of the measuring unit current at the end of the reporting period.

PART FOUR

PUBLIC COMPANY REPORTING

18

OPERATING SEGMENTS

INTRODUCTION

A publicly-held entity is required under IFRS (international financial reporting standards) to report various information at the operating segment level, which gives investors visibility into the entity's operations at a more granular level. This chapter describes how to determine which operating segments should be reported, as well as required disclosures.

DEFINITION OF AN OPERATING SEGMENT

An operating segment is a component of an entity that is a profit center, has discrete financial information available, and whose results are regularly reviewed by the entity's chief operating decision maker for purposes of performance assessment and resource allocation. An operating segment generally has a segment manager who is accountable to the chief operating decision maker for the results of the segment.

An entity's corporate headquarters is not considered an operating segment, nor are an entity's post-employment benefit plans.

CRITERIA FOR REPORTING OPERATING SEGMENTS

You must disclose information for an operating segment if it meets any of these thresholds:

- *Revenue*. Its external and inter-segment sales are at least 10% of the combined revenue of all segments.

- *Profit*. Its absolute profit or loss is at least 10% of the greater of the combined profit of all segments not reporting a loss and the combined loss of all operating segments reporting a loss.

- *Assets*. Its assets are at least 10% of the combined assets of all operating segments.

If the total external revenue reported by operating segments meeting these thresholds is less than 75% of the entity's revenue, then report on additional segments until you meet the 75% threshold, even if the extra segments are individually below the threshold criteria.

Example

Battle Star Corporation has six operating segments. The following table shows the operating results of the segments:

Segment Name	Revenue	Profit	Loss	Assets
A	€ 101,000	€ 5,000	€ –	€ 60,000
B	285,000	10,000	–	120,000
C	130,000	–	(35,000)	40,000
D	500,000	–	(80,000)	190,000
E	440,000	20,000	–	160,000
F	140,000	–	(5,000)	50,000
Totals	€1,596,000	€35,000	€ (120,000)	€620,000

Because the total reported loss of €120,000 exceeds the total reported profit of €35,000, the €120,000 is used for the 10% profit test. The tests for these segments are itemized in the next table, where test thresholds are listed in the second row. For example, the total revenue of €1,596,000 shown in the preceding table is multiplied by 10% to arrive at the test threshold of €159,600 that is used in the second column. Segments B, D, and E all have revenue levels exceeding this threshold, so an "X" in the table indicates that their results must be separately reported. After conducting all three of the 10% tests, the table shows that segments B, C, D, and E must be reported, so their revenues are itemized in the last column. The last column shows that the total revenue of all reportable segments exceeds the €1,197,000 revenue level needed to pass the 75% test, so that no additional segments must be reported.

Segment Name	Revenue 10% Test	Profit 10% Test	Asset 10% Test	75% Revenue Test
Test Threshold	€159,600	€12,000	€62,000	€1,197,000
A				
B		X		X	$285,000

(*continued*)

C		X		130,000
D	X	X	X	500,000
E	X	X	X	440,000
F				
			Total	€1,355,000

If an operating segment that was reported separately in the immediately preceding period has now dropped below the threshold criteria, management can still separately report its results if it believes the information is significant.

If a segment meets the threshold criteria for the first time, then report its results for any prior periods presented in the financial statements, unless the needed information is not available and would be excessively expensive to develop.

It is allowable to aggregate the results of smaller segments to create a reportable segment, but only if the segments have similar products, services, production processes, customers, distribution methods, and regulatory environments.

There is no precise limit to the number of reportable segments, but consider a reduction if the number exceeds ten segments.

If operating segments do not meet the threshold criteria just noted for separate reporting status, then combine them in an "all other segments" category.

WHEN TO RESTATE SEGMENT INFORMATION

If the entity changes its organizational structure sufficiently that it changes the composition of its reportable segments, then restate the corresponding information for earlier periods. This is not necessary if the required information is not available for the earlier periods and the cost of developing it would be excessive. However, the ability to create earlier information is made at the line-item level, so you may provide information for some line items and not for others. If you restate information for earlier periods, then disclose this fact.

If it is not possible to restate information for prior periods to reflect a change in organizational structure, then disclose the year in which the organizational change occurs. Also, provide segment information for both the old and new organizational structures for the current period, unless this information is not available and would be excessively expensive to develop.

DISCLOSURES OF SEGMENT INFORMATION

In general, you disclose segment information that enables financial statement users to evaluate the entity's business activities and economic environment. In more detail, this requires the following disclosures:

- *General information.* The factors used to identify reportable segments, and the types of products and services sold by each segment. Also note the basis of organization, which shows whether the organization is organized around products or services, geographic regions, regulatory environments, or some combination thereof.

- *Profit or loss information.* Revenues from external customers, inter-segment revenues, interest revenue, interest expense, depreciation and amortization, material expense items, equity method interests in other entities, income tax expense or income, and other material non-cash items, as well as the resulting profit or loss.

- *Asset and liability information.* Equity method investments, and the amounts of additions to non-current assets (other than insurance contract rights, post-employment benefits, deferred tax assets, and financial instruments).

Example

Amalgamated Green Products owns a number of subsidiaries that focus on reduced carbon emissions. It reports the results of its identifiable segments as follows:

(000s)	Electric Motors	Furnaces	LED Lighting	All Other	Totals
Revenues from external customers	€2,700	€4,500	€8,100	€900	€16,200
Inter-segment revenues		2,700	1,300		4,000
Interest revenue	400	650	230	50	1,330
Interest expense	100	120	90	10	320
Depreciation	180	80	40	20	320
Reportable segment profit	270	450	800	70	1,590
Reportable segment assets	1,800	3,200	3,700	800	9,500
Expenditures for reportable segment non-current assets	250	400	250	150	1,050
Reportable segment liabilities	900	1,600	2,000	400	4,900

These disclosures are only required if they are reported to the chief operating decision maker in order to make decisions about resource allocation and performance assessment.

You must provide an explanation of the measurements used when deriving segment information, which includes:

- *Inter-segment accounting.* The basis of accounting for any inter-segment transactions.

- *Measurement differences.* The reasons for any differences between segment-level profits and losses, assets and liabilities, and the same information in aggregate for the entire entity.

- *Inter-period differences.* The reasons for any differences between the measurement of profits and losses, assets and liabilities, and the same information in prior periods.

- *Asymmetrical allocations.* The reasons for using different allocations to different segments, such as the allocation of depreciation expense to one segment, but not to another.

DISCLOSURES OF RECONCILING INFORMATION

You should disclose reconciling information alongside the segment reporting that includes the following:

- *Comparisons.* The total of the revenues, profit and loss, and assets and liabilities for the reported segments in comparison to the entity's totals for the same items.

- *Other material items.* The total of any other material amounts for the reported segments in comparison to the entity's totals for the same items. Separately identify and describe each material item.

DISCLOSURES ABOUT PRODUCTS AND SERVICES

If you do not provide product and service information at the segment-reporting level, then do so for the entire entity. Do so for each product and service, or grouping thereof, unless this information is not available and would be excessively expensive to develop (in which case, disclose this fact).

Example

The Company operates in the consumer products industry, in which the Company designs, manufactures, markets, and distributes footwear, apparel, and accessories. For the year ending in December 31, 2010, the company sold £168 million of footwear, £19 million of apparel, and £11 million of accessories.

DISCLOSURES ABOUT GEOGRAPHICAL AREAS

If you do not provide geographical information at the segment-reporting level, then do so for the entire entity. This involves the disclosure of:

- *Revenues*. External revenues for the entity's country of domicile and the total for all other countries. If the revenues for an individual country are material, then disclose them separately. Also note the basis for attributing revenues to individual countries.

- *Assets*. Non-current assets located in the entity's country of domicile and the total for all other countries. If the assets in an individual country are material, then disclose them separately. This disclosure does not include deferred tax assets, financial instruments, insurance contract rights, or post-employment benefit assets.

Example

The Company operates a single business segment that includes the installation and servicing of oil rigs for independent oil exploration and production (E&P) companies. The following table summarizes the Company's revenues and assets in different countries:

	2010	2009
Revenues:		
Iraq	£ 67,000,000	£61,000,000
Nigeria	31,000,000	26,000,000
Other foreign countries	11,000,000	9,000,000
Total	£109,000,000	£96,000,000
Assets:		
Iraq	£ 29,000,000	£28,000,000
Nigeria	17,000,000	13,000,000
Other foreign countries	4,000,000	4,000,000
Total	£ 50,000,000	£45,000,000

Do not disclose this information if it is not available and would be excessively expensive to develop (in which case, disclose this fact).

The entity may also provide subtotals of geographic information about groups of countries, at its option.

DISCLOSURES ABOUT MAJOR CUSTOMERS

If you do not provide major customer information at the segment-reporting level, then do so for the entire entity. If revenues from a single customer are

10% or more of total entity revenues, then disclose that fact, as well as the total revenues for each such customer, and the identity of the segments reporting those revenues.

It is not necessary to disclose the identity of these major customers, nor the amount of revenues that each segment reports from them.

A group of customer entities under common control should be considered a single customer. Similarly, a government and entities controlled by that government are considered a single customer.

Example

The Company derives a significant portion of its net revenues from a limited number of customers. For the fiscal years ended December 31, 2010 and 2009, revenues from one client totaled approximately £15.7 million and £17.8 million, which represented 12% and 15% of total net revenues, respectively. For the fiscal year ended December 31, 2008, revenues from two clients totaled approximately £13.6 million and £10.9 million, which represented 16% and 12% of total net revenues.

19

EARNINGS PER SHARE

INTRODUCTION

An entity should report its earnings per share if its shares are traded in a public market, or if it is filing its financial statements with a regulatory organization to issue ordinary shares in a public market. Earnings per share are presented in two formats: basic earnings per share and diluted earnings per share. They are defined as:

- *Basic earnings per share*. The amount of earnings for a reporting period that are available to each share of common stock outstanding during that reporting period.

- *Diluted earnings per share*. The amount of earnings for a reporting period that are available to each share of common stock outstanding during that reporting period, and to each share that would have been outstanding, assuming that common shares had been issued for all dilutive potential common stock outstanding during the period.

Dilution is the reduction in earnings per share or increase in loss per share that results when you assume that convertible instruments are converted, that options and warrants are exercised, or that ordinary shares are issued if specified conditions are satisfied. *Anti-dilution* is the increase in earnings per share or decrease in loss per share that results when you assume the conversion of convertible instruments, the exercise of options and warrants, or that ordinary shares are issued if specified conditions are satisfied.

This chapter describes the various components of earnings per share, and how to calculate both basic and diluted earnings per share.

BASIC EARNINGS PER SHARE

Basic earnings per share is the simplest of the earnings per share calculations, and is the only one you need to calculate if the entity only has ordinary shares outstanding. An ordinary share is an equity instrument subordinate to all other equity classes. The basic earnings per share calculation follows:

Profit or loss attributable to ordinary equity holders of the parent entity

Weighted average number of ordinary shares outstanding during the period

---

This calculation is further split into the profit or loss from continuing operations attributable to the parent entity, and total profit or loss attributable to the parent entity.

Also incorporate the following adjustments into the numerator of the calculation of basic earnings per share:

- *Dividends*. For the calculation of basic earnings per share, deduct from the profit or loss in the numerator the after-tax amount of any dividends declared on non-cumulative preference shares as well as the after-tax amount of any dividends for cumulative preference shares, even if the dividends have not been declared; this does not include the amount of such dividends paid or declared during the current period that relates to previous periods.

- *Share repurchases*. If an entity repurchases preference shares at an above-market price, deduct the excess of the consideration paid over the fair value of the shares from the profit or loss in the numerator of the basic earnings per share calculation.

Also incorporate the following adjustments into the denominator of the calculation of basic earnings per share:

- *Contingent shares*. If shares are contingently issuable, treat them as outstanding as of the date when all necessary conditions are satisfied. If shares are contingently returnable, do not treat them as outstanding until whenever the shares can no longer be returned.

- *Issuance date*. Include shares in the denominator as of the date when cash is receivable for sold shares, when dividends are reinvested, when interest ceases to accrue on convertible debt instruments for which shares are issued, when a liability is settled in exchange for shares, when an acquisition is recognized in exchange for shares, and as services are rendered in exchange for shares. If there is a mandatorily convertible instrument, then include the related shares in the denominator as of the contract date.

- *Issuances without resource change.* If shares are issued without a corresponding change in resources, include them in the denominator as of the issuance date. Examples of such issuances are stock dividends, share splits, and reverse share splits.

- *Weighted average shares.* The calculation of the weighted average number of shares outstanding during the period is to adjust the number of shares outstanding at the beginning of the period for the number of ordinary shares repurchased or issued during the reporting period, adjusted by the number of days that the shares are outstanding as a proportion of the total days in the period.

Example

Rosco International earns a profit of £10 million after tax in Year 1. In addition, Rosco owes £250,000 in dividends to the holders of its cumulative preference shares, and there is also a £100,000 original issue premium on increasing rate preference shares. Rosco calculates the numerator of its basic earnings per share as:

£10,000,000 profit − £250,000 dividends − £100,000 original issue premium = £9,650,000

Rosco had 8 million ordinary shares outstanding at the beginning of Year 1. In addition, it sold 500,000 shares on April 1 and 800,000 shares on October 1. It also issued 1,000,000 shares on July 1 as part of a share true-up transaction to the shareholders of a former acquisition. Finally, it bought back 100,000 shares on December 1. Rosco calculates the weighted average number of shares outstanding as follows:

Date	Shares	Weighting (months)	Weighted Average
January 1	8,000,000	12/12	8,000,000
April 1	500,000	9/12	375,000
July 1	1,000,000	6/12	500,000
October 1	800,000	3/12	200,000
December 1	(100,000)	1/12	8,333
			9,083,333

Rosco's basic earnings per share is £9,650,000 adjusted profits ÷ 9,083,333 weighted average shares, or £1.06 per share.

DILUTED EARNINGS PER SHARE

The calculation of diluted earnings per share goes beyond the calculation of basic earnings per share to also include the effects of all dilutive potential ordinary shares. As a result, you increase the number of shares outstanding by the weighted average number of additional ordinary shares that would have been outstanding if all dilutive potential ordinary shares had been converted to ordinary shares. This dilutive change may also impact the profit or loss in the numerator of the earnings per share calculation. You calculate diluted earnings per share as follows:

$$\frac{\text{Adjusted profit or loss of the parent entity}}{\text{Weighted average number of ordinary shares outstanding during the period, plus all dilutive potential ordinary shares}}$$

This calculation is further split into the profit or loss from continuing operations attributable to the parent entity, and total profit or loss attributable to the parent entity.

Also incorporate the following adjustments into the numerator of the calculation of diluted earnings per share:

- *Dividends*. Adjust for the after-tax effect of dividends or other dilutive potential ordinary shares.

- *Interest expense*. Reverse any interest expense related to dilutive potential ordinary shares, since these shares are assumed to have been converted to ordinary shares, which eliminates the interest expense.

Also incorporate the following adjustments into the denominator of the calculation of diluted earnings per share; these adjustments are *in addition to* those already noted for basic earnings per share:

- *Contingent shares, general*. Treat contingently issuable ordinary shares as outstanding as of the beginning of the period, and therefore included in the calculation of diluted earnings per share, as long as the conditions required to issue the shares have been satisfied.

- *Contingent shares, future earnings*. If a contingent share issuance involves maintaining a specific earnings level past the current period, then assume that the related potential shares issued based on the amount of actual earnings at the end of the reporting period are the same as the amount at the end of the contingency period.

- *Contingent shares, future prices*. If a contingent share issuance depends on the future market price of ordinary shares, then base the potential share issuance on the market price at the end of the reporting period. If the issuance depends on the average market price over a period that has already started and extends into the future, then use the average price just for the period of time that has lapsed.

- *Contingent shares, other conditions*. If a contingent share issuance depends on another condition than future earnings or future share prices, then assume that the present status of the condition remains unchanged through the end of the contingency period.

- *Contracts settled in cash or shares.* If a contract can be settled in either ordinary shares or cash, assume that it will be settled in ordinary shares if the effect is dilutive.

- *Conversion effect.* Only convert potential ordinary shares to ordinary shares for the purposes of the dilutive earnings per share calculation if doing so will either decrease the earnings per share or increase the loss per share from continuing operations. Conduct this conversion review separately for each issue or series of potential ordinary shares, rather than in aggregate.

- *Convertible instruments.* Include the dilutive effect of convertible instruments in diluted earnings per share when they are dilutive. Convertible preference shares are anti-dilutive when the dividends on their converted shares exceeds basic earnings per share. Convertible debt is anti-dilutive when the interest expense on its converted shares exceeds basic earnings per share.

- *Dilutive shares.* Add to the denominator the weighted average number of ordinary shares that the entity would issue if all dilutive potential ordinary shares were converted. In the absence of other information, these additional shares are assumed to have been issued at the beginning of the reporting period.

- *Non-vested shares.* Treat non-vested shares with determinable terms as though they have vested. Thus, they become potentially dilutive shares as of their grant date.

- *Options and warrants.* Assume that all dilutive options and warrants are exercised at their exercise price, then convert the proceeds into the number of shares that would have been purchased at the average fair market value, and subtract this amount from the total amount that could have been exercised.

There is only a dilutive effect when this average market price is greater than the exercise price of the options or warrants.

Example

Pillory Corporation earns a net profit of €1 million, and it has 10 million ordinary shares outstanding. In addition, there is a €2 million convertible loan that has a 6% interest rate. The loan potentially converts to 3,000,000 of Pillory's ordinary shares. Pillory's incremental tax rate is 35%.

(*continued*)

(*continued*)

Pillory's basic earnings per share is €1 million ÷ 10 million shares, or €0.10/share. The following calculation shows the compilation of its diluted earnings per share:

Net profit	€1,000,000
+ Interest saved on €2,000,000 debt at 6%	120,000
− Reduced tax savings on foregone interest expense	(42,000)
Adjusted net earnings	€1,078,000
Ordinary shares outstanding	10,000,000
+ Potential converted shares	3,000,000
Adjusted shares outstanding	13,000,000
Diluted earnings per share (€922,000 ÷ 10,200,000)	**€0.08/share**

Example

Century Cellular earns a net profit of £1 million, and it has 10 million ordinary shares outstanding that had an average fair value of £20 during the past year. In addition, there are 3 million share options outstanding that are convertible to ordinary shares at £12 each.

Century's basic earnings per share is £1 million ÷ 10 million ordinary shares, or £0.10/share.

To determine Century's diluted earnings per share, first calculate the number of shares that would have been issued at the average fair value. To do so, multiply the 3 million share options by their exercise price of £12, resulting in a total payment for the options of £36 million. Then divide this amount by the £20 average fair value to arrive at 1,800,000 shares that could have been purchased with the option proceeds. Then subtract the 1,800,000 shares from the 3 million options originally exercised. Then add the difference of 1,200,000 shares to the 10 million ordinary shares already outstanding to arrive at 11.2 million diluted shares.

Century's diluted earnings per share is £1 million ÷ 11.2 million ordinary shares, or £0.09/share.

RETROSPECTIVE CHANGES TO EARNINGS PER SHARE

You should retrospectively adjust the calculation of basic and diluted earnings per share for all periods presented, if the number of shares outstanding changes due to a capitalization, share split, or reverse share split. Also, disclose the fact that the share calculations reflect these changes.

EARNINGS PER SHARE PRESENTATION

You should present basic and diluted earnings per share information in the statement of comprehensive income for every class of ordinary shares that has a different right to share in the period's profits, and for every period for which you present a statement of comprehensive income. If you present diluted earnings per share for at least one period, then you must report it for all periods presented. If the basic and diluted earnings per share are the same, then you can present them both as a single line item in the statement of comprehensive income.

If you report a discontinued operation, then separately disclose the basic and diluted earnings per share for that operation. You can include this information either in the statement of comprehensive income or its accompanying notes.

Example

Waterloo Wholesalers presents its earnings per share information using the following layout:

Combined earnings per year	20x9	20x8	20x7
	€	€	€
From continuing operations			
Basic earnings per share	2.09	1.89	1.75
Diluted earnings per share	2.04	1.84	1.70
From discontinued operations			
Basic earnings per share	0.53	0.29	0.10
Diluted earnings per share	0.49	0.25	0.08
From total operations			
Basic earnings per share	2.62	2.18	1.85
Diluted earnings per share	2.53	2.09	1.78

DISCLOSURES

You should disclose the following information regarding an entity's earnings per share:

- *Anti-dilutive items*. Any instruments not included in the diluted earnings per share calculation that could potentially dilute earnings per share in the future.

- *Numerators*. A reconciliation of the numerators used to calculate both basic and diluted earnings per share, noting all differences from the profit or loss attributable to the parent entity.

- *Shares*. A reconciliation of the weighted average number of ordinary shares used in the denominators of both basic and diluted earnings per share to each other.

- *Subsequent transactions*. Any subsequent share-related transactions occurring after the reporting period that would have significantly changed the number of ordinary or potential ordinary shares outstanding at the end of the period if they had occurred within the period. Examples are shares issued for cash, options issued, convertible instruments converted to shares, and conditions arising that would result in the triggering of convertible instruments. Do not adjust earnings per share calculations for these items.

20

INTERIM FINANCIAL REPORTING

INTRODUCTION

An interim period is a financial reporting period that is shorter than a full fiscal year. Interim financial reports are generally quarterly financial reports, and must be issued by publicly-held entities. Depending on which securities regulator or stock exchange is involved, an entity will be required to at least issue interim financial reports at the end of the first half of their fiscal year, and to do so no later than 60 days after the end of each interim period.

This chapter addresses the content of interim financial reports, as well as such related issues as materiality, the use of estimates, and the consistency of accounting policy application in interim periods.

CONTENTS OF AN INTERIM FINANCIAL REPORT

An interim financial report includes, for the reporting period in question, the following:

- Statement of financial position
- Statement of comprehensive income
- Statement of changes in equity
- Statement of cash flows

These reports can be in a condensed format. The statement of comprehensive income can be either a condensed single statement, or a condensed separate income statement and a condensed statement of comprehensive income. If you issue the reports in a condensed format, then the statements must include each of the headings and subtotals used in the most recent annual financial statements.

If the entity is normally required to present basic and diluted earnings per share in its annual financial statements, then it also includes this information in its interim financial report.

The interim financial report includes a statement of financial position as of the beginning of the earliest comparative period when an entity applies a retrospective restatement, reclassification, or accounting policy.

Finally, prepare the interim financial report on a consolidated basis if the entity's most recent annual financial statements were also presented in this manner.

ACCOMPANYING EXPLANATORY NOTES

The interim financial report includes a summary of significant accounting policies and other explanatory information. This may be less information than is provided in the annual financial statements; it is acceptable to only provide an update to the more complete information provided in the annual financial report, thereby avoiding duplication. Do not provide relatively insignificant updates to the information in the annual report. In general, include notes if their omission would make the condensed statements misleading.

Include the following explanatory notes in the interim financial report if they are material, and report it on a fiscal year-to-date basis:

- *Contingencies*. Any changes in contingent assets or liabilities since the last annual reporting period.

- *Dividends*. The amount of dividends paid, either in aggregate or per share, for ordinary shares and for other shares.

- *Entity composition*. The effect of changes in the entity's structure during the interim period, from such events as restructurings, discontinued operations, and business combinations.

- *Estimate changes*. Note the nature and amount of changes in any estimates from prior periods, if there is a material effect on the current period.

- *Item impact*. Explain the nature and amount of items having an unusual size, nature, or incidence, that impact any part of the financial statements.

- *Policies*. A statement that says the same accounting policies and computation methods used in the annual financial statements are being used in the interim statements. If not, then describe any changes.

- *Seasonality*. Explain any seasonality or cyclicality that impacts interim results.

- *Securities*. Note any issuances, repurchases, or repayments of securities.

- *Segments*. If segment reporting is required, then disclose for each segment the revenues from external customers, inter-segment revenues, profit or loss, total assets for which there has been a material change from the annual financial statements, differences in the basis of segmentation from the last annual financial statements, and a reconciliation of segment profit or loss to entity profit or loss. See the Operating Segments chapter for more information about segment reporting.

- *Subsequent events*. Disclose material events occurring subsequent to the end of the interim period.

Examples of these disclosable items are asset acquisitions, disposals and impairments, error corrections, inventory write-downs, litigation settlements, loan defaults, and related party transactions.

PERIODS OF PRESENTATION FOR INTERIM FINANCIAL STATEMENTS

You must include interim financial statements for the following periods:

- Statement of financial position for the current interim period and a comparative statement of financial position for the immediately preceding fiscal year

- Statements of comprehensive income for the current interim period and for the fiscal year-to-date, as well as comparative statements for the current and year-to-date periods of the immediately preceding fiscal year

- Statement of changes in equity for the current fiscal year-to-date and a comparative statement for the year-to-date period of the immediately preceding fiscal year

- Statement of cash flows for the current fiscal year-to-date, with a comparative statement for the year-to-date period of the immediately preceding fiscal year

MATERIALITY IN INTERIM PERIODS

You should assess the materiality of an item in relation to the financial data of the interim period. An item is material if its omission or misstatement could influence the economic decisions of users of the financial statements. The goal is to produce an interim financial report that includes all information relevant to understanding the entity's performance and financial position during and at the end of the interim period.

Example

The Uranium Detection Consortium has revenues of €12,000,000 in its first quarter, and will eventually generate revenues of €50,000,000 for its entire fiscal year. Uranium's controller traditionally has considered materiality to be 2% of revenues. In the first quarter, Uranium's Subatomic Detection subsidiary, which is designated as discontinued, earns a profit of €360,000. This is 3% of Uranium's revenues in that quarter, and so is material enough to be segregated for reporting purposes within the third quarter. However, it is less than 1% of Uranium's full-year results, so there is no need to segregate this information in Uranium's annual financial report.

CONSISTENCY OF ACCOUNTING POLICY APPLICATION

You should apply the same accounting policies from the annual financial statements to the interim financial statements. The exception is when you change an accounting policy after the last annual report, and expect to apply the new policy to the next annual report; in this case, apply the new accounting policy to the interim financial statements.

The consistency of accounting policies between interim periods means that the recognition of accounting transactions are made based on the expected results for the entire year, not just for a single interim period. This is known as the *integral view*. For example, an entity should recognize its income tax expense in an interim period based on its best estimate of the weighted average income tax rate that it expects to incur for the entire year. Also, you should accrue an expense provision within an interim period if an event has created a legal or constructive obligation where the entity has no realistic alternative other than to make a payment. If there is only an intention or necessity to incur expenses later in the fiscal year, this is not sufficient grounds to accrue an expense in the current interim period.

Example

Wave Energy Company creates electrical generators that are triggered by wave action. Wave incurs the following costs as part of its quarterly reporting:

- It pays €15,000 of trade show's fees in the first quarter for a green technology trade show that will occur in the fourth quarter.

- It pays €32,000 in the first quarter for a block of advertisements that will run throughout the year in *Energy Alternatives* magazine.

- The board of directors approves a profit sharing plan in the first quarter that will pay employees 20% of net annual profits. At the time of plan approval, full-year profits are estimated to be €100,000. By the end of the third quarter, this estimate has dropped to €80,000, and to €70,000 by the end of the fourth quarter.

Wave uses the following calculations to record these scenarios:

	Quarter 1	Quarter 2	Quarter 3	Quarter 4	Full Year
Trade show [1]				€15,000	€15,000
Advertising [2]	€8,000	€8,000	€8,000	8,000	32,000
Profit sharing [3]	5,000	5,000	3,000	1,000	14,000

[1] The trade show's expense is deferred until the show occurs in the fourth quarter.
[2] The advertising is proportionally recognized in all quarters as it is used.
[3] A profit sharing accrual begins in the first quarter, when the plan is approved. At that time, 1/4 of the estimated full-year profit sharing expense is recognized. In the third quarter, the total estimated profit sharing expense has declined to €16,000, of which €10,000 has already been recognized. When the profit sharing expense estimate declines again in the fourth quarter to €14,000, only €1,000 remains to be recognized.

This heightened level of accrual usage will likely result in numerous accrual corrections in subsequent interim periods to adjust for any earlier estimation errors.

If an asset no longer has any future economic benefits as of the end of an interim period, then charge it to expense at that time; do not wait for the end of the fiscal year to do so. Similarly, a recorded liability must still represent an existing obligation at the end of an interim period.

Example

Paris Bakeries writes down the value of its chestnut-flour inventory by €40,000 during the second quarter of its fiscal year, and reports the change in its

(continued)

> *(continued)*
> interim financial report for that period. During the third quarter, the market price of chestnut-flour increases somewhat, so Paris can justifiably reverse a portion of the original write-down; accordingly, it records a reversal of €28,000 in the third quarter, and reports the change in its interim report for that period.

RETROSPECTIVE ADJUSTMENT OF INTERIM FINANCIAL STATEMENTS

If you issue six-month or more frequent interim financial statements, you do not retrospectively adjust the information in the interim statements.

Example

Wave Energy Company is sued over its alleged violation of a patent in the hydraulic ram used in its wave generators. Under the settlement terms, which Wave agrees to during the fourth quarter of its fiscal year, it must retroactively pay a 4% royalty on all sales of the product to which the patent applies. Sales of the hydraulic ram were €20,000 in the first quarter, €35,000 in the second quarter, €10,000 in the third quarter, and €35,000 in the fourth quarter. In addition, the cumulative total of all ram sales in prior years was €400,000. Wave cannot restate its previously-issued quarterly financial results to include the royalty expense; instead, it reports the entire royalty expense, including the amount applicable to prior years, in the fourth quarter of the current fiscal year. The calculation follows:

	Quarter 1	Quarter 2	Quarter 3	Quarter 4	Full Year
Sales subject to royalty	€20,000	€35,000	€10,000	€35,000	€100,000
Royalty expense	0	0	0	4,000	4,000
Royalty related to prior year sales	0	–	–	16,000	16,000

RESTATEMENT OF INTERIM FINANCIAL STATEMENTS

If you implement a change in accounting policy, then restate the financial statements of prior interim periods of the current fiscal year, as well as the comparable interim periods of prior fiscal years that will be included in the annual financial statements. If it is impractical to do so, then apply the new accounting policy prospectively from the earliest practicable date.

THE USE OF ESTIMATES IN INTERIM FINANCIAL STATEMENTS

Some amount of estimation is required for both annual and interim financial reports, but you will likely need to rely on estimates to a greater degree when preparing interim financial information.

Example

The Suds Company only conducts a physical inventory count of its thousands of bath products at the end of its fiscal year. For its quarterly interim reports, Suds instead uses the 62% gross margin percentage that it recorded in the preceding fiscal year. In the current year's third quarter, Suds' controller believes that a fraud situation has resulted in an exceptional amount of inventory loss, and mandates an extra physical inventory count. The result is a year-to-date actual gross margin of only 51%. Suds then conducts its normal physical count at the end of the fiscal year, resulting in an actual full-year gross margin of 56%. As shown in the following table, Suds recognizes the entire amount of the additional expense in the third quarter that was detected as a result of the extra physical count in that quarter.

	Quarter 1	Quarter 2	Quarter 3	Quarter 4	Full Year
Revenues	€18,000,000	€21,000,000	€23,000,000	€32,000,000	€94,000,000
Standard gross margin percent	62%	62%			
Year-to-date actual gross margin			51%	56%	56%
Cost of goods sold	6,840,000	7,980,000	15,560,000	10,980,000	41,360,000
Gross margin	11,160,000	13,020,000	7,440,000*	21,020,000	52,640,000

*(€62,000,000 year-to-date revenues × 51% gross margin = €31,620,000) − €11,160,000 Quarter 1 gross margin − €13,020,000 Quarter 2 gross margin

PART FIVE

BROAD TRANSACTIONS

21

BUSINESS COMBINATIONS

INTRODUCTION

Accounting for a business combination can be one of the most complex transactions that an accountant ever deals with. In this chapter, we clarify the accounting for a business combination, resolving such issues as what to do with contingent liabilities, contingent consideration, step acquisitions, and acquisition-related costs. Also, we note the disclosure obligations of the acquiring entity.

DEFINITIONS

A *business combination* is a transaction in which the acquirer obtains control of another business (the acquiree). A *business* is an integrated set of activities and assets that can provide a return to investors in the form of dividends, reduced costs, or other economic benefits. A business typically has inputs, processes, and outputs. A development-stage entity may not yet have outputs, in which case you can substitute other factors, such as having begun operations and having plans to produce output, and having access to the customers who can purchase the outputs.

A business combination is not the formation of a joint venture, nor does it involve the acquisition of assets that do not constitute a business.

Goodwill is an asset that is not individually identified, is separately recognized, and which represents the future economic benefits arising from other assets acquired in a business combination.

ACCOUNTING FOR A BUSINESS COMBINATION

You should use the *acquisition method* to account for a business combination. Specifically, follow these five steps:

1. *Identify the acquirer.* This is the entity that gains control of the acquiree.

2. *Determine the acquisition date.* This is when the acquirer gains control of the acquiree, which is usually the deal-closing date, but which could be another date if so stated in the purchase agreement.

3. *Recognize and measure identifiable assets acquired and liabilities assumed.* These must be part of the business combination transaction, rather than from separate transactions. Measure these assets and liabilities at their fair values as of the acquisition date. More specifically:

   a. *Employee benefits.* Recognize a liability for any employee benefits assumed.

   b. *Held for sale assets.* Measure an acquiree's assets designated as held for sale at their fair value, less costs to sell.

   c. *Income taxes.* Recognize a deferred tax asset or liability associated with the other assets acquired and liabilities assumed.

   d. *Indemnifications.* The acquiree provides an indemnification to the acquirer for various issues related to the acquired business. For example, the acquiree may provide an indemnification against excessive accounts receivable bad debts. This is an indemnification asset, which the acquirer recognizes at its fair value at the same time it recognizes the indemnified item. However, do not recognize an indemnification if the related asset is not recognized.

   e. *Reacquired rights.* Measure a reacquired right as an intangible asset having a term tied to the duration of its remaining contractual term, irrespective of the potential for a contract extension.

   f. *Share-based payments.* Measure a liability or equity instrument to replace similar acquiree share-based payments.

4. *Recognize and measure any non-controlling interest in the acquiree.* Measure this non-controlling interest either at its proportionate share of the acquiree's net assets or at its fair value.

5. *Recognize and measure either goodwill or the gain from a bargain purchase.* Measure goodwill as follows:

   + Consideration paid, measured at fair value on the acquisition date
   + Non-controlling interests in the acquiree
   + Fair value of acquirer's previously-held equity interest in the acquiree
   − Net of identifiable assets and liabilities acquired

   = Goodwill

A bargain purchase occurs when the above calculation yields a negative goodwill amount. When this occurs, first review the goodwill calculation to ensure that all items were included. If they were, then recognize the gain resulting from the bargain purchase in profit or loss as of the acquisition date.

Example

Woodrow Reilly, a publicly-held consulting firm, acquires Foster Barrow, which is also a publicly-held consulting firm. The price to buy Foster Barrow is £7 million. Woodrow Reilly identifies assets at Foster Barrow having a fair value of £8 million, intangible assets with a value of £1 million, as well as £2 million of liabilities and £500,000 of contingent liabilities. Woodrow Reilly also owned an existing stake in Foster Barrow that has a fair value on the acquisition date of £3 million. Woodrow Reilly calculates the goodwill associated with the business combination as follows:

+ Purchase price	£7,000,000
+ Liabilities	2,000,000
+ Contingent liabilities	500,000
+ Existing stake in Finnegan	3,000,000
− Assets	(8,000,000)
− Intangible assets	(1,000,000)
= Goodwill	£3,500,000

If the acquirer pays with non-cash assets or liabilities, it should re-measure them as of the acquisition date and recognize any gains or losses in profit or loss. However, if the acquirer retains control of the assets or liabilities (as can happen if they are transferred to the acquiree rather than its owners), then only measure them at their carrying value, which precludes the recognition by the acquirer in consolidation of any gain or loss.

ACCOUNTING FOR CONTINGENT CONSIDERATION

If there is additional consideration payable by the acquirer based on conditions not yet met, the acquirer recognizes its fair value as of the acquisition date.

Example

Jet Mower Company, maker of the world's only lawn mower that runs on a Wankel rotary engine, acquirers Turbofan Concepts, maker of the only jet-engine powered lawn mower (for really big lawns). Jet Mower includes in the purchase agreement a contingent consideration payment of £4 million, payable over the next four years, if Turbofan achieves specific levels of profitability in each period. Jet's management believes that Turbofan will meet these targets, so it recognizes the full amount of the contingent consideration as of the acquisition date.

ACCOUNTING FOR AN ACQUIREE'S CONTINGENT LIABILITIES

A contingent liability is a possible obligation arising from past events whose existence can only be confirmed by uncertain future events that are not entirely under an entity's control. It may also be an obligation arising from past events, for which it is not possible to reliably measure an obligation. The acquirer should recognize a contingent liability if it can reliably measure the fair value of the liability as of the acquisition date, even if there is not a probable outflow of resources required to settle it.

ACCOUNTING FOR STEP ACQUISITIONS

An entity may already have a non-controlling equity interest in an acquiree, and then acquires a controlling interest in the acquiree. This is called a *step acquisition*. In this situation, the acquirer should re-measure its existing equity interest in the acquiree as of the date when it obtains control over the acquiree, and recognize any gain or loss in profit or loss.

If the acquirer had recognized any changes in the value of its non-controlling interest in other comprehensive income, it should now shift that amount into profit or loss.

Example

Bosnian Tile acquires 100% of Flamingo Mural Company in two stages, as noted in the following table:

Acquisition Date	Percent Acquired	Purchase Payment	Net Assets Fair Value
January 1, 20X1	15%	€ 2,000,000	€12,000,000
July 1, 20X2	85%	13,000,000	14,000,000
Totals	100%	€15,000,000	

Bosnian calculates the goodwill from the two transactions as follows:

Acquisition Date	(A) Purchase Payment	(B) % Acquired	(C) Net Assets Fair Value	A − (B × C) Goodwill
January 1, 20X1	€2,000,000	15%	€12,000,000	€ 200,000
July 1, 20X2	13,000,000	85%	14,000,000	1,100,000
				€1,300,000

The before-and-after statements of financial position for Bosnian and Flamingo, with adjustments, are as follows:

The before-and-after statements of financial position for Bosnian and Flamingo, with adjustments, are as follows:

	(A) Bosnian	(B) Flamingo	(C) Adjustments	A + B +/– C Consolidated
Cash	€400,000	€150,000		€550,000
Accounts receivable	9,250,000	7,000,000		16,250,000
Property, plant, and equipment	8,200,000	5,700,000	+ €2,000,000 (Note 1)	15,900,000
Investment in Flamingo	2,000,000	0	– €2,000,000 (Note 2)	0
Goodwill	0	0	+ €1,300,000 (Note 3)	1,300,000
Total assets	€19,850,000	€12,850,000		€34,000,000
Accounts payable	1,900,000	850,000		2,750,000
Revaluation surplus	0	0	+ €1,300,000 (Note 4)	1,300,000
Retained earnings	7,500,000	5,100,000		12,600,000
Issued equity	10,450,000	6,900,000		17,350,000
Liabilities and equity	€19,850,000	€12,850,000		€34,000,000

(1) Add back excess of €14,000,000 fair value on acquisition date over initial net assets (cash + accounts receivable + PP&E – accounts payable).
(2) Eliminate minority interest, since now owns 100% of Flamingo.
(3) See preceding goodwill calculation table.
(4) Bosnian's share of the increase in the net assets of Flamingo, as per the preceding goodwill calculation table.

THE MEASUREMENT PERIOD

The measurement period is the period following the acquisition date, which the acquirer uses to adjust the provisional amounts that it initially recognizes for a business combination. This typically includes the finalization of the identification of the acquiree's assets and liabilities, non-controlling interests, and goodwill. The measurement period does not exceed one year from the acquisition date.

If the acquirer cannot complete the accounting for a business combination within the initial reporting period, then report provisional amounts for any incomplete items. During the measurement period, the acquirer should retrospectively adjust the initial provisional amounts as it obtains new information that affects the measurement of the business combination. This can involve the recognition of additional assets or liabilities.

The measurement period ends as soon as the acquirer either:

- Finishes collecting information about the facts and circumstances existing at the acquisition date

- Determines that no more information is obtainable

- One year passes from the acquisition date

ADJUSTING FOR A PROVISIONAL MEASUREMENT

If you recognize a provisional amount for an asset, liability, or non-controlling interest and later need to alter it, the offsetting adjustment is to goodwill.

You should also revise comparative information for previous periods presented in the financial statements, so that adjustments are reflected in all comparative periods. If a change is to an asset that is being depreciated or amortized, retrospectively adjust the depreciation and amortization to reflect the revisions to the provisional amount.

ACCOUNTING FOR ACQUISITION-RELATED COSTS

An acquirer incurs a variety of acquisition-related costs to complete a business combination. Examples of these costs are advisory fees, finder's fees, legal and accounting expenses, valuation services, and the costs of maintaining an internal acquisitions department. You should charge all of these costs to expense in the period incurred.

SUBSEQUENT MEASUREMENT OF A BUSINESS COMBINATION

You should subsequently measure most assets and liabilities acquired through a business combination normally, in accordance with the applicable international accounting standards most applicable to those items. However, the following items require special measurement:

- *Reacquired rights*. Amortize the carrying amount of these rights over the remaining contractual period of the contract in which the right was granted.

- *Contingent liabilities*. Until settled, measure at the higher of the amount initially recognized less any cumulative amortization, or the amount that would be recognized as noted in the Provisions and Contingencies chapter.

- *Indemnification assets*. Measure at the end of every subsequent period on the same basis as the indemnified asset or liability, altered by any contractual limitations. If you are not measuring it at its fair value, use management's assessment of its collectability. You should derecognize it once the acquirer collects it, or sells it, or loses the right to it in some other manner.

- *Contingent consideration*. If there is a change in contingent consideration resulting from events *after* the acquisition date, it is not a measurement period adjustment. You should account for contingent consideration in three ways:

  - *Equity*. If the consideration was originally classified as equity, also make subsequent settlement entries to equity.

  - *Financial instruments*. If the consideration was originally classified as a financial instrument, then measure it at its fair value, and recognize the gain or loss in either profit or loss or other comprehensive income. See the Financial Instruments: Recognition and Measurement chapter for more information.

  - *Other assets and liabilities*. Account for them as indicated in the Provisions and Contingencies chapter.

DISCLOSURES

Generally, you should disclose sufficient information so that an entity's financial statement users can evaluate the nature and financial effect of a business combination occurring either in the current reporting period or following the period but before the period's financial statements are authorized for issuance. More specifically, disclose the following:

- *Assets*. The amounts recognized for each major class of assets acquired.

- *Bargain purchase*. If the combination is a bargain purchase transaction, note the amount of the gain, where in the financial statements it is recorded, and why the transaction resulted in a gain.

- *Consideration*. Fair value as of the acquisition date of the consideration paid, broken down by class of consideration.

- *Contingent consideration*. The recognized amount of contingent consideration arrangements and indemnification assets, a description of these arrangements, how the payment amounts were determined, and an estimate of the undiscounted range of outcomes. If there is no maximum payment, note this point. If it is not possible to determine a range of possible payments, note this point and the reasons why the determination cannot be made.

- *Contingent liabilities*. All standard disclosures are needed for recognized contingent liabilities. See the Provisions and Contingencies chapter for more information.

- *Control method*. How the acquirer attained control over the acquiree.

- *Date*. The acquisition date.

- *Description*. The name and description of the acquiree.

- *Equity interest*. The percent voting equity interest acquired.

- *Financial results–acquiree*. The acquiree's revenue and profit or loss since the acquisition date.

- *Financial results–consolidated*. The combined entity's revenue and profit or loss in the current period, adjusted as though all acquisitions in the year had been as of the beginning of the fiscal year.

- *Goodwill–detail*. The factors making up goodwill, such as intangible assets not qualifying for separate treatment, and expected synergies from the business combination.

- *Goodwill–deductible*. The amount of goodwill that you expect will be deductible for tax purposes.

- *Liabilities*. The amounts recognized for each major class of liabilities assumed.

- *Non-controlling interests*. If the acquirer does not own 100% of the acquiree, note the amount of the non-controlling interest, how that amount is measured, and the valuation methods and inputs used to calculate the value of the non-controlling interests.

- *Reasons*. The main business reasons for the acquisition.

- *Receivables*. For acquired receivables, note their aggregate fair value, the gross amounts receivable, and the best estimate of receivables that will not be collected.

- *Separate transactions.* If there are transactions recognized separately from the business combination, provide a description of each transaction, how it was accounted for, the amounts recognized, and the financial statement line item in which it is located. If it settles a pre-existing relationship, note the method used to determine the settlement amount. Also note the amount of acquisition-related costs, identified by the amounts expensed and not expensed.

- *Staged combination.* If a business combination has occurred in several stages, note the fair value of the acquirer's equity interest just prior to the acquisition date, the gain or loss it recognized when it re-measured to fair value just prior to the acquisition date, and where that gain or loss is recognized.

If a business combination is completed after the reporting period but before the financial statements are authorized for issuance, disclose all of the preceding information to the extent practicable. If not practicable, note which disclosures were not made, and why.

In addition, you should disclose information that allows financial statement users to evaluate the effects of adjustments recognized in the current period relating to business combinations that occurred either in the current or previous reporting periods. Specifically, disclose the following for each material business combination, and in aggregate for those business combinations that are individually immaterial:

- *Contingent consideration.* For each reporting period until settled, note the recognized changes in contingent consideration, the reasons for and amounts of any changes in the range of undiscounted outcomes, and the valuation methods and inputs used to measure the contingent consideration.

- *Gains and losses.* The amounts of and reasons for any recognized gains or losses related to the assets acquired and liabilities assumed as part of a business combination, if they are relevant to understanding the financial statements.

- *Provisional items.* If the accounting for a combination is provisional, then state why it is incomplete, which specific items are incomplete, and describe any adjustments made during the reporting period.

- *Reconciliation.* Reconcile the carrying amount of goodwill at the beginning and end of the period, highlighting changes in the gross amount, impairment losses, additional goodwill recognized, adjustments caused by tax asset recognition, inclusion in a held-for-sale group, net exchange rate differences, and any other items.

22

CHANGES IN ACCOUNTING POLICIES, ESTIMATES, AND ERRORS

INTRODUCTION

Financial statements include a combination of solidly fact-based transactions and estimates regarding expenses that should be recorded within the reporting period, but which have not yet actually occurred. Thus, no financial statement will be exactly correct as issued, and may in retrospect vary significantly from actual results. Inaccuracies are caused by one of the following factors:

- *Changes in accounting estimate*. This is an assessment of the current and future status of the benefits and obligations associated with assets and liabilities, resulting in a modification of the carrying amount of either an asset or a liability, or the periodic consumption of an asset.

- *Material omission or misstatement*. This is material if it could influence the economic decisions that users of financial statements make. The size or nature of the item (or both) may be relevant to the determination.

- *Prior period error*. This is an omission from or a misstatement of prior period financial statements that was caused by the failure to use or the misuse of information that was available when the financial statements were authorized for issuance, and which could have been expected to be obtained. Examples of a prior period error are fraud, calculation mistakes, factual misinterpretations or oversights, and mistakes in applying accounting policies.

Should you restate financial statements to account for these problems, and if so, which ones? This chapter provides the answers.

RETROSPECTIVE APPLICATION AND RESTATEMENT

Retrospective application is the application of a new accounting policy as if that policy had always been applied, while a *retrospective restatement* is the correction of financial statements as if a prior period error had never occurred.

It is impractical to implement a retrospective policy change when an entity cannot apply it after making reasonable efforts to do so. It is impractical to make a change for a specific prior period when its effects are not determinable, or it requires assumptions about what management's intent would have been in that period, or it requires an estimate of significant amounts *and* it is impossible to distinguish information about the estimates on the measurement dates that would have been available when the financial statements for that period were authorized for issuance.

On the other hand, there are no restrictions on *prospective application*, where you apply a new accounting policy to transactions and recognize the effect of changes in accounting estimates on a go-forward basis.

If you plan to retrospectively apply a change in accounting policy or an accounting error, the following information must have been available in the prior periods that you plan to adjust:

- Evidence of circumstances that existed when the transaction, condition, or event occurred

- Evidence that would have been available when the prior period financial statements were authorized for issuance

It is not acceptable to use hindsight when applying a change in accounting policy or an accounting error, since this implies the use of information and knowledge of circumstances that were not available when the original financial statements were assembled.

ACCOUNTING POLICY CHANGES

It is acceptable to change an accounting policy only when required by an international financial reporting standard (IFRS), or when the change will result in financial statements that provide more relevant information in the financial statements.

The key issue when revising an accounting policy is whether the change results in more relevant information in the financial statements. Some policy changes have a significant impact on reported results, and so are worthy of considerable review prior to implementation. This should involve not only a discussion among the entire management team, but also with the company auditors. Furthermore, document the basis for the change and archive the document, to ensure that the entity can justify its position at a later date.

If an accounting policy change is mandated by an IFRS, then do so in accordance with any specific transitional provisions noted in the IFRS. If there are no specific transitional provisions listed in the IFRS, then apply the change retrospectively to all presented financial statements. If you voluntarily change an accounting policy, then apply the change retrospectively to all presented financial statements. Early application of an IFRS is not considered a voluntary change in accounting policy.

Example

London Pottery Company originally tracked its hand-thrown ceramic products in inventory on an individual basis. However, with increased sales volume, this method proves impractical to continue, so London elects to change its accounting method to the first-in, first-out (FIFO) method.

London presents two years of financial statements. For Year 1, the impact of the change was an inventory increase of £28,000, and the impact in Year 2 was an inventory decrease of £12,000. The changes to London's income statement are as follows:

	Year 1			Year 2		
	Prior to Adjustment	Adjustment	Restated	Prior to Adjustment	Adjustment	Restated
Revenue	£2,475,000		£2,475,000	£3,100,000		£3,100,000
Cost of sales	1,485,000	£(28,000)	1,457,000	1,860,000	£12,000	1,872,000
Other expenses	750,000		750,000	868,000		868,000
Net profit*	£ 240,000	£(28,000)	£ 268,000	£ 372,000	£12,000	£ 360,000

*No impact on income taxes is assumed in this example.

When making a retrospective adjustment to the financial statements for prior periods, adjust the opening balance of each affected equity account (usually retained earnings) for the earliest prior period presented, as though the new policy had always been applied.

Do not implement a retrospective accounting policy if it is impractical to determine either the period-specific or cumulative effects of the change. If this is the case, apply the policy to the carrying amounts of assets and liabilities as of the beginning of the earliest period for which this treatment is practicable.

ACCOUNTING ESTIMATE CHANGES

Many business activities involve accounting estimates, since their ultimate outcomes may not be resolved for some time. Examples of transactions requiring estimates are reserves for bad debts, inventory obsolescence, and warranty obligations, as well as the useful lives of property, plant, and equipment, and the fair value of financial assets or liabilities.

A change in measurement basis is a change in accounting *policy*, not a change in accounting *estimate*. However, when it is difficult to distinguish between changes in accounting policy and accounting estimate, treat the issue as a change in accounting estimate. If you make a change in accounting estimate, the revision does not relate to prior periods.

It may be necessary to change an accounting estimate if there is new information about the circumstances upon which the most recent estimate was based. Recognize a change in accounting estimate for transactions, other events, and conditions beginning in the period of the change. If the change in estimate alters the carrying amount of assets or liabilities, recognize these changes in the period of the change.

Example

Mirror Laminates International uses vacuum deposition to deposit a thin-film coating on periscope lenses. It originally depreciates the vacuum deposition equipment using an estimated useful life of ten years, with no residual value. Thus, it depreciates the €10,000,000 carrying amount of the equipment at the rate of €1,000,000 per year.

After five years, Mirror Laminates determines that the equipment now has a remaining useful life of eight years. It therefore depreciates the remaining carrying amount of €5,000,000 at a revised rate of €625,000 per year. There is no retrospective change in prior periods.

ACCOUNTING ERROR CHANGES

You should correct a prior period material error retrospectively. Restate the amounts for the prior periods in which the error occurred, or, if the error occurred before the earliest period presented, then restate the opening balances of the affected accounts for the earliest period presented. Exclude the correction of a prior period error from the current reporting period's profit or loss.

If it is impracticable to determine the period-specific or cumulative effect of an error, then do not make a retroactive restatement. Instead, restate the opening balances of the current accounts for the earliest period for which the restatement is practicable.

Example

Paris Bakeries acquires Lyon Bakeshop. Two years later, Paris discovers that it has not amortized any of the intangible assets that it booked as a result of the acquisition. The amortization expense should have been €30,000 in the first year (a partial year) and €75,000 in the second year. The changes to Paris' income statement are as follows:

	Year 1			Year 2		
	Prior to Adjustment	Adjustment	Restated	Prior to Adjustment	Adjustment	Restated
Revenue	€5,220,000		€5,220,000	€5,612,000		€5,612,000
Cost of sales	3,760,000		3,760,000	4,040,000		4,040,000
Gross margin	1,460,000		1,460,000	1,572,000		1,572,000
Amortization	0	€30,000	30,000	0	€75,000	75,000
Other expenses	897,000		897,000	882,000		882,000
Other income before taxes	563,000		533,000	690,000		615,000
Income taxes	195,000	(10,000)	185,000	240,000	(25,000)	215,000
Net profit	€ 368,000	€20,000	€ 348,000	€ 450,000	€50,000	€ 400,000

Paris adds the following disclosure to its financial statements:

The amortization of intangible assets acquired as part of the Lyon Bakeshop acquisition was not included in the financial statements for Year 1 or Year 2. The financial statements for the past two years have been restated to correct this error. The effect of the restatement on those financial statements is summarized below:

	Year 1	Year 2
Increase in amortization expense	€(30,000)	€(75,000)
Decrease in income tax expense	10,000	25,000
Decrease in profit	€(20,000)	€(50,000)
Decrease in equity	€(20,000)	€(50,000)

IMMATERIAL CHANGES

If the effect of applying an international financial reporting standard (IFRS) is immaterial, then you do not need to apply it. However, do not depart from an immaterial IFRS in order to create a particular presentation of the financial statements.

There are cases where the decision to not implement an IFRS will be highly judgmental; one person may rule in favor of doing so, and another may not. Other cases are more clearly in favor of implementation, but an entity does not do so, either because it is unaware of the standard, or because someone wants to avoid the financial reporting consequences of the implementation. The following controls can mitigate these issues:

- *Formal review*. Create a review committee that examines how standards apply to an entity, and whether they are immaterial. Document its proceedings to show how the group voted on each issue.

- *Scheduled reviews*. Schedule a review of all new or updated standards at least once a year. Consider consulting with an auditing firm for advice, since they are most likely to be cognizant of changes that may impact the entity.

DISCLOSURES

When applying an IFRS that has an effect on past, present, or future financial statements, disclose the following:

- Title of the IFRS

- Whether the change is made in accordance with the transitional provisions of the IFRS

- The nature of the policy change

- The transitional provisions of the change, and any provisions that may affect future periods

- The amount of the adjustment for the current and prior periods (if practicable), and the adjustment amount for each line item affected, including basic and diluted earnings per share (if applicable)

- The adjustment amount for periods prior to those presented (if practicable)

- Why retrospective application is not possible for a prior period or for periods before those presented, as well as from what period the policy change was applied

When a voluntary accounting policy change affects past, present, or future financial statements, disclose the following:

- The nature of the policy change

- The reasons why the change provides more reliable and relevant information

- The amount of the adjustment for the current and prior periods (if practicable), and the adjustment amount for each line item affected, including basic and diluted earnings per share (if applicable)

- The adjustment amount for periods prior to those presented (if practicable)

- Why retrospective application is not possible for a prior period or for periods before those presented, as well as from what period the policy change was applied

Disclose the nature and amount of a change in an accounting estimate that affects the current period or is expected to impact future periods. Do not disclose this information for future periods if it is impractical to estimate the effect, but disclose that fact.

If there is a prior period error, disclose the nature of the error, the amount of the correction for each line item affected in each prior period presented, and the change in basic and diluted earnings per share (if applicable). Also note the amount of the correction at the beginning of the earliest period presented. If it is impracticable to have a retrospective restatement, disclose the circumstances causing that condition, when the error was corrected, and how it was corrected.

23

DISCONTINUED OPERATIONS AND NON-CURRENT ASSETS HELD FOR SALE

INTRODUCTION

There are separate accounting classifications and accounting treatment of assets listed as discontinued operations, and for non-current assets held for sale. This chapter describes the circumstances under which an asset is categorized as either a discontinued operation or held for sale, and the related accounting.

DEFINITION OF A DISCONTINUED OPERATION

A discontinued operation is a component of an entity that has either already been disposed of or is held for sale. It also falls into one of the following three categories:

- *Separate business*. It is a separate and major line of an entity's business, or comprises a geographical area of operations.

- *Disposal plan*. It is part of a plan to dispose of a separate and major line of an entity's business, or a geographical area of operations.

- *Resale acquisition*. It is a subsidiary that the entity originally acquired exclusively to resell it.

> **Example**
>
> Singapore Motors suffers an apparently permanent and substantial decline in its automobile sales along the Pacific Rim, due to an increase in mass transit systems in Singapore's markets. Accordingly, Singapore plans to stop producing its Copra sedan by the end of the year, and close the facility that produces the car. Singapore should account for the Copra product line as a discontinued operation.

ACCOUNTING FOR A DISCONTINUED OPERATION

Do not depreciate a discontinued operation while it retains that classification. If the discontinued designation is later removed from an operation, then measure the operation at the lower of its recoverable amount or its carrying amount before the operation was classified as discontinued, adjusted for any depreciation or revaluations that would otherwise have taken place while it was designated as discontinued. Thus, no longer being designated as discontinued subjects an operation to a "catch up" event for depreciation in arrears. The entity records this adjustment in profit or loss as soon as the operation is no longer designated as discontinued.

CLASSIFYING A NON-CURRENT ASSET AS HELD FOR SALE

You should classify all of the assets and liabilities of a subsidiary as held for sale when you are committed to a sales plan involving loss of control of the subsidiary, even if you will retain a non-controlling interest after the sale. You should only use this classification on a subsidiary if you expect that its carrying amount will be recovered through its sale, rather than through its continuing operations, and also if the subsidiary's sale is highly probable and it is ready for immediate sale in its present condition.

For an asset sale to be highly probable, management must be committed to sell it, and is actively searching for a buyer to acquire it at a price that is reasonable in relation to its fair value. Further, the transaction should qualify for recognition within one year of the classification date.

> **Example**
>
> Rowe Company, maker of custom sea-going rowboats for the fishing industry, acquires Seagoing Rowboats, and elects to merge both entities in
> *(continued)*

Seagoing's facilities, leaving empty its warehouse complex in Margate. Rowe advertises the Margate facility for sale at a below-market price. Rowe can classify its Margate facility as held for sale, since it is ready for immediate sale and that sale is highly probable.

There is a real estate market crash one week later, and building prices in Margate drop by 50%. Rowe does not reduce its offer price to the new market rate. Since the offer price is well above the market price, the warehouse is no longer available for immediate sale, and Rowe should discontinue its classification as held for sale.

If you cannot meet the designated criteria for reporting a non-current asset as held for sale, then you cannot assign this classification to the related asset in the financial statements related to that period. However, if you can meet the criteria after the reporting period but before the statements are authorized, then disclose this fact in the accompanying notes.

If circumstances prolong the sale period to beyond one year, it is still acceptable to use the held for sale designation, as long as the cause of the delay is beyond the entity's control and the entity remains committed to selling the asset.

Example

Braston Brick Company decides to sell a brick production facility, and classifies it as held for sale. Braston markets the property at a competitive price. It fails to find a buyer, and market conditions deteriorate during the ensuing year. Braston continues to drop its offer price to match the market rate. In this scenario, market conditions are beyond Braston's control, and so it can continue to designate the facility as held for sale, so long as it continues to offer the facility at or below the market price.

ACCOUNTING FOR ASSETS CLASSIFIED AS HELD FOR SALE

If you classify an asset as held for sale, apply the following accounting to it:

- *Carrying cost.* Measure the asset at the lower of its carrying amount or its fair value less costs to sell, and charge any impairment loss to profit or loss. If it will take longer than one year to sell an asset classified as held for sale, then measure the costs to sell at their present value. Later, if there is a gain on any subsequent increase in the asset's fair value less costs to sell, recognize the gain only to the extent of any cumulative impairment loss.

If you classify an asset as held for sale that you acquired as part of a business combination, then measure it at its fair value less costs to sell.

If you classify an asset as held for distribution to owners, measure it at the lower of its carrying amount or its fair value less costs to distribute (which are any incremental costs directly attributable to the distribution, not including finance costs and income tax expenses).

- *Depreciation*. Stop depreciating the asset as of the classification date.

- *Assets and liabilities*. If it is a multi-asset group, present the related assets and liabilities separately in the statement of financial position.

Example

Pillory Pottery designates its Kitchener Ceramics subsidiary as held for sale. At this point, Pillory must measure the subsidiary at the lower of its carrying amount or its fair value less costs to sell. The carrying amount of the Kitchener subsidiary is 2 million Canadian dollars. Its fair value is 1.8 million Canadian dollars, and the costs to sell are 100,000 Canadian dollars. Thus, Pillory should record an impairment loss of 300,000 Canadian dollars in profit or loss, which is Kitchener's fair value less its costs to sell.

If an asset no longer meets the criteria for being designated as held for sale, then stop classifying it as such. At the time of conversion away from the held for sale designation, measure the asset at the lower of its recoverable amount or its carrying amount before the asset was classified as held for sale, adjusted for any depreciation or revaluations that would otherwise have taken place while it was held for sale. Thus, no longer being held for sale subjects an asset to a "catch up" event for depreciation in arrears. The entity records this adjustment in profit or loss as soon as the asset no longer meets the held-for-sale criteria.

If an entity removes a single asset or liability from a disposal group that is currently classified as held for sale, the remaining assets and liabilities within the disposal group must still qualify as held for sale, or else they too must be treated as just noted, at the lower of their recoverable amounts or their carrying amounts before being classified as held for sale, adjusted for any depreciation or revaluations that would otherwise have taken place while they were held for sale.

DISCLOSURES

Generally, an entity should disclose information that enables users of its financial statements to evaluate the financial effects of discontinued operations and held-for-sale items. Specifically, you should disclose the following information in the statement of comprehensive income:

- *Adjustments to discontinued operations.* Any current-period changes to previously classified discontinued operations that are related to their disposal in a prior period. Examples are the resolution of purchase price adjustments, indemnification issues, product warranty obligations, and benefit plan obligations.

- *Assets.* Separately present the major classes of assets of a disposal group in the statement of financial position. Do not offset these assets against the liabilities of the disposal group. Separate asset disclosure is not necessary if it relates to a newly acquired subsidiary that was classified as held for sale upon acquisition. Also, do not separately present this information for prior periods if the held-for-sale classification occurred in the current period.

- *Cash flows.* The net cash flows related to the operating, investing, and financing activities of the discontinued operation. Present this information either in the notes to the financial statements or within the statement of comprehensive income.

- *Ended classification.* If you no longer classify an operation as held for sale, then reclassify its operational results back into the entity's continuing operations for all periods presented, and describe the amounts for prior periods as being re-presented. Any gain or loss on re-measurement of such an operation is also included in profit or loss from continuing operations.

- *Income linked to owners.* The income from discontinued operations and separately from continuing operations that is attributable to the owners of the parent entity. Present this information either in the notes to the financial statements or within the statement of comprehensive income.

- *Liabilities.* Separately present the major classes of liabilities of a disposal group in the statement of financial position. Do not offset these liabilities against the assets of the disposal group. Separate liability disclosure is not necessary if it relates to a newly acquired subsidiary that was classified as held for sale upon acquisition. Also, do not separately present this information for prior periods if the held for sale classification occurred in the current period.

- *Profit or loss summary.* The post-tax profit or loss on discontinued operations, and the post-tax gain or loss on either the adjustment to fair value less costs to sell, or on final disposition.

- *Profit or loss detail.* Break down the summary-level profit or loss into the revenue, expenses, pre-tax profit or loss, related income tax, and the pre- and post-tax gain or loss on either the adjustment to fair value less costs to sell, or on final disposition. Present this information either in the notes to the financial statements, or separately identified within the statement of comprehensive income. Also present the same information for the discontinued operation in all presented previous periods, even if the operation was not discontinued in the earlier periods.

Example

The following is a sample layout of a statement of comprehensive income, with the results of discontinued operations included:

Continuing operations	
Revenue	1,000
Cost of sales	600
Gross profit	400
General and administrative expenses	300
Profit before tax	100
Income tax expense	40
Profit from continuing operations	60
Discontinued operations	
Profit from discontinued operations	20
Profit for the period	80
Profit attributable to:	
Owners of the parent	
Profit from continuing operations	15
Profit from discontinued operations	0
Profit attributable to owners of the parent	15
Non-controlling interests	
Profit from continuing operations	45
Profit from discontinued operations	20
Profit attributable to non-controlling interests	65
Total profit from all sources	80

When identifying non-current assets classified as held for sale in an entity's statement of financial position, enter them as a separate line item after current assets, entitled "Non-current assets classified as held for sale." When identifying liabilities that are associated with such assets, enter them as a separate line item entitled, "Liabilities directly associated with non-current assets classified as held for sale."

In addition to the above information, which is disclosed within an entity's financial statements, also disclose the following information in the accompanying notes:

- *Classification change.* If an asset or disposal group is no longer classified as held for sale, describe the reason for the change, and the effect of the change on the results of operations for both the current period and prior periods presented in the financial statements.

- *Description.* A description of the non-current asset or disposal group that is held for sale.

- *Fair value changes.* Any gain or loss from changes in the fair value of the asset or disposal group.

- *Sale information.* The circumstances of the expected sale, including its manner and timing.

- *Segment.* The reportable segment (if applicable) in which the non-current asset or disposal group is presented.

24

EFFECTS OF FOREIGN EXCHANGE RATE CHANGES

INTRODUCTION

If an entity buys or sells with a foreign currency, then it must translate the foreign currency transactions into the currency it uses to report its financial results. This chapter shows how to make such translations, as well as how to disclose foreign exchange transactions in the financial statements.

DEFINITIONS

A *functional currency* is the currency used in the primary economic environment where an entity operates. This is the environment in which an entity primarily generates and expends cash. You should consider the following *primary* factors in determining an entity's functional currency:

- The currency that primarily influences sales prices (usually the currency in which prices are denominated and settled).

- The currency of the country whose competition and regulations primarily influence sales prices.

- The currency that primarily influences labor and other costs of goods sold (usually the currency in which prices are denominated and settled).

An *exchange rate* is the ratio at which two currencies are exchanged. The *spot exchange rate* is the exchange rate at which a currency can be delivered immediately. The *closing rate* is the spot exchange rate at the end of a reporting period.

A *monetary item* is an item containing a right to receive or deliver either a fixed or determinable number of units of currency.

ACCOUNTING FOR A FOREIGN CURRENCY TRANSACTION

To initially account for a transaction denominated in a foreign currency in an entity's functional currency, apply the spot exchange rate between the functional currency and the foreign currency as of the transaction date.

Example

Crevasse Designs is a German exporter of climbing equipment, whose functional currency is the Euro. On November 30, it sells an order of ice-climbing gear to a United States outdoor retail chain that is denominated in U.S. dollars, in the amount of $80,000. The spot rate on the November 30 shipment date was €1:$1.25, so Crevasse records the following entry in Euros (calculated as $80,000 ÷ $1.25 exchange rate).

Accounts receivable	€64,000	
Sales		€64,000

The receivable is still outstanding on December 31, which is Crevasse's fiscal year-end. On December 31, the exchange rate has changed to €1:$1.15, so the receivable is now worth €69,565 (calculated as $80,000 ÷ $1.15 exchange rate). This represents a foreign exchange gain of €5,565, which Crevasse records with this entry:

Accounts receivable	€5,565	
Foreign currency exchange gain		€5,565

The customer wires payment to Crevasse on the following day, when the exchange rate remains at €1:$1.15. Crevasse records the following entry to recognize the receipt of cash:

Cash	€69,565	
Accounts receivable		€69,565

INCORPORATING EXCHANGE RATES INTO THE FINANCIAL STATEMENTS

When preparing financial statements, an entity should follow these three general steps in order to properly incorporate the effects of foreign exchange rates:

1. Determine the entity's functional currency.

2. Translate foreign currency items into the functional currency. If an entity has a number of subsidiaries, associates, or joint venture investments, it must convert the results and financial position of each of these entities into the reporting entity's functional currency.

3. Report the effects of this translation.

If the financial statements of a foreign operation are issued on a different date than those of the reporting entity, it is best to have the foreign operation prepare additional statements matching the date used by the reporting entity. If this is not possible, then use a different date, but with no more than three months difference, with adjustments being made for the effects of significant transactions occurring between the different dates. When there is a date differential, translate the foreign entity's assets and liabilities at the exchange rate at the end of the foreign operation's reporting period.

ACCOUNTING FOR A FOREIGN CURRENCY TRANSACTION IN LATER PERIODS

Use the following transactions to account for foreign currency items in subsequent periods:

- *Foreign currency monetary item.* Translate it at the end of each reporting period using the closing rate at the end of the period.

- *Non-monetary item at historical cost.* If measured in a foreign currency, translate it using the exchange rate on the transaction date.

- *Non-monetary item at fair value.* If measured in a foreign currency, translate it using the exchange rate on the date of fair value determination.

Example

Firestone Candy obtains a $1,000,000 mixer for the corn syrup used in its blisteringly hot candies from a supplier in the United States on October 31,

(continued)

(*continued*)

when the British Pound to U.S. Dollar exchange rate is £1:1.50. Firestone also sells 200,000 of its signature Combustion Candy to a United States retail chain on November 30, when the exchange rate is £1:1.65. Both the payable and receivable are not yet settled as of year-end, when the closing exchange rate is £1:1.40. Firestone's functional currency is the British Pound.

The accounts payable for the corn syrup mixer is a foreign currency monetary item, and so must be translated at the end of the period, using the closing rate. On the October 31 purchase date, Firestone records the mixer as an asset, having a carrying cost of £666,667 (calculated as $1,000,000 payment due ÷ $1.50 exchange rate), along with a matching account payable. At year-end, Firestone has not yet settled the payable, so it recognizes a foreign exchange loss of £47,619 (calculated as (($1,000,000 payment due ÷ $1.40) − £666,667)).

The account receivable for the Combustion Candy sale is a foreign currency monetary item, and so must be translated at the end of the period, using the closing rate. On the November 30 sale date, Firestone records the sale at £121,212 (calculated as $200,000 ÷ $1.65 exchange rate), along with a matching account receivable. At year-end, Firestone has not yet settled the receivable, so it recognizes a foreign exchange gain of $£21,645 (calculated as (($200,000 receivable ÷ $1.40) − £121,212)).

ACCOUNTING FOR EXCHANGE DIFFERENCES BETWEEN PERIODS

You should recognize the difference between exchange rates on the settlement or translation of items differently, based on the type of transaction. Here are the scenarios:

- *Monetary items*. For foreign exchange rate differences between the end of the current reporting period and their initial recognition, recognize the difference in profit or loss in the period in which they arise.

- *Non-monetary items*. When you recognize a gain or loss on a non-monetary item in other comprehensive income, then also recognize any exchange-rate component of that gain or loss in other comprehensive income. When you recognize a gain or loss on a non-monetary item in profit or loss, then also recognize any exchange-rate component of that gain or loss in profit or loss.

- *Net investment in a foreign operation*. If there is an exchange rate difference on a monetary item that is part of a net investment in a foreign operation, then recognize the difference in the profit or loss of either the reporting entity or the foreign operation, as appropriate. If the reporting entity issues consolidated results that include the foreign operation as a subsidiary, it instead recognizes the difference in other comprehensive income, and then reclassifies it to profit or loss when it disposes of the net investment.

TRANSLATING FROM A FUNCTIONAL CURRENCY TO A PRESENTATION CURRENCY

A *presentation currency* is the currency in which an entity presents its financial statements. If this currency is not the same as an entity's functional currency, it translates its financial statements into the presentation currency. Use the following three-step procedure to do so:

1. Translate assets and liabilities at the closing rate on the date of the statement of financial position.

2. Translate revenues and expenses at the exchange rates on the transaction dates. It is acceptable to use an average exchange rate, unless the rates fluctuate significantly.

3. Recognize all resulting exchange differences in other comprehensive income. These differences arise from translating revenues and expenses at the exchange rates on the transaction dates, versus using the closing rate to translate assets and liabilities, as well as from translating opening net assets at a period-closing rate that differs from the previous period-closing rate.

Example

Swiss Style, maker of stylish women's clothing, uses the Euro as its functional currency, but wishes to use the U.S. Dollar as its presentation currency. The exchange rate between Euros and U.S. Dollars at the beginning of the year was one Euro to $1.25 U.S. Dollars, which changed to $1.75 U.S. Dollars at the end of the year (closing rate), and averaged $1.50 U.S. Dollars during the year. The conversion of its financial statements follows:

Profit and Loss Statement (P&L)

(000s)	In Euros	Comment	Exchange Rate	In U.S. $
Revenues	90,000	Average rate	1.50	135,000
Cost of sales	39,000	Average rate	1.50	58,500
Gross profit	51,000			76,500
Other expenses	34,000	Average rate	1.50	51,000
Profit	17,000			25,500

(*continued*)

(continued)
Balance Sheet

(000s)	In Euros			In U.S. $
Assets				
Cash	8,000	Closing rate	1.75	14,000
Accounts receivable	23,000	Closing rate	1.75	40,250
Inventory	18,000	Closing rate	1.75	31,500
Plant and equipment	11,000	Closing rate	1.75	19,250
Total Assets	60,000			105,000
Liabilities and Equity				
Accounts payable	19,000	Closing rate	1.75	33,250
Other liabilities	9,000	Closing rate	1.75	15,750
Retained earnings	17,000	From P&L	1.5	25,500
Exchange difference	–			4,250
Share capital	15,000	Closing rate	1.75	26,250
Liabilities and Equity	60,000			105,000

DISCLOSURES

A reporting entity should disclose the following information about the effects of foreign exchange rate changes:

- *Change in functional currency.* When there is a change in the functional currency of either the reporting entity or a significant foreign operation, note the fact and why the entity changed the currency.

- *Differences in other comprehensive income.* The net amount of exchange differences that it recognized in other comprehensive income. Also reconcile changes in the beginning and ending balances of these exchange differences.

- *Differences in profit or loss.* The amount of exchange differences that it recognized in profit or loss.

- *Different currency.* When the financial statements or other financial information is displayed in other than an entity's functional or presentation currency, then state that the financial statements comply with all IFRS. If they do not, then identify the information as supplementary, the currency in which it is displayed, the functional currency, and the translation method used to create the supplementary information.

- *Presentation currency differs.* When the presentation currency differs from the functional currency, note this fact. Also disclose the functional currency, and why the entity is using a different presentation currency.

25

LEASES

INTRODUCTION

Lease accounting can be one of the more complex areas of accounting, since it is not always obvious when an arrangement constitutes a lease, or what type of lease it may be. This chapter describes the various types of leases, shows how to determine when an arrangement contains a lease, and how to account for it from the perspectives of both the lessor and the lessee.

DEFINITIONS

A lease is an arrangement where the lessor agrees to allow the lessee to use an asset for a stated period of time in exchange for one or more payments. A *finance lease* is one in which the lessee assumes substantially all risks and rewards associated with the asset, while an *operating lease* is any lease other than a finance lease. Examples of situations that could lead to a lease being classified as a finance lease are:

- *Additional lease*. The lessee can continue the lease for an additional period at a rate substantially lower than the market rate.

- *Cancellation*. If the lessee can cancel the lease, the lessee pays the lessor's losses associated with the cancellation.

- *Fair value changes*. Gains or losses from fair value changes accrue to the lessee.

- *Ownership*. The lease transfers asset ownership to the lessee by the end of the lease.

- *Present value*. The present value of minimum lease payments substantially equals the asset's fair value at lease inception.

- *Purchase option*. There is an option for the lessee to purchase the asset at a price expected to be sufficiently below fair value on the option date for it to be reasonably certain that the lessee will exercise the option.

- *Specialized nature*. The asset is so specialized that only the lessee can use it without major modifications.

- *Term*. The lease term covers the major part of the economic life of the asset, even if title is not transferred.

Additional terms relevant to a discussion of leases include the following:

- *Economic life*. The period over which an asset is expected to be economically usable.

- *Gross investment in a lease*. The minimum lease payments receivable by the lessor, as well as any unguaranteed residual value accruing to the lessor.

- *Interest rate implicit in a lease*. The discount rate at which all minimum lease payments and the unguaranteed residual value equal the sum of the asset's fair value and any initial direct costs incurred by the lessor.

- *Minimum lease payments*. Those payments over the term of a lease agreement that the lessee will be required to make. This excludes contingent rent and any payments made by the lessee that will be repaid by the lessor or a third party.

- *Net investment in a lease*. The gross investment in the lease, discounted at the interest rate implicit in the lease.

- *Non-cancelable lease*. A lease that can only be cancelled with the permission of the lessor, if the lessee enters into a new lease with the same lessor, upon the occurrence of a remote contingency, or upon payment of an amount that makes continuation of the lease reasonably certain.

- *Residual value*. This is comprised of guaranteed residual value and unguaranteed residual value. *Guaranteed residual value* is that portion of a leased asset's residual value that the lessee or a third party guarantees to the lessor; thus, if the actual residual value declines below the guaranteed residual value, the lessee or a third party will pay the lessor for the difference. The *unguaranteed residual value* is that portion of a leased asset's residual value for which the lessor has no assurance of realization.

- *Unearned finance income*. The difference between the gross and net lease investments.

- *Useful life*. The estimated remaining period over which an entity expects to consume the economic benefits of an asset.

DETERMINING WHEN AN ARRANGEMENT CONTAINS A LEASE

Assessing whether an arrangement contains a lease requires an assessment of whether the arrangement conveys a right to use an asset, and whether fulfilling the arrangement is dependent upon the usage of a specific asset or group of specified assets.

An arrangement contains a right to use the asset if it conveys to the purchaser the right to control the use of the asset. The right of control occurs in any of the following situations:

- *Access*. The purchaser can control physical access to the asset while controlling more than an insignificant part of its output or utility.

- *Operation*. The purchaser can operate the asset in a manner it determines while controlling more than an insignificant part of its output or utility.

- *Output*. There is a remote chance that a third party will take more than an insignificant amount of its output or utility, and the price the purchaser pays for the asset's output is not fixed by the agreement, nor is the price equal to the current market price.

If the supplier is allowed under the arrangement to use assets not specified in the arrangement, then the arrangement does not contain a lease. However, an arrangement permitting the supplier to substitute other assets may not preclude lease treatment prior to the date of asset substitution. If the supplier owns only one asset with which to fulfill the arrangement and it is not feasible to use other assets, then it is assumed that the asset has been specified in the arrangement.

Example

Verdun Automotive enters into an agreement with Swedish Energy, whereby Swedish Energy constructs a wind farm next to the Verdun radiator construction

(continued)

(continued)

facility. Under the agreement, Swedish Energy will provide a minimum fixed amount of electricity to the facility for the next five years from the wind farm. Swedish Energy has ownership of and control over the wind farm, and also is responsible for repairing and maintaining it. Swedish Energy could use the facility to supply electricity to other customers, but it intends to operate it solely for the use of Verdun Automotive. Verdun Automotive must pay a fixed minimum fee for the electricity, as well as a variable fee if its usage exceeds a specified amount.

This arrangement contains a lease, because it specifically identifies the wind farm and states that the electricity is sourced from the wind farm. Given Swedish Energy's intent to devote the wind farm to the Verdun facility, there is only a remote chance that other parties will use its output. Also, pricing is not based on the market rate at the time of delivery.

ACCOUNTING BY A LESSEE FOR A FINANCIAL LEASE

The lessee recognizes a financial lease at the commencement of the lease term. The lessee recognizes a financial lease as an asset and a liability to pay future lease payments, at an amount equal to the leased asset's fair value, or if lower, the present value of the minimum lease payments. Also, add any initial lessee direct costs to the amount recognized as an asset, such as the costs of negotiating and securing a lease.

Example

Clear Bonding enters into a five-year finance lease to lease a polycarbonate bonding machine from another party. The fair value of the machine is €200,000. The present value of minimum lease payments at the lease inception is €184,000, and the machine has an unguaranteed residual value in five years of €25,000.

Clear Bonding records the machine asset and lease liability at the minimum lease payment present value of €184,000, which is the lower of the machine's fair value or present value of minimum lease payments. The difference between the €25,000 unguaranteed residual value and the €16,000 difference between the machine's fair value and the present value of minimum lease payments is the present value of the unguaranteed residual value.

Use the discount rate implicit in the lease for the present value calculation. If it is not practicable to determine the implicit rate, then use your incremental borrowing rate instead.

In addition, the lessee should record depreciation expense for the asset. If there is no reasonable certainty that the lessee will obtain ownership of the asset by the end of the lease, then fully depreciate it over the shorter of the lease term and its useful life. See the Property, Plant, and Equipment chapter for more information about systems of depreciation.

ACCOUNTING BY A LESSEE FOR SUBSEQUENT FINANCIAL LEASE PAYMENTS

Whenever the lessee makes a lease payment, it apportions the payment between a finance charge and a reduction of the outstanding liability. The finance charge should result in a constant periodic interest rate on the remaining liability balance.

Example

United Munitions leases a munitions loading machine that has a fair value of €250,000. The lease term is four years and involves four equal payments of €75,480, one at the end of each year. There is no assumed residual value. The implied interest rate in the lease is 8%, and the present value of the minimum lease payments is €250,000 (€75,480 annual payment × 3.31213 present value factor for an ordinary annuity of 1 per period).

United records the lease using the following table.

Payment	Balance	Finance Charge	Payment	Lease Liability
1	€250,000	€20,000	€75,480	€194,520
2	194,520	15,562	75,480	134,602
3	134,602	10,768	75,480	69,890
4	69,890	5,591	75,480	0

United records the initial asset acquisition with the following entry:

Leased equipment	€250,000	
Lease obligation		€250,000

United records the first lease payment with the following entry:

Lease obligation	€55,480	
Interest expense	20,000	
Cash		€75,480

(continued)

(*continued*)

United also depreciates the munitions loading machine. It chooses to do so on the straight-line method, so it records the following entry in each of the four years of the lease term to fully depreciate it by the end of the lease term:

Depreciation expense	€62,500	
Accumulated depreciation		€62,500

At the end of the lease period, the munitions loading machine reverts back to the lessor. United has already drawn the Lease Obligation balance down to zero with its four lease payments. The only remaining step is to eliminate the asset and its offsetting accumulated depreciation, which United accomplishes with the following entry:

Accumulated depreciation	€250,000	
Leased equipment		€250,000

ACCOUNTING BY A LESSOR FOR A FINANCIAL LEASE

A lessor recognizes an asset held under a financial lease at an amount equal to its net investment in the lease. The lease payment receivable is a repayment of principal, as well as finance income.

The lessor includes initial direct costs in the initial measurement of the finance lease receivable. Direct costs include commissions, legal fees, and internal costs that are directly and incrementally attributable to negotiating and arranging a lease. Do not include in the measurement of the finance lease receivable any of these direct costs if they involve a manufacturer or dealer lessor; in these cases, charge the direct leasing costs to expense at the same time that the lessor recognizes the selling profit (normally when the lease commences).

The lessor recognizes finance income based on a pattern that reflects a constant periodic rate of return on its investment in the lease. As each lease payment arrives from the lessee, the lessor applies the payment against the gross investment in the lease to reduce both the principal and unearned finance income.

ACCOUNTING BY A MANUFACTURER OR DEALER LESSOR FOR A FINANCIAL LEASE

A manufacturer or dealer lessor recognizes a selling profit or loss in the period when the lease commences. The revenue it recognizes is the lower of the fair value of the asset or the present value of minimum lease payments (using a market discount rate). The cost of sales is the cost or carrying amount of the asset being leased, less the present value of any unguaranteed residual value.

If the lessor incorporates an artificially low rate of interest in the lease, then it must reduce its selling profit to the amount that would apply if it had charged a market rate of interest.

Example

The Neptune Boat Company has issued a seven-year lease to the Adventure Yachting Company (AYC) on a boat for its yacht rental business. The boat cost Neptune €450,000 to build, and should have a residual value of €75,000 at the end of the lease. Annual lease payments are €77,000. Neptune's implicit interest rate is 8%. The present value multiplier for an ordinary annuity of €1 for seven years at 8% interest is 5.2064. The present value multiplier for €1 due in seven years at 8% interest is 0.5835. The initial journal entry is constructed with the following calculations:

- *Lease receivable.* This is the sum of all minimum lease payments, which is €539,000 (€77,000/year × 7 years), plus the actual residual value of €75,000, for a total lease receivable of €614,000.

- *Cost of goods sold.* This is the asset cost of €450,000, minus the present value of the residual value, which is €43,763 (€75,000 residual value × present value multiplier of 0.5835).

- *Revenue.* This is the present value of all minimum lease payments, or €400,893 (€77,000/year × present value multiplier of 5.2064).

- *Inventory.* Neptune's book value for the yacht is €450,000, which is used to record a reduction in its inventory account.

- *Unearned interest.* This is the lease receivable of €614,000, minus the present value of the minimum lease payments of €400,893, minus the present value of the residual value of €43,763, which yields €169,344.

Based on these calculations, the initial journal entry is as follows:

	Debit	Credit
Lease receivable	€614,000	
Cost of goods sold	406,237	
Revenue		€400,893
Boat asset		450,000
Unearned interest		169,344

(*continued*)

(*continued*)

The next step is to determine the allocation of lease payments between interest income and reduction of the lease principle, which is accomplished through the following effective interest table:

Year	Annual Payment	Interest Revenue	Reduction in Lease Obligation	Remaining Lease Obligation
0				€444,656
1	€77,000	€35,572	€41,428	403,228
2	77,000	32,258	44,742	358,486
3	77,000	28,679	48,321	310,165
4	77,000	24,813	52,187	257,978
5	77,000	20,638	56,362	201,616
6	77,000	16,129	60,871	140,745
7	77,000	11,255	65,745	75,000

The interest expense shown in the effective interest table can then be used to record the allocation of each lease payment between interest revenue and principal reduction. For example, the entries recorded for Year 4 of the lease are as follows:

	Debit	Credit
Cash	€77,000	
Lease receivable		€77,000
Unearned interest	€24,813	
Interest revenue		€24,813

Once the lease expires and AYC returns the boat to Neptune, the final entry to close out the lease transaction is as follows:

	Debit	Credit
Boat asset	€75,000	
Lease receivable		€75,000

ACCOUNTING BY A LESSEE FOR AN OPERATING LEASE

The lessee normally recognizes an expense on a straight-line basis for lease payments under an operating lease. It is possible to recognize the expense using a method other than straight-line, if the other method is more representative of the lessee's usage of the asset.

ACCOUNTING BY A LESSOR FOR AN OPERATING LEASE

A lessor recognizes lease income from an operating lease in income on a straight-line basis over the term of the lease. It is acceptable to use another method than the straight-line method if it is more representative of the usage pattern of the asset.

Recognize the depreciation associated with the asset over the term of the lease. As was the case with the related revenue, recognize the depreciation on a straight-line basis unless there is another method more representative of actual usage. The lessor should use a depreciation method that is consistent with its normal depreciation policy for similar assets.

If the lessor incurs any direct costs in negotiating and arranging an operating lease, the lessor adds these costs to the carrying amount of the leased asset and recognizes it as an expense over the term of the lease, on the same basis used to recognize lease income.

A manufacturer or dealer lessor does not recognize a selling profit upon initiation of an operating lease, since the transaction is not the equivalent of a sale.

ACCOUNTING FOR INCENTIVES ASSOCIATED WITH AN OPERATING LEASE

The lessor may grant an incentive to a lessee to enter into an operating lease. Examples of incentives are an up-front cash payment or the assumption of leasehold improvements. You should include all of these incentives in the total amount of consideration for the use of the leased asset.

The lessor recognizes the cost of incentives as a reduction of rental income over the term of the lease. The lessee recognizes the incentive benefit as a reduction of rental expense over the lease term. The lessor and lessee should recognize the incentives on a straight-line basis, unless another method is more representative of asset usage.

Example

Ajax Company enters into a new building lease arrangement with Norwegian Properties, where it will build custom sea-going rowboats for the fishing industry. Norwegian agrees to give Ajax free rent for the first year of the agreement as an incentive for entering into the lease. The new lease has a term of ten years, at a fixed rate of €50,000 per year after the first year of free rent.

The total payment over the 10-year term of the arrangement is €450,000. Both Ajax and Norwegian should recognize the €450,000 over the full 10-year period, using a standard amortization method.

ACCOUNTING FOR A SALE AND LEASEBACK TRANSACTION

A sale and leaseback transaction occurs when an entity (the seller-lessee) sells an asset to a third party and then leases it back. The accounting for this transaction varies depending on the type of lease that results. For example:

- *Finance lease*. The seller-lessee defers and amortizes over the lease term any excess of sales proceeds over the carrying amount of the asset.

- *Operating lease*. The seller-lessee can immediately recognize a profit or loss if the transaction is established *at* fair value. If the sale price is *above* fair value, then the seller-lessee defers and amortizes over the lease term the excess amount over fair value. If the sale price is *below* fair value, the seller-lessee immediately recognizes any profit or loss on the sale (the difference between its carrying amount and fair value); however, if the loss compensates for future lease payments that are below the market rate, then the seller-lessee defers and amortizes the loss in proportion to the lease payments over the asset usage period.

The table in Exhibit 25.1 shows the various treatments accorded to a sale and leaseback transaction under different scenarios.

Exhibit 25.1   Sale and Leaseback Decision Matrix

Recognition Scenario	Carrying Amount = Fair Value	Carrying Amount < Fair Value	Carrying Amount > Fair Value
Sale Price at Fair Value			
Profit recognition	No profit	Recognize profit upon lease commencement	Not applicable
Loss recognition	No loss	Not applicable	Recognize loss upon lease commencement
Sale Price Below Fair Value			
Profit	No profit	Recognize profit upon lease commencement	No profit; recognize a loss for the difference upon lease commencement
No loss compensation with reduced future lease payments	Recognize loss upon lease commencement	Recognize loss upon lease commencement	Recognize a loss for the difference upon lease commencement

(continued)

Loss compensation with reduced future lease payments	Defer and amortize loss	Defer and amortize loss	Recognize a loss for the difference upon lease commencement
Sale Price Above Fair Value			
Profit recognition	Defer and amortize profit	Defer and amortize excess profit; recognize excess of fair value over carrying amount upon lease commencement	Defer and amortize profit; profit is the difference between fair value and sale price
Loss recognition	No loss	No loss	Recognize a loss for the difference upon lease commencement

DISCLOSURES–BY A LESSEE FOR A FINANCIAL LEASE

For each class of asset, the lessee should disclose the following information:

- *Balances.* For each class of asset, report the net carrying amount at the end of the reporting period.

- *Contingent rent.* Disclose the contingent rent recognized in the period.

- *Future payments.* Disclose total future minimum lease payments and their present value at the end of the reporting period, as well as for not later than the next year, later than one year and not later than five years, and later than five years.

- *Lease terms.* Describe the general terms of all material leasing arrangements, including the basis on which contingent rent payments are determined, the terms of any renewal, purchase, or escalation clauses, and any restrictions imposed by lease arrangements.

- *Reconciliation.* Reconcile between the total future minimum lease payments at the end of the reporting period and their present value at the end of the period.

- *Subleases.* Disclose the total of all future minimum sublease payments that the entity expects to receive under non-cancelable subleases.

DISCLOSURES–BY A LESSOR FOR A FINANCIAL LEASE

A lessor discloses the following information for a financial lease:

- *Bad debt allowance*. The accumulated allowance for uncollectible minimum lease payments receivable.

- *Contingent rent*. The amount of any contingent rent recognized as income in the period.

- *Finance income*. The amount of any unearned finance income.

- *Future payments*. The gross investment in the lease and the present value of minimum lease payments receivable at the end of the reporting period, as well as for not later than the next year, later than one year and not later than five years, and later than five years.

- *Lease terms*. The general terms of all material leasing arrangements.

- *Reconciliation*. Reconcile the gross investment in the lease at the end of the reporting period to the present value of its minimum lease payments.

- *Residual values*. The amount of any unguaranteed residual values that accrue to the lessor.

DISCLOSURES–BY A LESSEE FOR AN OPERATING LEASE

A lessee should disclose the following information for an operating lease:

- *Future payments*. The total of future minimum lease payments under non-cancelable operating leases for not later than the next year, later than one year and not later than five years, and later than five years.

- *Subleases*. The total of all future minimum sublease payments that the entity expects to receive under non-cancelable subleases.

- *Current expense*. The amount of all lease and sublease payments expensed in the period, separately disclosing the amounts for minimum lease payments, contingent rents, and sublease payments.

- *Lease terms*. The general terms of all material leasing arrangements, including the basis on which contingent rent payments are determined, the terms of any renewal, purchase, or escalation clauses, and any restrictions imposed by lease arrangements.

DISCLOSURES–BY A LESSOR FOR AN OPERATING LEASE

A lessor should disclose the following information for an operating lease:

- *Contingent rent*. The amount of any contingent rent recognized as income in the period.

- *Future payments*. The future minimum lease payments under noncancelable operating leases, both in aggregate and for not later than the next year, later than one year and not later than five years, and later than five years.

- *Lease terms*. The general terms of the lessor's leasing arrangements.

Index

Accounting estimate changes, 228–229

Accounting policy changes, 226–228

Accounting profit, 43

Acquisition method, 215–217

Acquisitions, *see* Business combinations

Actuarial gains and losses, 17, 23

Actuarial discount rate, 27

Admission fees, 3

Advance payments, 3

Advertising barter, 7–8

Asset revaluation, tax effect of, 54

Associates
  Accounting for, 88–89
  Definition, 175
  Disclosures, 91–92
  Investing in, 87–88
  Transactions with, 91

Available-for-sale investment, 61

Barter exchange, 4

Basic earnings per share, *see* Earnings per share

Bill and hold, 4

Business combinations
  Accounting for, 215–211
  Disclosure of, 221–223
  Recognition of intangible assets, 119–120
  Subsequent measurement of, 220–221
  Tax effects of, 52–53

Byproducts, accounting for, 101

Carry back tax loss, 54

Cash on delivery terms, 4

Cash flow hedge, 71–73

Cash generating unit, 129

Closing rate, 242

Common control, 175

Compensated absence, accounting for, 19

Construction revenue, 8–11

Contingent assets
  Accounting for, 149–150
  Disclosures, 150
Contingent consideration,
  217
Contingent liabilities
  Accounting for, 143
  Acquiree, 218
  Disclosures, 150
Curtailments, accounting for,
  25–26
Customer disclosures,
  194–195
Customer loyalty programs,
  11–13

Deferred payment, 4–5
Deferred tax assets and liabil-
  ities, 43
Defined benefit plan
  Accounting for, 21–22
  Definition, 17
  Disclosures, 30–32
  Present value method,
  27–28
Defined contribution plan
  Accounting for, 20–21
  Definition, 18
Depreciation
  Assets not subject to, 110
  Time period, 111–112
  Methods, 112–113
  Of revalued assets, 113
Derecognition
  Accounting for, 113–114
  Definition, 61
Derivative, definition of,
  61–62

Diluted earnings per share, see
  Earnings per share
Diminishing balance method,
  112–113
Disclosures
  Accounting adjustments,
  230–231
  Associates, investments in,
  91–92
  Business combinations,
  221–223
  Contingencies and provi-
  sions, 150
  Defined benefit plan, 30–32
  Discontinued operations,
  236–239
  Earnings per share,
  203–204
  Events after the reporting
  period, 181
  Financial instruments,
  74–77, 78–79
  Financial statements,
  165–168, 173–174
  Foreign exchange transac-
  tions, 246
  Hedging, 77
  Hyperinflationary economy
  reporting, 186
  Impairment, 139–141
  Income tax, 56–57
  Intangible asset, 127–128
  Inventory, 102
  Joint venture, 86
  Lease, 257–259
  Operating segment,
  192–195
  Policy changes, 230

Property, plant, and equipment, 114–115
Related party, 175–177
Revenue recognition, 15
Share-based payment, 40–41
Discontinued operations
Accounting for, 234
Definition, 233–234
Disclosure of, 236–239
Dividends
Declared after the reporting period, 180
Tax withholdings on, 55

Earnings per share
Basic, calculation of, 198–199
Diluted, calculation of, 199–202
Disclosures, 203–204
Presentation of, 203
Retrospective changes to, 202
Effective interest method, 64–66
Equity method, when to stop using, 90–91
Estimate changes, 228–229
Events after reporting period
Accounting for, 179–181
Disclosures, 181
Exchange rate, 241

Fair value
Definition, 93
Disclosure, 78
Hedge, 70–71

Family member, 175
Financial lease, 247, 252–252, 257–258
Financial asset or liability
Accounting for, 62–63, 67–68
Cash flow hedge, 71–73
Derecognition, 63–64
Disclosures, 74–79
Fair value derivation of, 66–67
Fair value hedge, 70–71
Impairment of, 68–70
Net investment hedge, 73
Risks, 78–79
Financial statements
Consolidated, 169–173
Contents of, 154
Definitions, 153–154
Disclosures, 165–168, 173–174
First in, first out method, 95–97
Fixed assets, *see* Property, plant, and equipment
Foreign exchange transactions
Accounting for, 242–246
Disclosure of, 246
Franchise fees, 13–14
Functional currency, 241

Geographical area disclosures, 194
Going concern issue, 181
Goodwill
Definition, 129
Disclosures, 141

Goodwill (*Continued*)
　Impairment, 135–139
　Less than its tax base, 54–55
Group administration plan, 18

Hedge effectiveness, 62
Hedging, 62, 70–74, 77
Held for sale assets
　Accounting for, 235–236
　Classification of, 234–235
Held-to-maturity investment,
　62
Hyperinflationary economies
　Designation as, 183–184
　Disclosure of, 186
　Reporting in, 184–186

Immaterial changes, 230
Impairment
　Disclosures, 139–141
　Goodwill, 135–139
　Loss reversal, 135
　Testing, 130–135
Income tax disclosures,
　56–57
Individual control, 175
Initiation fees, 5
Installation fees, 5
Installment sales, 5
Intangible assets
　Amortization of, 126
　Definition of, 117–118
　Disclosures, 126–128
　Recognition of, 118–120,
　　122–123
　Revaluation of, 123–124
　Useful life of, 124–126
Interim financial reports

Consistency of policy
　application in, 208–210
Contents of, 205–206
Estimates in, 211
Materiality in, 208
Notes to, 206–207
Presentation periods, 207
Restatement of, 210
Retrospective adjustment
　of, 210
Inventory
　Cost to include in, 94
　Definition, 93
　Disclosures, 102
　Measurement systems, 95–98
　Overhead cost allocation to,
　　98
　Write down, 100–101
Investments, tax effect of,
　53–54

Joint ventures
　Accounting for, 82–86
　Definition, 176
　Contributions to, 84–85
　Disclosures, 86
　Types of, 81–82

Key management, definition
　of, 176

Lay away sales, 6
Lease
　Accounting by lessee,
　　250–252, 254
　Accounting by lessor,
　　252–254, 255
　Assessment of, 249–250
　Disclosures, 257–259

Financial, 250–252
Operating, 254–255
Terminology, 247–249
Long-term employee benefits,
    accounting for, 29–30

Monetary item, 242
Multi-employer plan, 18, 20

Net investment hedge, 73
Net realizable value, 94

Operating lease, 247,
    254–255, 258–259
Operating segments
    Criteria for, 189–191
    Definition, 189
    Disclosures, 192–195
    Restatement of, 191
Overhead cost allocation,
    98

Past service cost, 18, 24
Policy changes, 226–228
Post-employment benefit
    plan, 18
Professional services, *see*
    Services revenue
Profit sharing, accounting for,
    20
Property, plant, and
    equipment
    Cost to include in, 104–106
    Definition, 103
    Depreciation, 110–113
    Derecognition, 113–114
    Disclosures, 114–115
    Exchanges, 108

Interest costs to include in,
    106–108
Residual value, 108
Revaluation of, 109–110
Subsequent measurement
    of, 109
Provisions
    Accounting for, 144–145
    Disclosures, 150
    Measurement of, 145–146
    Reimbursement of, 147
    Restructuring, 148–149
Purchase option, 248

Recoverable amount, 129,
    132–133, 140–141
Related party
    Definitions, 175–176
    Disclosures, 176–177
Research and development
    expenditures, 121–122
Residual value, 248
Retail method, 96
Retrospective application, 226
Revenue recognition
    Disclosures, 15
    Rules, 3–6
Royalties, 6

Sale and leaseback transac-
    tions, 256–257
Services revenue, 14–15
Servicing fees, 6
Settlements, 25–26
Share-based payment
    Disclosures, 40–41
    Fair value determination,
        36–37

Share-based payment
(*continued*)
  Reload feature, 39
  Settled with cash, 34–35
  Settled with cash alterna-
    tives, 35–36
  Settled with equity, 33–34
  Taxes on, 55
  Terms modification, 38–39
  Vesting impact, 37–38
Short-term employee benefits
  Accounting for, 19
  Definition, 18–19
Significant influence, 81
Special purpose entity,
    consolidation of, 172
Spot exchange rate, 241–242
Standard cost method, 95–96
State plan, 18
Statement of cash flows, con-
    tents of, 163–165
Statement of changes in
    equity, contents of, 162
Statement of comprehensive
    income, contents of,
    158–162
Statement of financial position,
    contents of, 155–158

Step acquisitions, 218–219
Straight-line method, 112
Subscription revenue, 6

Tax assets and liabilities,
    46–47, 55
Tax base, 43–44
Tax liability, recognition of,
    55
Tax planning, 46
Taxable profit, 45
Temporary difference, 45–46,
    48–51
Termination benefits,
    accounting for, 30
Total comprehensive income,
    153
Tuition revenue, 6

Useful life, 249

Value in use, 130
Vested benefits, 18

Website development costs,
    120–121
Weighted average method,
    95–99